Heaviness in Metal Music

Heaviness in Metal Music

Stephen S. Hudson

OXFORD
UNIVERSITY PRESS

OXFORD
UNIVERSITY PRESS

Oxford University Press is a department of the University of Oxford.
It furthers the University's objective of excellence in research, scholarship,
and education by publishing worldwide. Oxford is a registered trade mark of
Oxford University Press in the UK and in certain other countries.

Published in the United States of America by Oxford University Press
198 Madison Avenue, New York, NY 10016, United States of America.

Library of Congress Cataloging-in-Publication Data
Names: Hudson, Stephen S. author
Title: Heaviness in metal music / Stephen S. Hudson.
Description: [1]. | New York, NY : Oxford University Press, 2026. |
Includes bibliographical references and index. |
Identifiers: LCCN 2025049439 (print) | LCCN 2025049440 (ebook) |
ISBN 9780197774960 paperback | ISBN 9780197774953 hardback |
ISBN 9780197774991 | ISBN 9780197774984 epub
Subjects: LCSH: Heavy metal (Music)—History and criticism |
Heavy metal (Music)—Analysis, appreciation |
Heavy metal (Music)—Philosophy and aesthetics
Classification: LCC ML3534 .H824 2026 (print) | LCC ML3534 (ebook) |
DDC 782.42166—dc23/eng/20260107
LC record available at https://lccn.loc.gov/2025049439
LC ebook record available at https://lccn.loc.gov/2025049440

DOI: 10.1093/9780197774991.001.0001

Paperback printed by Marquis Book Printing, Canada
Hardback printed by Lightning Source, Inc., United States of America

The manufacturer's authorized representative in the EU for product safety is
Oxford University Press España S.A. of Parque Empresarial San Fernando de Henares,
Avenida de Castilla, 2 – 28830 Madrid (www.oup.es/en or product.safety@oup.com).
OUP España S.A. also acts as importer into Spain of products made by the manufacturer.

Contents

Epilogue: The Promise of Post-Extreme Metal   194

Acknowledgments

Like many first-time authors, I owe a heartfelt thanks to virtually every friend, colleague, and family member I've had since I began studying in academia. Each one of you has, through your support, enabled me and helped me to develop my ideas, grow as a writer, and acquire and keep the academic positions that have allowed me to do this kind of work.

But there are also quite a few people that contributed more directly to this book, whom I should thank individually. Ashlie Sandoval read early versions of ideas that eventually became several chapters of this book while we were both in graduate school. Jasmine E. Johnson taught a class I took about Black Dance and encouraged me to pursue a term paper that, ten years later, eventually became Chapter 5. Anthony Sparacino and Kylie Korsnack were my fellow travelers in learning about book proposals during the pandemic while I was at the University of Richmond. Myles Schaller of Secret Passage Editing helped me revise the book proposal. Norm Hirschy at OUP reached out to me after my SMT talk in 2021 to ask about the book project I mentioned in my bio, and then was the most supportive acquisitions editor I could have asked for, guiding me through the book proposal process. Lori Burns and Brad Osborn both went above and beyond as copyeditors for my first two journal articles, which became the basis for Chapters 8 and 10. David Carter and Ramona Gonzalez read drafts of Chapters 4 and 6 at critical moments and their feedback was enormously helpful. Janet Bourne has welcomed me to the small SoCal music theory community and has been a great friend as we celebrate milestones of writing our first books at the same time. Olivia Lucas, Brad Osborn, Calder Hannan, Michael Dekovich, and Megan Creek read drafts of the entire book and gave incredibly thorough feedback, for which I am so grateful. I have been blessed to work with several talented and tireless editors at OUP during the production process, including Rachel Ruisard, Meredith Taylor, and Elakkia Bharathi, who are primarily responsible for any degree of order and consistency in the book as it is printed. Any errors which remain are my own.

I was fortunate to have several wonderful opportunities to workshop chapters from this book as I was finishing the manuscript. I should thank everyone involved in the AMS Popular Music Study Group's Junior Faculty Symposiums in 2020 and 2022, where I was able to workshop early drafts of what became Chapters 3 and 4—but especially Brian Wright and Amy Coddington. Special thanks to two colleagues in Germany, Daniel Suer and Florian Heesch, who arranged a conference on metal and dance that will be published in a special issue in *Metal Music Studies*, my contribution to which has been repurposed as Chapter 5. Walter Clark and the other music faculty at UC Riverside invited me to give a colloquium talk as I was editing Chapters 3, 4, and 5. The SEM Cognitive Ethnomusicology Special Interest Group, led by Alex Rossi and Gina Fatone, invited me to workshop a draft of Chapter 6 as part of their symposium series.

I should also thank a few mentors. Beth Levy, D. Kern Holoman, and Christopher Reynolds at UC Davis taught me the basics of writing, encouraged me to write about metal music, and helped me get into graduate school. Mark Butler, my PhD advisor at Northwestern, took a chance letting me into the program and I will be forever grateful. I must also thank Bruno Alcalde and Jeff Riehl for hooking me up with my first job at the University of Richmond, which was a wonderfully supportive environment while I got my career off the ground. David Kasunic led the hiring committee at Occidental College and was the most supportive and protective department chair I could have asked for in my first two years at my current position, which was absolutely critical in allowing me to get the book proposal out and finish the manuscript.

I also want to thank my colleagues in metal music studies, who have all helped or encouraged me over the years, and had conversations with me about ideas or conference papers that have become part of this book, including Calder Hannan, Olivia Lucas, Lori Burns, Brad Osborn, Guy Capuzzo, Meghan Creek, Florian Walch, Steve Waksman, Harris Berger, Kevin Fellesz, Eric Smialek, Michael Dekovich, Lewis Kennedy, Ross Hagen, Edward Banchs, Jeremy Wallach, and many, many others. It's been really cool to get to be a part of such a rapidly growing research area and I can't wait to see what happens next!

Finally, thanks to Mom, Dad, my brother Andrew, and my wife Bruna— without your love and support this book never would have happened. Mom helped me workshop the book's title. Bruna has been my constant consultant on book matters throughout the last three years and has gently persuaded me to keep going every time I'm about to give up.

PART I

WHAT IS HEAVINESS?

Introduction

It's possible to quickly get a sense of the importance of heaviness in metal music, its stunningly vast range, and its visceral impact on listeners, by considering two contrasting songs with "heavy" in the title. "Heavy Metal Mania" (1981) by the somewhat obscure Scottish heavy metal band Holocaust begins with a major-key guitar line like a bugle call. It slowly builds intensity with twin guitar lines at 0:45, in contrary motion vaguely reminiscent of the eighteenth-century Italian composer Vivaldi (or more directly, Vivaldi's admirers in 1970s hard rock and heavy metal, like Deep Purple and Randy Rhoads).[1] Then the guitarists slowly descend to their lowest strings to start a loud, distorted rock riff at 1:14 (reminiscent of earlier biker songs like Steppenwolf's "Born to Be Wild"), eventually culminating in an enthusiastic shout-along chorus. Here, heaviness evidences the sonic power that characterizes the genre, and serves as a metonym for youthful exuberance about music and music-related homo-social male bonding.

"The Heaviest Matter in the Universe" (2006) by the French progressive extreme metal band Gojira manifests heaviness differently. Without any kind of introduction, the band jumps directly into a rapid, bludgeoning riff with continuously shifting rhythms and squealing pinch harmonics, that sounds like a machine run amok—as if the groove metal of Lamb of God and Sepultura, the asymmetrical riffs of Meshuggah, and the brutal metalcore breakdowns of Killswitch Engage were chopped to bits and reassembled in an unholy Frankenstein order that maximized chaos. At 0:37, the singer screams "Lay down / fall away," but we hardly need to be told; the wild intensity and chaotic riffing hardly give one the option to do anything else. This abrupt start sets the tone for an unrelenting song which describes, in abstract but evocative terms, an experience of paralysis and utter despair. Here, heaviness manifests as a suffocating intensity that affords no reprieve to its listeners, no space to collect their thoughts.

To understand these two songs through the same concept, "heaviness," is to reveal some underlying commonalities that hold the metal genre together,

---

[1] See Walser (2014 [1993], 57–107).

Heaviness in Metal Music. Stephen S. Hudson, Oxford University Press. © Oxford University Press 2026.
DOI: 10.1093/9780197774991.003.0002

but also at the same time to map out the divergence of the genre's many styles, periods, and communities. The goal of this book is to understand the forces that make metal music work: What makes the music feel so visceral and compelling to its fans? Why do they like these intense experiences so much? Why is the genre is shaped the way it is, and how did it come to be that way? Heaviness, the central aesthetic quality of the genre (after which the genre's classic style "heavy metal" is named), is a large part of the answer to each of these questions.[2]

Defining Heaviness

In some ways, heaviness in music works like heaviness in the physical domain. Heaviness is often a relative distinction—there's no specific weight threshold that distinguishes between a "heavy" object and a "light" one. Instead, a lot depends on context and comparison. A half-ounce lead bullet feels heavy for its size, while a ten-pound bag of straw is surprisingly light compared to the mulch next to it at the hardware store. Like physical objects, what counts as "heavy" in metal music depends on what you're comparing it to. If you're used to listening to Van Halen, Iron Maiden, and Mötley Crüe, Metallica's 1991 album *Metallica* (often known as the "Black album" because of its monochromatic cover) sounds ominous, muscular, and powerful (Hudson 2021b). But if you're comparing it to extreme metal releases from the same year by bands like Entombed or Death, it might sound restrained, rock-oriented, and rather commercial.

The most crucial, determining factor in physical heaviness is what you're trying to do with an object. Half a pound is sadistically burdensome for a pair of eyeglasses, but a laughable feather weight for bicep curls at the gym. A lot has to do with the person's prior experiences, too: a ten-pound paving stone might feel heavy for someone who doesn't normally do their own yard work, but not for a landscaper who moves paving stones every week. Additionally, we can even have an experience of heaviness without actually touching any object: we all know that a jet engine would be astoundingly heavy, even though

---

[2] Like all genre labels, the terms "metal" and "heavy metal" have always been contested and in flux (Walser 2014 [1993], 4–7). Originally, these terms may have been interchangeable, but in recent years, "heavy metal" has increasingly referred to a specific older style that characterized the genre's early years (think Black Sabbath, Van Halen, Iron Maiden), while "metal" invokes the whole genre. The most partisan extreme metal fans, however, say that the older "heavy metal" style no longer counts as "metal," or just barely, and that "metal" proper begins in the 1980s with early thrash metal bands such as Metallica. But as the qualifier "heavy" has gradually dropped from the genre label, heaviness has not declined in importance—if anything, it has become more exaggerated and central.

few of us have ever tried to lift one. A big part of how we experience heaviness, then, is imaginative—how heavy we think something is, or should be, based on how it looks or what it's made out of. By analogy, to understand heaviness in metal music, we have to understand how people relate to the music, who the people are, where they're coming from, how they behave while listening, what they're thinking about, and what they've listened to before.

For the purpose of this book, I define heaviness fairly broadly as a listener's experience of embodied impact. This means that my discussions of "heaviness" include some music and moments that might not be called "heavy" in other contexts. A lot of hard rock might be called "hard," not "heavy," and a lot of power metal might more accurately be described as "powerful." But while these genres don't weigh down their listeners like some of the darker metal styles, they certainly share a lot of parameters that contribute to the music's impact: loudness, drum patterns, guitar distortion and playing techniques, fantastical lyrics, mythological or futuristic imagery, headbanging, and so on. When I say "heavy," I have in mind this broader palette of power and impact, which a broad collection of metal and metal-adjacent subgenres each draw on in their own ways.

Several previous writers have defined heaviness primarily as a quality of guitar timbre (Berger and Fales 2005; Herbst 2018; Miller 2022; Herbst and Mynett 2022, 2023a, 2023b, 2023c), but I fear that this definition will inevitably constrain our understanding of heaviness to narrow ranges of expression within attributes of sound, and performance or recording techniques. To contrast, in the first book-length academic study of heavy metal, Deena Weinstein argues that this music's impact is multisensory—and that listeners themselves play a crucial part.

> Ecstasy at a heavy metal concert requires more than the music. There must also be a great deal of excitement generated by non-sonic means. There are many ways of creating excitement, and all three actors that constitute the concert—the band, the backstage crew, and the audience—do their part [. . .] A heavy metal concert is a multisensory experience [. . .] Each of the senses is simultaneously receiving variegated but constant stimulation, with a mutually reinforcing impact. (Weinstein 1991, 214)

In my book, I have sought to frequently center the experiences of music consumers, not just music producers; and I have sought to analyze music as an event, not just a text. Throughout the book, I argue that each listener (and this includes performing musicians, who are usually also listening) participates in creating or construing their own experiences of heaviness, through their listening practices, their dancing, and the metaphors and social imagination they apply to what they hear. Heaviness is not just an objective quality of the music—it is also a subjective experience in the mind and the body of the beholder, something that listeners participate in creating. If we want to understand heaviness, and metal music more broadly, we have to study its culture and context, how listeners think about the music and interact with it and each other, not just internal properties of "the music itself."

To understand heaviness as both an embodied experience and a genre-wide aesthetic, and to understand how and when it emerged, and how it has shaped the metal genre, I have drawn on an interdisciplinary variety of ideas and methods. To capture and analyze aspects of the listening experience, I have drawn on ideas from music theory, performances studies, embodied cognitive science, and phenomenology—especially Harris Berger's concept of "stance" (Berger 2009) and Diana Taylor's conceptions of "scenario" and "repertoire" (Taylor 2003). I use music analysis and historical musicology tools to identify document common musical structures, trace their origins, and study how performers and listeners understand and interact with them. These methods are not used separately but woven together throughout the book.

Defining Metal

A book that was just about heaviness might explore a wider selection of styles throughout rock and beyond (see Moores 2021), but since my purpose in studying heaviness is to understand the metal genre I've focused more narrowly. That said, I have defined the book's scope rather inclusively. If a band or album has ever been called "heavy metal" or "metal" by a significant number of people, I consider it part of the scope of this book. While I was still a student, I often had the experience of telling an older relative or family friend that I was studying metal, and they would start asking me about Kiss or AC/DC or Twisted Sister—bands which few metalheads today would consider part of their genre, and which were distant from what I was writing about at the time (extreme metal like Meshuggah and Death). Younger friends were more likely to ask about mainstream, rock-oriented bands (like Avenged Sevenfold or System of a Down), which are also often considered marginal or peripheral to metal. This broader range of bands form a significant part of how the world understands metal music, so they should be included as part of metal's story, even if metal insiders today often don't consider them part of the genre.

If I decide what's heavy and what's not, what's metal and what's not, then that would unfairly flatten the subjective experience of a diverse community to my own perspective. Since I've defined heaviness as a feeling of embodied impact that listeners help create, it's important to center fans' own experiences. But I also want to question received wisdom and open up new perspectives or ways of listening—to cast new light on the genre's history, and highlight the consequences of deciding to hear a song as part of it—and I want to leave as much as I can up to you, the reader. There's inevitably some consequence that I have selected certain specific bands to talk about instead of others, but my goal is not to define a particular canon of bands, or enshrine a particular aesthetic or way of listening; instead, I want to provide you with concepts and tools to explore the experience of heaviness and the history of metal on your own terms.

For example, rather than picking Black Sabbath as the first metal band, it's more provocative to leave that an open question, and listen to a wide range of bands as potential pioneers. Black Sabbath is often credited as the first to combine the sounds that would come to define metal music—namely, power chord riffs on highly distorted guitars—with ominous supernatural topics. But that's not the only way to define the origin of metal. In an interview commemorating the 35th anniversary of the band's eponymous debut album, Ozzy Osbourne recalled:

> We were four local kids that played in a jazz-blues band [...] Someone went to a movie theater and said, "Isn't it strange that people pay money to have the s—scared out of them?" We thought, why don't we scare people with music? Then, Tony came up with those demonic riffs. (Farber 2013)

But his idea of scaring people with blues music had a precedent: Screamin' Jay Hawkins' 1956 hit "Put a Spell on You," which today is better known through Nina Simone's 1965 cover version. According to legend, Jay Hawkins was an ordinary blues singer when he and his band were getting drunk one night and, as a joke, recorded a wildly overdone take of a refined ballad his band had been working on. Hawkins' label released this take as a novelty single, and it became an unlikely hit, compelling Hawkins to develop a full character (Screamin' Jay Hawkins) based on his performance, with a spectacular stage show including outlandish outfits and props that crossed campy gothic horror with voodoo exoticism—such as a fake tusk piercing his nose and a skull-topped shaman staff. What would it mean to listen to "Put a Spell on You" as early heavy metal? What new insight might that perspective give us about the formation of the genre, or its nature today?

Metal is often stereotyped as music performed by and for White straight men, but I argue that this framing distorts and limits our understanding of the history and expressive potential of a genre centered on heaviness. Each of these three stereotypes (Whiteness, masculinity, heteronormativity) is reductive. As I show in Chapters 4 and 5, heavy metal emerged out of the highly racialized blues and rock scenes of the 1950s and 1960s, and many of metal's core ideologies and values to this day have been shaped by Blackness, ideas about Blackness, and the politics of White encounters with Blackness—including heaviness itself. Metal music is, in many ways, an extension of Black musical traditions (see Fellezs 2011). Further, Black artists have always been part of the genre, but have been playing increasingly prominent roles within the last two decades. Women have also always been a part of the metal genre, but it has often been assumed that metal's aggressive intensity is inherently masculine, and not a natural domain for female artists or fans (see Hill 2016). But as I argue in Chapter 6, a growing number of prominent female artists continue to demonstrate new ways in which the pursuit of heaviness can be compatible with femininity, even within the most extreme styles and performance techniques. Amber Clifford-Napoleone (2016) has shown that metal's supposed heteronormativity is, at the very least, easily and frequently subverted or bent, if it is not itself fundamentally queer. Whiteness, masculinity, and heteronormativity—which Keith Kahn-Harris (2016, 27) has called the "metal identity triad"—are often described as "defaults" in metal scholarship, in ways which too often reinforce these biases, and I aim to help unwind them instead.

I've organized the book into three parts. Part I focuses on defining heaviness and mapping out the ideas and practices that contribute to creating these experiences. Chapter 1 shows how sound can appear "heavy" by appealing to theories of cognitive metaphors, which argue that almost all human cognition depends on cross-domain analogies (like transferring qualities from heavy physical objects to musical sounds). It also introduces an idea called "stance" (Berger 2009), which I use to build a framework to understand how experiences of heaviness and the meanings they carry are shaped by the relationships listeners imagine between themselves, the sound, and other listeners. Chapter 2 uses the power chord as a case study to illustrate how the experience of heaviness often depends on hearing metal music as something more powerful and impactful than what is literally being played, a phenomenon I call "the basic illusion of heaviness." Chapter 3 explores the idea that heavier music is more authentic, and that the genre must get heavier over time to stay relevant—a kind of "progressionism" which has been perennially influential throughout metal's history.

Part II uses heaviness as a lens for genre criticism and historiography. Chapter 4 demonstrates that the progressionism studied in Chapter 3 in fact predates metal and was inherited from White blues music of the late 1960s, foregrounding how racialized thinking shaped heavy metal's emergence and determined the direction in which the genre grew for much of its history. Chapter 5 applies the ideas of Chapter 4 to dance, showing how headbanging emerged alongside heaviness from White encounters with Black music, as a distortion and exaggeration of a practice of nodding that White audiences thought was an appropriate response to Black music. Chapter 6 shows how metal's fantastical vocals have a similar racial history, and theorizes a kind of mishearing in which we hear a mundane human singer invoking beyond-human identities or power. This dynamic of mishearing has complex consequences for non-male singers, since these fantastical vocal techniques are often heard as inherently masculine.

Part III focuses in on musical structures and listening practices that fans and musicians use to create heaviness, showing how those practices have shaped the expansion of the metal genre. Chapter 7 is a case study of progressionism, showing how Metallica championed a new extreme metal paradigm through their cover songs and original compositions, but also through their roles as fans, collectors, and tastemakers. Chapter 8 explores how metal fans amplify or add to their experiences of heaviness through headbanging, exploring the agency they have in coordinating with common drum patterns. Chapter 9 builds on Chapter 8 to show how conventional song form in metal music creates ritual spaces for the (re)enactment of extreme dance practices and experiences of heaviness. Chapter 10 shows how the very conventionality of these song-form patterns enables a diverse range of style distinctions and qualities of heaviness to be discerned and experienced. The book ends with an epilogue in which I argue that we should understand metal as a genre centered on heaviness, rather than extremity—a shift in perspective which seems to reflect recent trends in the genre, and interprets these trends optimistically as a sign of the genre's continued growth, increasing maturity, and thriving future.

1
Experiencing Heavy Timbres Through Metaphors

Buzzsaw Tone

Metal fans and musicians often describe their music as if it has compelling, tangible power to create visceral experiences of physical impact. But in a literal sense it is just sound, and under normal circumstances, sound hardly has any physical consequence at all. When metal fans hear their music as powerful, some of that power is real physical impact, but some of it is amplified in the listener's imagination through cognitive metaphors—the same kind of transfers or analogies across sensory domains that allow us to describe sour flavors as "sharp" and colors as "warm" or "cool." This metaphorical dimension is no less real in human experience than the measurable, physical, objective dimensions of the world around us, and realizing this is the key to understanding how metal can feel so serious and urgent even when it escapes into imaginary realms, and also why the genre's flightiest fantasies continue to be caught up in real-world problems of race, gender, popularity, and authenticity. In this chapter, I identify some of the main metaphors involved in the experience of heaviness, and I argue that these metaphors interact across different imaginative and social dimensions that allow heaviness to take on a diverging, prismatic spectrum of meanings and embodied impacts.

The intertwined relationship between metaphor and heaviness, and the way they shape our experiences of metal, can be understood through the story of a guitar distortion pedal called the Boss Heavy Metal-2 (HM-2)—a story which is arguably the founding myth of the Swedish death metal scene. According to legend—authoritatively confirmed by the scene insider and historiographer Daniel Ekeroth (2008)—in the late 1980s, the teenage guitarist Leif Cuzner, who at the time was part of the band Nihilist, was experimenting with the Boss HM-2 pedal when he got the crazy idea of turning all the knobs up to the maximum at the same time. One might expect such a reckless, artless setting to produce unusable noise, but instead, Cuzner discovered what came to be known as the "buzzsaw tone," a sound which seemed to be just

Heaviness in Metal Music. Stephen S. Hudson, Oxford University Press. © Oxford University Press 2026.
DOI: 10.1093/9780197774991.003.0003

the right sort of distorted timbre to push metal to new depths of heaviness. In the world of guitar tone, equipment combinations and settings are like alchemical formulas, arcane recipes which are illegible to laypeople but proudly shared among initiates. Although Cuzner's band Nihilist broke up after recording a few demos, several other band members immediately reformed as the band Entombed, bringing with them the secret of the maxed-out HM-2 guitar pedal. Entombed used the HM-2 pedal when they recorded their debut album *Left Hand Path* (1990), which played a key role in establishing the Swedish death metal style and has turned out to be one of the most enduring and highly regarded metal albums ever.

Part of why this story is so compelling is that the unrestrained extremity of turning every knob up to the maximum resonates with metal's aesthetic of sonic excess, immortalized in *This Is Spinal Tap*'s famous joke about changing the numbers on volume knobs to go up to eleven instead of merely ten. Metal fans are already primed to think of metal in terms of heaviness and maximal volume, and the buzzsaw metaphor helps fans hear heaviness in a new way, taking that experience of heaviness to a new level. This creates a kind of virtuous cycle: metal is already heavy, so it activates metaphors associated with heaviness, but then these metaphors make our listening experience even heavier.

In a review piece about the HM-2 pedal that compiled perspectives from influential scene members, Anders Nyström (who founded the band Katatonia) tells his version of the story as if this timbre itself generated the whole scene.

> Believe me, the impact was so brutal that I was fucking nailed to my seat! It really dawned on me right there, that has gotta be the ultimate death metal guitar tone! It literally sounded like someone was playing notes on an actual buzzsaw, delivering Swedish death metal as we know it. (Gus 2017)

The prolific multi-band songwriter Rogga Johansson confirms that the buzzsaw tone is "the source of the sound for an entire part of the death metal scene" (Gus 2017). This tone, Nyström reports, "felt so much more raw and brutal than, for instance, what the entire Florida [death metal] scene had going on" at that time (Gus 2017), by which he means early releases by bands like Obituary, Cannibal Corpse, and Morbid Angel. This new type of sonic heaviness gave Swedish death metal of the early 1990s a distinctive musical identity. The buzzsaw tone was subsequently imitated widely by bands outside Sweden and continues to be used in new death metal recordings (although today this timbre carries nostalgic "old-school" connotations it did not have thirty years ago).

The word "buzzsaw" and various violent adjectives used to describe the timbre of the maxed-out HM-2 pedal might strike some readers as empty hype words from a journalist's thesaurus, but this buzzsaw metaphor actually communicates some important aspects of musical experience. The use of these terms creates an analogy that transfers some qualities of dangerous power tools over to the Boss HM-2 tone, as exemplified by the opening of the review piece I mentioned earlier:

> Buzzsaw. It's doubtful there's ever been a single word more on-the-nose for describing a guitar's tone. It metaphorically captures the violent brutality of the music associated with it, but at the same time literally describes the timbre and pitch of the tone. (Gus 2017)

This opening resonates with Nyström's later wording, "It *literally* sounded like someone was playing notes on an actual buzzsaw" (Gus 2017). Joe Anastasio, who produces a handmade pedal based on the HM-2, describes the sound more specifically as "a throttled chainsaw" (Gus 2017). In other words, "buzzsaw" is not a hyperbolic extended metaphor; instead, it directly represents how fans and musicians hear and think about guitar tone.

Chainsaws and buzzsaws are not randomly chosen power tools, but ones which resonate with concepts of power and danger. Besides their practical use in workshops and forestry, portable power saws are widely associated with human dismemberment throughout popular culture—videogames, comic books, and horror films. By describing the HM-2 guitar tone as a buzzsaw or chainsaw sound, these associations transfer over to the timbre of Swedish death metal, a genre whose lyrics revel in scenes of carnage, which in turn heighten our imagination of the timbre's gruesome power. In other words, the sound of Swedish death metal's timbre, the discourse about the scene, and the imagery in lyrics and album art all mutually reinforce one another to invest this music with the power of imagined destruction. Metaphor and metaphoric listening are the mechanisms of this cross-domain feedback.

Experiencing Heaviness Through Metaphorical Listening

But how do metaphors work in listening? Metaphor is often thought of as a poetical use of language that imaginatively diverges from reality. We sometimes say a best-selling book is "flying off the shelves," but we all know that books don't actually fly. However, cognitive scientists argue that metaphor isn't *completely* detached from reality, but contains some kernel of truth, some useful point of comparison. In the metaphor above, the books are moving off the shelves at such a speed it's *almost as if* they had wings and were flying away as fast as they could. This is what Deidre Gentner (1983) calls "analogical transfer": even though books and flying things are completely different categories (there's no book that is also a flying thing, and vice versa), some aspect of our knowledge about flying things transfers into the domain of book sales. While the metaphor is not literally true, it does add some useful new insight or meaning: one particular title is disappearing from the shelves in a way that books usually don't.

The way metal fans talk about and experience heaviness is saturated with metaphors that make analogical transfers between music and other domains of experience, and these metaphors have a much deeper impact than just serving as heightened descriptive language. A school of thought called "cognitive metaphor theory" has been built around an argument made famous by George Lakoff and Mark Johnson (1980): that metaphors are more than just figurative language. Instead, metaphors reveal how cognition is almost always analogical, meaning that we are always understanding things around us in terms of concepts from other domains of experience. For example, the concept that "argument is war" is not only used in our figurative language around taking sides, giving up ground, and "winning" or "losing" a verbal argument, but also shapes our *experience* and *enactment* of arguments as conflicts which can feel antagonistic or violent even when no physical threats or blows are exchanged. In other words, metaphors are a fundamental part of the human conceptual system; they are more than "just" language, because they shape how we perceive the world and interact with it.

Metaphors about heaviness describe the physical feeling or impact of metal's sound, but metaphorical thinking can also add to the heaviness we experience, amplify it, or expand it in new directions. The "buzzsaw tone" metaphor describes some aspects of the timbre's literal sound: the rip of the chainsaw's teeth tearing through wood or flesh, the metal-on-metal rattle of the drive chain, and the ear-splitting growl of the two-stroke engine. But this analogy also directs one's attention to these saw-like qualities of the sound, highlighting the timbre's harshness and amplifying the buzzsaw-like qualities one would experience listening to this tone without that metaphor in mind. And thinking of the guitar tone as a buzzsaw invites an analogical transfer of the buzzsaw's mechanical and destructive power onto the music, encouraging us to think of the guitar tone as more than just guitar tone.

From the perspective of cognitive metaphor theory, the analogical thinking described above is not merely a "special effect" invoked only when someone explicitly mentions metaphorical words like "buzzsaw tone"; instead, analogical thinking is *always* part of how we experience heaviness. In a recent book, the music production and cognition scholar Mads Walther-Hansen explains how we experience most timbres through tactile and visual qualities, using metaphorical thinking to understand musical sound in terms of our previous non-musical experiences with objects that are heavy, big, rough, warm, and so on (Walther-Hansen 2020, 2–3). In other words, *all* our experiences of musical timbre are inherently physical. While metal might be exceptional as a "sonic contact sport,"[1] what makes it exceptional is not the fact that it is physical, but the overwhelming intensity of its physicality and the centrality of this physicality in discourse about the genre by musicians and fans.

Physicality is central to Walther-Hansen's definition of the "light/heavy" metaphor, which provides a good starting point for developing a more complex understanding of heaviness. Walther-Hansen emphasizes "cross-modal mappings" or "entailments," which are the qualities and associations that transfer from heavy objects to heavy sounds through this metaphor.

> Heavy objects weigh more than light objects and they ... are more powerful than light objects.... Moreover, heavy objects do not move easily.... Sounds with a lot of low-frequency content are considered heavy.... Since the experience of heaviness is often linked with weighty and firmly grounded objects, sounds floating in reverberation or sounds that appear at a distance often appear less grounded and lighter. High volume, a flattened dynamic envelope, and distorted amplification are also considered important parameters of perceived heaviness. (Walther-Hansen 2020, 106)

A rapidly growing literature goes far beyond Walther-Hansen's brief account of the acoustics of heaviness, by explaining the electroacoustic processes that create guitar distortion (Scotto 2016), exploring how it impacts consonance and dissonance in harmonies (Lilja 2009; Herbst 2018), and documenting the production techniques used to make guitar distortion especially heavy (Mynett 2012, 2017; Herbst 2017; Herbst and Mynett 2023a, among others), but most of this literature does not discuss heaviness's metaphorical dimensions. Walther-Hansen suggests that heaviness always involves metaphors of physicality; metal's low, loud, and distorted guitar riffs

---

[1] The British music critic Ian MacDonald once disparaged heavy metal by writing that it was "more of a sonic contact sport than a musical experience," and while I must insist on metal's musicality, his comparison of metal to contact sports is evocative in the context of my definition of heaviness as a feeling of physical impact.

and drums feel heavy because they automatically invoke our previous human experiences with powerful, weighty, and firmly grounded objects.

Heaviness is more than just physical impact, though. It also has connotations of seriousness and emotional intensity that are foundational dynamics for many metal bands. This sense of "heaviness" actually predates the metal genre. Hippies in the 1960s established "heavy" as a synonym for "serious, thought-provoking, or profound" and carried this sense into psychedelic rock music, a style which then became a big influence on heavy metal (McCleary 2004, 240). One prominent early example is the Beatles' "I Want You (She's So Heavy)," which doesn't have the power chords that are a central characteristic of the metal genre but does have metal's sense of ominous fatefulness and immense physicality. John Lennon, who wrote the song, told *Rolling Stone* it was about his overwhelming, all-encompassing love for his wife Yoko Ono: "When you're drowning, you don't say, 'I would be incredibly pleased if someone would have the foresight to notice me drowning and come and help me.' You just *scream*" (Wenner 2000 [1971], 83). The sense of "heavy" as "emotionally intense" isn't exactly separate from the sense of "heavy" as physically weighty. Heavy emotions are a weight to bear; they use up our energy and make us feel like action requires great effort, as if we were physically heavy. This sense of emotional intensity continues into metal, in which the heaviness metaphor often indexes emotional intensity alongside material and tactile dimensions.

The Many Senses of Heaviness

Walther-Hansen describes heaviness as a multimodal metaphor, in which various parameters of timbre and loudness activate associations with physical size and power, which gives us a good starting point for understanding heaviness. But this definition is just the starting point, because, as several scholars have argued, heaviness is not just one thing. Berger and Fales connect heaviness to several different kinds of metaphorical experiences.

> "Heaviness" signifies a range of meanings and qualities in addition to, or beyond, power and intensity. In English, the word "heavy" literally denotes great physical weight and can be used to connote a range of affective or valuative qualities dear to the speed/thrash tradition—seriousness, gravitas, grimness, threat, implacability, and durability. (Berger and Fales 2005, 194–95)

In other words, heaviness is not just one metaphor, but a collection or network of related metaphors. These different affective qualities are different versions of heaviness, which are often connected to different metal styles or subgenres.[2] Different listeners draw on different parts of this network of metaphors in different ways, leading to a diverse range of experiences of heaviness.

For example, Cryptopsy's "Benedictine Convulsions" and Pallbearer's "I Saw the End" have completely different kinds of heaviness. Their heavinesses manifest in different (or even opposing) musical characteristics, invoke different metaphors and cross-domain mappings, and feel different in listening. "I Saw the End" is expansive, stable, relaxed, ponderous, resonant, sorrowful, and monumental. "Benedictine Convulsions" is nearly the opposite: claustrophobic, chaotic, tense, hurried, relentless, animalistic, and heretical. Both songs activate parameters of lowness, power, large size, weight—the same metaphorical resources described in Walther-Hansen's definition of "heaviness." But these two songs take this background metaphor in opposite directions, highlighting different aspects of heaviness and combining heaviness with different related metaphors. Here's another way to think of it: HEAVY is an underlying idea throughout most metal, but there are more specialized or specific flavors of heaviness that we experience in the foreground of our awareness, each of which inherits from the broader background metaphor.[3]

In other words, heaviness can't be completely captured with a single, simple definition. Instead, we might describe it as a large network of varied metaphors which each draw on a different mixture of size, physicality, effort, excess, danger, power, and other parameters and associations. The cognitive linguist Ronald Langacker suggests that this is also true of most words, grammatical constructions, and familiar phrases, a broad category that he calls "lexical items."

> Most lexical items have a considerable array of interrelated senses, which define the range of their conventionally sanctioned usage. These alternate senses are conveniently represented in network form.... The precise configuration of such a network is less important than recognizing the inadequacy of any reductionist description of lexical meaning. A speaker's knowledge of the conventional value of a lexical item cannot in general be reduced to a single structure, such as the prototype or the highest-level schema. For one thing, not every lexical category has a single, clearly determined prototype, nor can we invariably assume a high-level

---

[2] Jeremy Wallach et al. make a similar statement: "To listeners unfamiliar with the music, metal may seem to focus solely on the expression of rage and aggression. Closer inspection, however, reveals a far broader palette of affective valences, and this is key to the music's meaning. Rage and aggression are certainly present in metal, but songs and performances also offer sadness, fear, depression, grandeur, drama, and a kind of affectively neutral but intensely powerful energy" (Wallach et al. 2011, 14).

[3] Following Walther-Hansen's usage, I'll put a sound quality in all caps when it is functioning as a background cognitive metaphor.

schema fully compatible with the specifications of every node in the network. (2002, 2–3)

I'll unpack the significance of Langacker's argument slowly. First, heaviness also involves a "considerable array of interrelated senses." Metal fans use a thesaurus full of terms to describe the music's power and impact, like "fune-real" or "buzzsaw" or "brutal," and these terms draw on both the main back-ground metaphor of HEAVY and several other background metaphors for experiencing sound, like ROUGH, HARD, and DARK. Multiple background metaphors can overlap and contribute to the same song (e.g., Girlschool's "Demolition Boys" is both HARD and ROUGH, while Nightwish's "Noise" is both HEAVY and DARK).

A more rigorous picture of this resonance or overlap between background metaphors can be built by examining how Walther-Hansen's definition of HEAVY involves many entailments that overlap with his definitions for DARK, HARD, and ROUGH. For example, HEAVY, HARD, and ROUGH sounds all entail apparent force or effort; HEAVY and DARK sounds both tend to be low in pitch; and so on. In fact, there is no single entailment or correlate that is associated only with HEAVY; every single physical or sonic quality associated with HEAVY in Figure 1.1 is also associated with one of these other three background metaphors. The solid lines in Figure 1.1 rep-resent the entailments mentioned by Walther-Hansen, but I have added a couple more connections in dotted lines. ROUGH sounds are also often loud (or at least, associated with loudness); and "heavy metal" and "hard rock" are usually bad/evil, so in the context of these music styles it might make sense to

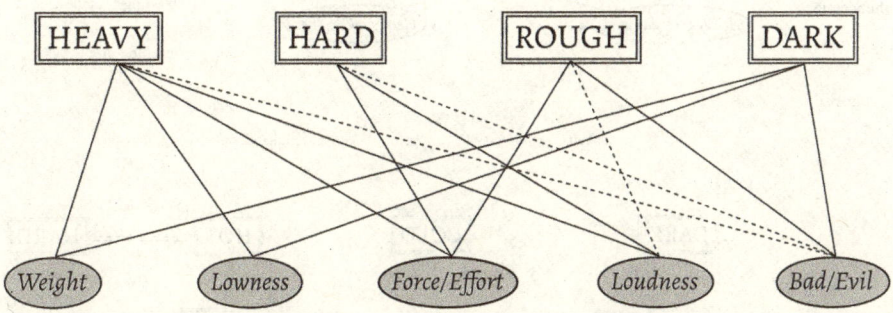

Figure 1.1 Four cognitive metaphors with their overlapping entailments. Top row, cognitive metaphors for sound quality; bottom row, entailments / characteristics from other domains of experience. Based on the work of Walther-Hansen (2020, Chapter 4). Diagram adapted from Hudson 2022b.

say that HEAVY and HARD background metaphors activate an association with badness and/or evil.

Within this collection of interrelated and overlapping background metaphors, there is a dense network of more specific senses of "heaviness" that are also interrelated with each other and with the background metaphors. Heaviness is the broad governing metaphor which serves as a kind of schema for all these individual terms, in that it passes on many entailments to each of these senses (like size, weight, impact, etc.). But many of these individual senses resonate with other background metaphors simultaneously. For example, "grim" could be described as a finer distinction of two background metaphors in combination, HEAVY and COLD. Figure 1.2 takes a handful of the myriad senses of HEAVY and groups them into two broader senses of "heavy & fast" and "heavy & slow," as well as showing connections to several other background metaphors. Double dotted lines show closely related background metaphors. Dotted lines with arrows at both ends show oppositions between contrasting pairs of Slow/Fast, and Organized/Chaotic. Single solid lines show how these categories inherit from the background metaphors, and single dotted lines show how individual senses like "funereal" or "machine-gun" inherit from several background metaphors or large categories.

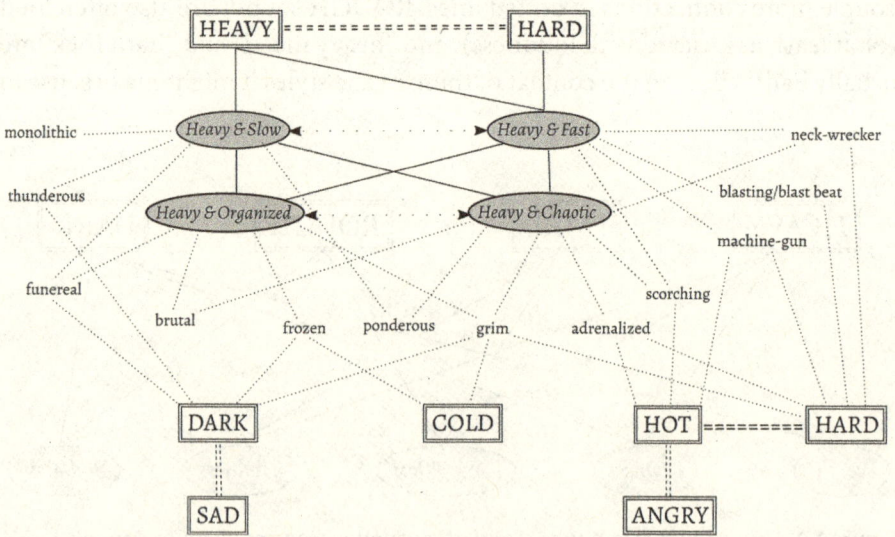

Figure 1.2 A small number of terms that draw on the HEAVINESS metaphor, and some of the senses of heaviness and other background metaphors they invoke. Expanded from a figure in Hudson 2022b.

Echoing Langacker, the precise organization in Figure 1.2 is less important than the conclusion it demonstrates: HEAVINESS has a colorful lexicon of senses that each have their own distinct connotations and associations, and they cannot all be collapsed together into a single definition. Even within the small list in Figure 1.2, there are many near opposites. "Neck wrecking" and "ponderous" are one such pair. "Machine-gun" and "funereal" are another. But speed isn't the only factor of opposition; "explosive" and "grim" are also almost irreconcilable, and both could be applied to a wide range of tempos. This diagram could also have included an additional background metaphor WET with senses "swampy" (DARK, COLD) and "sweltering" (HOT).[4] In sum, we can understand each of these metaphors as a kind of HEAVINESS, but these individual metaphors all pull HEAVINESS in their own divergent directions. HEAVY is a metaphor that connects many different experiences and sensory modes, and no single definition of heaviness or list of required features can neatly define this category of experience.

Introducing Stances: Social Dimensions of Heaviness

Many different sound qualities invoke the physical impact and imagined power I call "heaviness," and many cognitive metaphors recruit our bodies in our experience of timbre's visceral impact. But even given the same exact sound and the same metaphors for understanding the physicality of this sound, you can still have radically different experiences of heaviness, depending on what you imagine the sound to represent and what kind of relationship they imagine it has to yourself. People listening to Swedish death metal and thinking in terms of the metaphor "buzzsaw tone" could have a wide range of experiences varying along at least three different dimensions:

1. They could imagine "buzzsaw" as representing a terrific machine tool for gleeful destruction, or a defensive weapon in a zombie invasion, or an instrument of terror wielded by a horror villain—or, less likely, a mundane professional tool of foresters or construction contractors.
2. They could experience "buzzsaw tone" in the third person as an action involving other people, in the second person as a sound they inflict, or in the first person as a sound they experience impacting their own body.

---

[4] WET is a common metaphor in sound production discourse. A dry sound is a sound captured right at the source, in an acoustically dead space, so there is no reverb or "room sound." A wet sound has natural reverb or other effects, such as artificial reverb, distortion, or equalization. See Walther-Hansen (2020, 124–26).

3. They could imagine the people involved to have different ranges of consent or comfort, with the effect of "buzzsaw tone" ranging from a surge of empowering energy (Gamble 2022) to an abrasive or even violent skull-splitting intrusion.

Cross these three variables and you get a dizzying range of different relationships that afford different experiences of heaviness. These social and associational dimensions of heaviness have been mentioned by previous scholars writing about heaviness (e.g., Herbst and Mynett 2022, 2023a, 2023b; Miller 2022), but remain barely explored. However, since I define heaviness as an experience of impact (rather than just the timbre or sound quality which might create that impact), I consider these social and associational dimensions to be foundational to understanding how heaviness is created, experienced, and described by metal fans.

These different relationships we can have with buzzsaw tone are "stances," a term coined by the ethnomusicologist and metal scholar Harris Berger. Berger defines stance as "the valual qualities of the *relationship* that a person has to a text, performance, practice, or item of expressive culture" (2009, 5; emphasis mine). By "valual," Berger means that these relationships we have with things, or our stances toward them, shape both how we value (or evaluate) these things and how we experience them. The kind of relationship we have with metal music, the purpose we imagine for the music, and the way we fit into the social context we imagine around it shape the values it represents for us and the kind of listening experiences we can have.

Stance is also wrapped up in our own identities and how we align ourselves with artists and genre communities, what Berger calls "stance qualities of identity" (2009, 30). A song about Viking warriors might be more or less accessible to listeners depending on whether they are comfortable picturing themselves as Vikings. A song with graphic sexual violence might feel different to people of different sizes, backgrounds, and genders—especially if they identify as a victim, or a likely target, of harassment or assault. I'll have more to say about these personal aspects of stance and heaviness in later chapters. For now, I want to map out some possible stances toward heaviness, and explore their aesthetic, social, and political consequences.

One of the most powerful factors in experiences of heaviness is rooted in the tendency for very loud sounds to be felt as impacts on or inside the body; the stance we take toward this physical onslaught or intrusion has dramatic impacts on heaviness's meanings and significance in our experience. Heller describes the more extreme end of this phenomenon as "listener collapse," in which the sounds' vibration of the body is so intense that it dulls or numbs one's sense of separation between one's own body and the environment around it (Heller 2015, 45). In his account, Heller mentions two distinct phases of this experience that I identify as different stances toward heaviness.[5] Heller cites Olivia Lucas's article about the extreme drone metal band SunnO))) (pronounced "sun"), and David Novak's work on Japanese noise music, arguing that "both authors make reference to listener collapse's ability to evoke experiences of the sublime—an encounter with an object of such force and power that it defies attempts at measured or detached comprehension" (Heller 2015, 46). Novak relays his friend's description of two separate phases in their experience of this overwhelming force of loud sound: "At first you're just shrinking back, until you overcome that and let it go, and then you're in it and you're just being blown away" (Novak 2013, 46). This reaction begins with "shrinking back," a physical aversion to the intensity of the sound. Many non-fans have this reaction to metal and other noisy or extreme music genres: to try to escape it by turning it off or leaving the space where it is playing. A similar stance to "shrinking back" is something like "fighting back," striving to maintain one's own individuality by resisting and enduring the sound's power. (I'll return to this stance below.)

But "shrinking back" or "fighting" the sound is only one option, and other stances can lead to radically different experiences. In the next moment, Novak's friend reports giving in to the noise. This experience involves embracing the blurring of selfhood that the loudness creates, rather than rejecting it. Lucas separates these two stances more explicitly in her description of a concert by SunnO))).

> I recall how stressed and nearly ill I felt when the music first began. When my body stopped fighting the overload, however, and submitted, I discovered a state of freedom and relaxation so intense as to be soporific. In this environment, the listener must either fight or submit, and most seem to take the latter route, letting the sound fill their bodies and gently rock them to and fro. (Lucas 2014)

There's even another finer distinction within this category of submission: you could enjoy being adrift in the sound, as a kind of passivity, allowing the sound to wash over and through you; or you might imagine your own dislocation or destruction, "being blown away." It's the distinction between feeling

---

[5] These are "meta-stances"; that is, instead of a direct stance toward the music, these are stances toward an experience of heaviness which is itself created through other stances. Stances toward heaviness, stance qualities of identity, and many other types of stance interact in complex and contingent ways to create a listener's "total stance" (Berger 2009, 32).

like you're joining the sound, and feeling like the sound is a separate force obliterating you.

Another more personalized version of listener collapse is worth discussing here because it can have a unique, positive, therapeutic impact. Starting in the 1990s, the much-maligned nu-metal genre often had songs with lyrics about negative personal experiences and emotions; for example, Korn's frontman Jonathan Davis frequently sang about his own childhood sexual abuse and his subsequent pain and social maladjustment. While many critics have described the music of Korn and other nu-metal bands as whiny and self-involved, fans often describe it as providing a healthy way to work through personal trauma. One student I had told me that he liked listening to the band Slipknot because it felt almost like he was the one screaming when the lead singer screamed, giving him an outlet to work through his feelings about having an alcoholic parent. Similarly, many fans across the decades have testified that their own lives have been saved by Metallica's ballads "Fade to Black," "One," and "Welcome Home (Sanitarium)," which dwell on experiences of loss, isolation, depression, anguish, and helplessness. Listener collapse can create a blurring of the boundaries between listener and singer, a chance for listeners to experience the singer's expressions of sorrow and therapeutic explorations of trauma as their own catharsis.

The Negative Side: Loudness as Violence

Loudness and listener collapse can be much more negative experiences if they are inflicted on listeners as a form of violence. At extreme volumes, sound crosses the "threshold of pain," beyond which sound becomes "an experience of direct physical touch, force, or torment" (Heller 2015, 42). Metal and other loud music has even been used in US military psychological torture (or, in the words of the Bush administration, "enhanced interrogation") programs (Daughtry 2014; Cusick 2006). J. Martin Daughtry proposes a conceptual framework he calls "thanatosonics" to explain how wartime sounds have the power to cause intense trauma in the mind and body. Daughtry's account of these catastrophic effects closely parallels Eric Heller's account of listener collapse: both are founded in the same properties of loud sounds, which occupy space, penetrate the body, and overwhelm conscious rationalization. In extreme volumes, sound damages hearing and can lead to tinnitus and other neurological conditions. Daughtry summarizes these properties as "the similar way that sound and violence move through the world" (2014, 27). Listener collapse, when violently forced upon a listener, can become a terrifying, destructive force, capable of violating the body's boundaries and shattering its autonomy, even when it does not cause physical harm.

Metal culture has a complex, ambivalent relationship with the malignant side of loudness. On one hand, every fan I've ever talked to about the subject disapproves of the use of their music for military torture. But on the other hand, fans sometimes joke about forcing their music on others, such as the novelty T-shirt that says, "My neighbors listen to Motörhead ... whether they like it or not." Similarly, many rock and metal news sites gleefully shared a 2013 story about an elderly couple in Sweden who were facing harassment charges after they blasted Iron Maiden all night for weeks on end to get revenge on their neighbors. These jokes reflect fantasies of oppositional confrontation between fans and non-fans that run deep in the metal genre, fantasies which are sometimes acted out in music videos depicting non-fans being forced to listen to metal music with apparent displeasure, including Ghost's "Cirice," Lamb of God's "Redneck," and others.

Scholarship on music and violence has often focused on the use of music for violent ends, but I argue that in metal, these similarities work in the opposite direction as well: simulated violence is used for musical ends, to create additional heaviness. In addition to describing the blunt trauma caused by the loudness of wartime sounds, Daughtry identifies a more insidious harm that occurs when wartime sounds "ventriloquize civilian sounds, taking advantage of their similarity to the sounds of violence itself" (2014, 44). Wartime sounds directly represent instruments of violence and the mortal danger they create. Civilian sounds which happen to resemble wartime sounds (like loud bangs, engines, sirens, nail guns, and more) activate wartime associations. This "auditory haunting" (2014, 28) can trigger memories of violence to bubble up unbidden in a listener's mind, causing distress and disruption in everyday life, when no violence is occurring. It is a "ventriloquizing" because the civilian sounds inflict violence's force at a (temporal) distance from violence's original destructive impact. Daughtry's description provides a compelling account of metal: metal is a civilian sound that—aided by metaphorical listening—fosters the impression that violence is acting through it, by taking advantage of the similarities between the sounds of violence and the sounds of distorted guitars, pummeled drums, and screamed vocals.[6] Metal

---

[6] Production practices in metal amplify this impression of violence or threat, as argued by Jan-Peter Herbst and Mark Mynett:

  guitars and drum cymbals are usually panned wide in a metal mix, and sometimes psycho-acoustic measures are applied to make the sound appear even wider than the stereo field naturally allows. Such widening not only creates the impression of greater size but also heightens

co-opts the sounds of violence and trauma, appropriating the power of violence to create experiences of heaviness.

The use of violent imagery to create experiences of threat and horror is common in all styles of metal, and even further into the genre's prehistory. Black Sabbath declared that they wanted to make music that scared people, and metal bands have followed their lead ever since. Imagery of violence has been widespread in the genre throughout its history, ranging from Sabaton's historical accounts of bloody military battles, through Metallica's bleak depictions of electrocution and nuclear apocalypse and Mercyful Fate's disturbing tales of demonic rites, to Cannibal Corpse's stomach-churning collages of decontextualized gore. And violence does not remain in the text but is also performed with varying degrees of reality: GWAR fans lining up to be "eaten" on stage, Turisas singing about real historical Vikings while dressed in armor and covered in fake blood, or depraved murders and arson perpetrated by members of the pioneering Norwegian black metal band Mayhem. A metal band's performances of violence are often key elements in the band's mythology. Any metal fan could probably easily list a dozen more examples of real or simulated violence inflicted by famous metal artists.

Violence isn't just something musicians invoke; fans and critics also draw on violent descriptors in their listening and discussion. The metaphor of the buzzsaw tone in Swedish death metal appropriates the power of violence to produce heaviness in music, and many of the other cognitive metaphors for timbre I discussed earlier also have violent or destructive connotations. For example, Olivia Lucas uses terms of violence to describe a performance by the band SunnO))): "they scream, wail, growl, rumble, batter, assault, roar and, occasionally, sing" (Lucas 2014). Rosemary Overell reports that in the Melbourne grindcore scene, good bands are "brutal" and "killed" in their performances (Overell 2012, 202). These descriptions are by no means exceptional but illustrate a common tendency among fans and critics of all metal subgenres to use language saturated with bellicose overtones.

The most generous reading of this symbiosis of music and violence is a sympathetic one: metal creates a space in which threats and traumas are invoked and summarily dispelled, to help participants deal with their own horrific memories and fears. And plenty of metal fans report that metal music fulfills this need for them—both in songs which mention traumas directly, and in

proximity to the listener. […] Such enhanced width and proximity add to aggression and contribute to heaviness because of the threatening nature of a close sound. (Herbst and Mynett 2022, 6)

songs which activate them indirectly through references to struggle, darkness, depression, or hate. But a more cynical reading is that metal appropriates representations of violence as a vocabulary of power deployed to inflate its own grandiosity and impact—which arguably is neither respectful nor considerate of real victims of violence. In both readings, violence is entangled with metal's broader constructions of transgression, authenticity, and seriousness that shape the genre's power, status, and fan appeal.

Loudness as a Mechanism for Toxic Masculinity and Far-Right Politics

Some stances toward heaviness involve a problematic type of toxic masculinity. Zachary Wallmark sees death metal sound as the opposite of listener collapse, instead describing it as an onslaught listeners must endure to exert their control. Wallmark describes death metal timbres as creating a "trick" or a "simulation" of violence, an explanation that runs in parallel to my description of metal's ventriloquizing of violence above.

> We are "tricked" into hearing the high-tension timbres of the guitar and the voice as instantiations of actual physical danger, when in fact they are carefully controlled and regulated. This element of simulation is crucial to the symbolic function of timbre in the socio-ritual space of the music; indeed, these timbres are able to radically tear the listener out of "music-listening" mode, forcing him or her to actually feel the horror. (Wallmark 2018, 75)

Wallmark describes audience members being coerced or tricked into believing in the evilness or threat of death metal timbres, but his quotation marks around words like "trick" seem to suggest that, in fact, nobody is actually deceived. Wallmark claims that the most extreme, bleeding-edge death metal timbres are necessary to "force" this trick, but from my perspective, the "trick" is no trick, and requires no such force; listeners are able to hear metal timbres as a simulation of violence throughout the metal genre, including in older or more mainstream metal, through the power of imagined loudness. (I discuss these issues of illusion and agency more in Chapter 2.)

This also invokes a dynamic similar to the first phase of Heller's "listener collapse," but one that involves fighting against (and, ultimately, overcoming) the dissolving of self; domination of the threat instead of submission. As he puts it, "only the strong can withstand the ugliness and brutality of this *sui generis* timbre" (Wallmark 2018, 72). Wallmark then constructs an elaborate reading of death metal as a ritual of symbolic sonic violence, in which listeners perform their mastery and control in spite of the sounds' "threat," drawing terms from the French philosopher and cultural critic René Girard.

> Violence is extracted (in the form of loudness, timbral brutality, and moderated physical aggression), accumulated (around the ugly, noisy object of sacrificial focus), then purged (controlled or sacrificed). A successful ritual-concert, like an efficacious sacrifice, curbs and rechannels individuals' violent energies into a feeling of physical energy, ecstasy, and release. (Wallmark 2018, 81)

Wallmark's metaphoric reading of death metal as a ritual assumes that listeners take this particular stance toward heaviness. But this doesn't represent my personal experience with metal music; and in fact, I'm troubled by how comfortably Wallmark's language resonates with macho attitudes lurking in some corners of the metal scene that tolerate or embrace hyperaggression and misogynistic exclusion. (For example, Rosemary Overell has documented misogynistic rhetoric and representation in Australian grindcore, although she also argues that some of it is "undermined and ironized in various ways" [Overell 2012, 198].) Wallmark's warrior stance toward heaviness, through which a listener proves their strength by withstanding heaviness, is certainly a noticeable presence in metal culture, but it's only one stance a listener can take, and a relatively problematic one.

Another stance within the phenomenon of "listener collapse" can have even more sinister sociopolitical outcomes. In a recent conference paper, Jillian Fischer argued that heaviness and loudness played a unique role in so-called national socialist black metal, a small fringe of bands in the black metal scene who openly advocate for white-supremacist, far-right cultural and political values. According to Fischer, the overwhelming loudness and harsh timbres of black metal might allow "bands working within neo-Nazi ideological frameworks to manipulate this affective charge to push listeners towards political extremes" (Fischer 2021). Listeners interested in exploring politically transgressive ideas and imagery might have their critical reactions slowed or numbed by the effect of listener collapse, so that the musicians' far-right positions and iconography could become habituated or normalized to listeners who otherwise might have rejected them outright.[7]

---

[7] Compare with the discussion of "reflexive anti-reflexivity" by Keith Kahn-Harris (2007, 145).

Conclusion

This brief survey of some of the stances one could take toward heaviness shows how heaviness is not only a sound quality in the music, but also a subjective experience listeners help create. Two recent articles (Miller 2022; Herbst and Mynett 2022) have made similar arguments to my claim that there are multiple kinds of heaviness with contradictory sound qualities, but their explanations of heaviness locate it primarily within the music. Jason Miller (2022, 71) claims quite directly that there are multiple types of heaviness, that "part of what makes the term 'heavy' conceptually inarticulable, if not irreducible, has to do with the radically different, sometimes incompatible, musical properties present in perceptions of musical heaviness." Jan-Peter Herbst and Mark Mynett (2022) make essentially the same argument but are even more explicit in prioritizing properties of sound over social and metaphorical ("associative") dimensions.

> This article, therefore, aims to elaborate a framework of *musical* heaviness in the metal genre by identifying its constituent components and their relationships. Sociological, emotional, and associative components … are secondary. Extramusical factors … are disregarded, as is the low-fidelity aesthetic characteristic of some styles of black metal, which according to Ian Reyes (*Sound*, "Blacker") and [Ross] Hagen is characterized by a different form of heaviness. (Herbst and Mynett 2023b, 17; citing Reyes 2013 and Hagen 2011)

In both articles, heaviness is ultimately located in the music; the reason why a song is heavy is explained by pointing to details within the song, including dimensions of timbre, lyrics, rhythm, and mixing.

But this previous scholarship doesn't sufficiently explore the subjectivity of heaviness—the agency fans have to shape their own experience through stances, metaphoric listening, headbanging, and other listening practices. Miller (2022) and Herbst and Mynett (2023b) each start leaning in this direction by showing that heaviness can be subjective, evaluated differently by different listeners. Herbst and Mynett gesture even closer toward my position in their comment on Calder Hannan, who describes an analogical transfer from HEAVINESS to complex rhythms—specifically, rhythms that are hard to understand or imitate.[8] Hannan argues that in rhythmically difficult metal

---

[8] Hannan (2022) develops his theory of the effects of difficulty and complexity further in his article about "structural density and clarity" in technical death metal.

music, such as songs by Meshuggah or Dillinger Escape Plan, "it is easy to get lost in the middle of a song section" (Hannan 2018, 445).

> The song section metaphorically becomes "bigger," bigger than the listener's ability to keep track of it.... Its unusual shapes draw attention to themselves and feel unwieldy, harder to understand, larger, and ultimately metaphorically heavier; just as low, slow attacks parallel the acoustic properties of large, heavy physical objects. (Hannan 2018, 445)

Hannan further argues that "by innovating in their use of rhythm, bands claim transgressive subcultural capital and their music becomes serious and therefore heavy" (Hannan 2018, 455). In short, Hannan invokes cognitive metaphors of size, difficulty, and transgression in addition to the metaphors for timbre and speed that I've discussed. Herbst and Mynett admit that "Hannan's considerations suggest that perception of heaviness is partly associative and that associations can be influenced by musical structures, performance qualities, and the listener's ability to appreciate these" (Herbst and Mynett 2023b, 28), but I would go further. Cognitive metaphor theory indicates that heaviness is *fundamentally* associative (i.e., metaphorical, involving analogical transfer), not just "partly," and that listeners' abilities and appreciation are foundational components of heaviness, not just layers of subjective influence. As I hope to show throughout this book, heaviness is a physical experience of impact that listeners help create by drawing on or enacting cognitive metaphors, dance practices such as headbanging (Hudson 2022a), aesthetic ideologies, genre and subgenre judgements and distinctions, and other behaviors and ways of thinking.

2

Power Chords and the Basic Illusion of Heaviness

Hearing Something More Powerful Than Reality

Power chords might be the most ubiquitous musical structure in metal and are the keystone in metal's sonic manifestations of heaviness. A power chord usually consists of two notes forming an interval of a perfect fifth (or more rarely, a perfect fourth), but in more recent years, guitarists sometimes add additional octaves of one or both of these notes. For example, an E power chord is usually played with an open E string (the sixth and lowest string on a guitar in standard tuning) and a second-fret B on the next string up (Figure 2.1a), but one can also add a second-fret E on the fourth-highest string (Figure 2.1b) or even a fourth-fret B on the third-highest string (Figure 2.1c), and an uncommon variant omits the lowest note (Figure 2.1d). The power chord, especially when played on a guitar with distortion, has a big, heavy, powerful sound, which can also be intense, grating, or guttural depending on the techniques or processing effects used. Through the kind of metaphorical cognition explored in the previous chapter, with the right rhythm this sound can be heard and experienced as a roaring motorcycle engine (Steppenwolf's "heavy metal thunder"), a terrific buzzsaw rending through flesh and bone, a sonic manifestation of crackling electricity or magical power, or the thundering gallop of a horse carrying a warrior or demigod.

But in addition to these metaphorical aspects of our experience, power chords also create an acoustic special effect of weight and lowness, and their loudness and power are tangible and measurable. In other words, the heavy physical impact of power chords is partly real and partly imagined. One of these parts isn't prior to the other; in Deena Weinstein's evocative description of the multisensory nature of a heavy metal concert, "one source [of excitement] will reinforce and heighten others, ideally producing an upward spiral" in which several experiential components combine to create a "mutually reinforcing impact" (1991, 214). This chapter draws on basic acoustics, studies of timbre perception, and horror theory, to show how a combination

Heaviness in Metal Music. Stephen S. Hudson, Oxford University Press. © Oxford University Press 2026.
DOI: 10.1093/9780197774991.003.0004

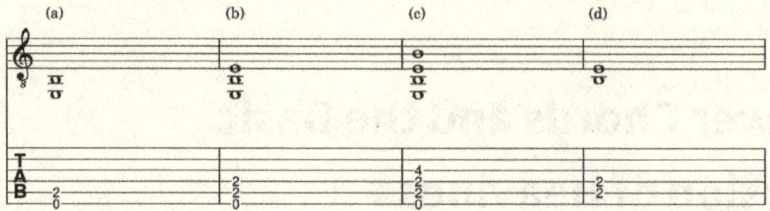

Figure 2.1 Various E power chords, in staff notation and guitar tablature.

of real, material power and imagined power (which in many cases are not easily separated) creates what I call the "basic illusion of heaviness"—an illusion which is powerful when it works and ridiculous when it fails.

Perceptualization

Power chords and heaviness are not unique in the broader world of sound cognition; most human sound perception involves some degree of imaginative (re)construction by the listener. In her study of timbre, Cornelia Fales (2002) explores how sound perception is subjective, meaning that different ways of listening can draw out different features from the same sound, sometimes even leading to substantial differences in what a listener recognizes as the sound's source, substance, or meaning (one instrument instead of two, a single note instead of a full chord, a bird song instead of a piano, etc.). She calls this phenomenon "perceptualization."

> At an extreme, the effects of perceptualization may be created almost entirely from the cognitive substance of listeners' minds—that is, from pre-existing information or structures in the perceived world—but they must implicate the acoustic world to some degree at least—else auditory perception becomes auditory hallucination. (Fales 2002, 65)

Fales mostly discusses literal identification of sounds, but more metaphorical listening is also a type of perceptualization: a lot of the heaviness that metal listeners experience is a perceptualization effect, an imagined impact that adds to or amplifies the actual physical impact that the music has on their bodies. But like all perceptualizations, heaviness is not just a hallucination; it is grounded in culture and our previous experiences, and it is triggered and shaped by the sound itself. In other words, heavy metal's metaphors and ways of thinking can't be arbitrarily applied to just any kind of music;

fans' perceptions of heaviness are activated by the sounds and social context of metal.

You can see the transformative power of perceptualization in different experiences of power chords, which are often heard as notes other than the ones played. Power chords sound loud and bold on acoustic instruments, but when played through distortion, power chords sound even bigger through a sonic effect called "resultant tones." Robert Walser describes how individual notes played in combination can generate resultant tones which are lower than the actual notes played.

> The strongest resultant tone is produced at the frequency that is the difference between the frequencies of the main tones. If, for example, the open A string on the guitar (which vibrates at a frequency of 110 cycles per second, or 110 Hz) and the E above it (165 Hz) are played as a power chord, then the A an octave lower (165 - 110 = 55 Hz) will sound very prominently as a resultant tone [See Figure 2.2]. If the A is played with a fourth above instead of a fifth, D (147 Hz), the D two octaves lower (37 Hz) will be produced. These resultant tones are often at frequencies lower than the instrument itself can normally produce; both of these examples result in the production of pitches far below the actual range of the guitar. (Walser 2014 [1993], 43)

By playing two higher notes that fit into a particular harmonic series, the musician generates an acoustic illusion in which the fundamental tone of that series seems audible even though it is not being played. Such effects have been known for centuries to advanced violin players (who call them "Tartini tones" after Giuseppe Tartini, composer of the fiendishly difficult *Devil's Trill Sonata*). The music theorist Esa Lilja has demonstrated that guitar distortion manifests this illusory resultant tone into material, measurable sound spectra (Lilja 2009). This low resultant tone is often doubled by the bass guitar's actual notes but is clearly audible in the guitar's sound alone. The many notes and harmonics actually being played tend to merge into a single gestalt in human perception, so that what most listeners hear is only the lowest resultant tone

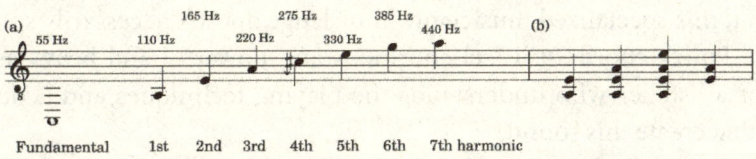

Figure 2.2 (a) The series of harmonics over low A = 55 Hz; (b) Open-A (110 Hz) power chords, which each approximate the harmonic series of low A.

as a fundamental tone, with the other notes being played functioning as harmonics above that fundamental.

You don't need to understand the sound physics to understand the key point: although there are a variety of ways to voice a power chord, it usually sounds like a single note instead of a collection of several distinct pitches. Power chords are often used in parallel, so even when the individual notes that make up a single power chord can be distinguished by ear, a series of power chords creates the effect of a single melodic line rather than a counterpoint of independently moving voices. Additionally, the effects of distortion cause the notes of the chord to merge into a single perceived pitch, so that they "blur the traditional distinction between harmony and melody" (Pillsbury 2006, 210n50). In this sense, power chords aren't really chords: instead, what most listeners perceive is more like one enormous composite sound, one single note that seems impossibly powerful and low—in other words, impossibly heavy.

At a larger level of scale, the rhythm guitars and bass in metal often merge together to act as a single "meta-instrument" (Mynett 2017, 145–46). In the studio, the band might record four or eight guitar parts, and two or more bass parts, and through various production techniques these tracks can be carefully mixed together to create the impression of a single impossibly large and loud instrument, rather than several separate takes. Herbst and Mynett (2025) describe many of these techniques and argue that they are especially characteristic of more recent generations of metal producers.

But some listeners can distinguish the separate notes of the power chord, and some listeners can hear the multiple takes that are laminated together to create most modern recordings. Skilled players familiar with the sound of the guitar strings and the effects of distortion can distinguish the specific notes, instruments, and playing techniques that comprise a power chord in a given recording, even under chaotic conditions with fast note changes and high amounts of distortion. This difference in hearing is not just a matter of choice or awareness; merely knowing about the existence of power chords didn't help me identify them reliably under high distortion levels. I often have to try to play a power chord riff myself before I am able to hear the fifth clearly and to distinguish the sound of the bass guitar from the rhythm guitar tone. However, this specialized musicianly knowledge doesn't necessarily spoil the illusion. Power chords still feel enormous and powerful and heavy as hell, even for a listener who understands the playing techniques and acoustical effects that create this sound.

The magic trick of perceptualization isn't unique to music, but music seems to be especially good at creating such tricks. Or maybe it would be more accurate to put it this way: when we are listening to music, we are more willing to play along than we are in other domains of listening, more willing to hear a sound as if it were something other than what it objectively is. Fales suggests that two elements are necessary to create this "disruption" of objective listening, "the skill of the musician and the willingness of listeners" (Fales 2002, 65). Fales is talking about fairly literal sound illusions—like a cello imitating a singer's voice, a songbird's call, or a harp arpeggio—but I think heaviness works in the same way: the impact of heaviness depends on both the performers' impressive presentation and a kind of willingness or eagerness from the listeners.

Like all perceptualizations, heaviness is somewhere between structure and subjectivity. It's something that is construed in the mind of a listener, but it's not just an "auditory hallucination." We have some agency over heaviness, and not everyone experiences it in the same way. But the kind of agency we have may only allow us to craft a listening practice over time rather than change our in-the-moment experiences on a whim. Heaviness is something listeners create in their own minds, but how we perceive heaviness is often a subconscious act rather than a conscious choice.

Loudness, Real and Imagined

Our sense of loudness indexes a large proportion of heaviness's concrete and metaphorical effects. Loudness in the most objective sense is the decibel level of a sound, the amount of energy or power in the pressure wave that physically constitutes a sound. But loudness is also a subjective impression shaped by our understanding and imagination of what we think the sounds represent; acoustic instruments and whispering often seem quieter than electric guitar and shouted vocals, even when they are amplified to the same decibel levels. In live concerts, metal is played at extreme volumes that penetrate the skull, jostle the body, and shake the floor. This literal loudness becomes a kind of sense memory associated with all things metal, leading to more metaphorical senses that Michael C. Heller calls "imagined loudness" (2015, 46).

Heller is not the first scholar to suggest that metal's loudness is partly imagined. He quotes Walser, who wrote two decades earlier that

the nature of metal and the needs and pleasures it addresses demand that it always be heard loud. Even when it is heard from a distance, or even softly sung to oneself, metal is imagined as loud, for volume is an important contributor to the heaviness of heavy metal. Robert Duncan writes of the "loudestness" of heavy

metal, its perceived status as the most sonically powerful of musical discourses.
(Walser 2014 [1993], 45)

Even when metal is played at a quiet volume, it can still have the power and
physical impact of loudness if we imagine it to be loud—if we imagine it to be
a quiet version of something that is actually loud, or imagine that it represents
loudness, even when it is literally quiet. In short, metal fans can *imagine loudness into metal*. And this imagined loudness can be just as consequential as
actual loudness in creating experiences of heaviness.

But imagined loudness is not entirely imagined—instead, imagined loudness is usually grounded in (or triggered by) metal's timbres and performance
techniques, which clearly *represent* or *signify* loudness even when played at
quieter volumes. The first distorted timbres in recorded music were accidents,
occurring when a sound signal overrode the capacity of an electrical channel,
which resulted in cutoff of the peaks in a signal that transformed the sound's
timbre. Walser makes an analogy between this electronic distortion and
more organic distorted vocal sounds like screams and growls common in
metal music.

> Not only electronic circuitry, but also the human body produces aural distortion
> through excessive power. Human screams and shouts are usually accompanied
> by vocal distortion, as the capacities of the vocal cords are exceeded. Thus, distor-
> tion functions as a sign of extreme power and intense expression by overflowing
> its channels and materializing the exceptional effort that produces it. (Walser 2014
> [1993], 42)

This insight has been measured empirically by the music psychologist Chen-
Gia Tsai, who found correlations between the perception and production of
growl-like timbres and the activation of deep abdominal muscles involved in
fight-or-flight responses (Tsai et al., 2010). Heller argues that through such
associations between sound and physical sensations, "distorted timbres can
arouse a perceptual impression of loudness even when reproduced at softer
levels, evoking the haptic memory of [overwhelming loudness]" (Heller 2015,
47). Even when the loudness evoked by distortion is imagined or metaphorical rather than literal, it can still have an enormous, visceral—in other words,
heavy—physical impact.

While metal's loudness can be amplified by imagination, it is also often a
tangible objective fact: at high enough volume it has concrete, physical power
and consequences. The louder sound is, the more we experience it as a physical force rather than a heard pitch, as a vibration within the body rather than

a sound in the air outside the body. Loud sound blocks rational thought and blurs one's ability to distinguish their own body and perspective from the sounding environment around them. Heller describes how these direct effects of loudness reduce a sound's capacity to carry symbolic or representational meaning, preventing contemplative and analytical listening and turning that sound into a physical force we can only react to on a more automatic level (Heller 2015, 43–45). In a very literal sense, loud sound exerts power over listeners, acting as a heavy blanket that fills their senses and weighs down conscious thought.

Buying In: Heaviness and Stephen King's Suspension of Disbelief

Metal's heaviness, then—its impact on listeners—is usually a combination of varying degrees of material power (loudness, physical impacts) and imagined power (imagined loudness, imagined impacts). But where does imagined power come from, and how does it work? What are the conditions under which the illusion of heaviness succeeds, and when does it fail? Heller poses similar questions about imagined loudness.

> Is it a desire? An association? A delusion? A projection? Though it cannot be described as physical, its phenomenological potency is sufficient to satisfy a metal fan's aesthetic requirement for loud experience (and, perhaps, listener collapse), even at moments where further amplification would be impractical. (Heller 2015, 47)

Imagined loudness is only one dimension or component of heaviness, but the same ontological questions apply. Heaviness is something more creative than a mere association, but more tightly bound to reality than a delusion or hallucination. The threat of violence and transgression is tied into the power of metal music, and part of the music's effectiveness lies in a kind of belief in the power of this threat, even when we know that this threat is not material. This is not just true for metal's fans; sometimes the most prominent critics of the genre, especially those associated with the satanic panic of the 1980s, seem to believe that the genre has real power to seduce and harm young people.[1] I call this willingness to believe "buying in."

---

[1] For more on the heavy metal moral panics of the 1980s, and specifically the Parents Music Resource Center's criticism of heavy metal music, see Walser (2014 [1993], chapter 5), Weinstein (2000 [1991], chapter 7), and Hill and Savigny (2019).

The proof that listeners have to "buy in" at some level to experience heaviness is everywhere in metal music, but it's especially clear in moments when some listeners think a particular strain of music is awesomely heavy while others can't take it seriously.[2] Harris M. Berger observes a divergence of this kind between death metal and power metal fans: death metal fans "interpret death metal as the cutting edge of heaviness. On the contrary, many power metal devotees find death metal to be unpleasant nonsense rather than incarnate heaviness" (1999, 61). These power metal fans clearly are enthusiastic about the heaviness of metal music, and Berger even points out in a later article that virtually all metal fans (including power metal devotees) will agree that death metal is objectively "heavier" than earlier styles.[3] And yet, death metal apparently sounds like just "unpleasant nonsense" to them.

This is more than just partisan hostility between genres described in hyperbolic language. I've had similar listening experiences, and I suspect most other metal fans have too. Sometimes a song has plenty of cues for heaviness but doesn't grip me, doesn't produce the thrilling experience of weight and impact. Simply put, death metal does nothing for Berger's power metal fans; in their experience, death metal has none of that captivating power of heaviness that makes it so appealing to death metal fans. How could this be the case if everyone agrees that death metal is objectively heavier? It's because death metal fans have bought in to death metal in a way that power metal fans haven't: death metal fans have become habituated to listening to this music as a weighty, threatening, and serious matter—but if you're not a death metal fan, death metal is none of these things; it's just a needlessly intense style that doesn't hold your attention.

Another example showing the impact of "buying in" on our experiences of heaviness is a review of the notoriously over-the-top power metal band Manowar, printed in 1999 in the extreme metal and hardcore punk magazine *Terrorizer*. "Manowar is more than just a band. It's a need, a calling, a way of life ... a fucking *legend*. Some people don't understand this. They

---

[2] Jason Miller describes the common example of lyrics interfering with some listeners' experience of heaviness:

> A peculiarity of heavy metal music is that the intention to express heaviness through lyrical seriousness all too frequently fails. And when it does fail, the effect is not neutral. Lyrics are a wager on heaviness: if won, they advance the aim of the music; when lost, they set the music behind. This phenomenon—call it the "Spinal Tap effect"—happens when the seriousness of lyrical content gets expressed in particularly corny or cliched lyrics that in turn end up diminishing rather than contributing to the perception of heaviness in music. Different listeners will of course have different tolerance thresholds, but the Spinal Tap effect is familiar to metalheads: the audible experience of heaviness ruined by bad lyrics. (2022, 78)

[3] "It is worth noting that while lite metal adherents are generally uninterested in underground metal and its pursuit of heavier tones, almost all would agree that underground guitar timbres have gotten heavier over time" (Berger and Fales 2005, 187).

look at the furry loincloths, the leather waistcoats and the swords, and they laugh. But to mock is to miss the point completely" (Greg Whalen, quoted in Kahn-Harris 2006, 151, ellipsis in original). The reviewer doesn't deny that Manowar is mockable; but "to mock is to miss the point." The message is that even someone who is aware that Manowar's costume is preposterous can still take the band seriously at some level—and by taking the band seriously, one can have an impactful experience of power (falling within my definition heaviness), which is presumably what makes the band "a legend."

Of course, this quote also seems to be half-kidding, which is a paradox that is especially common in extreme metal music: the insistence on seriousness despite ridiculous details, even while treating this seriousness itself partially as a joke. Keith Kahn-Harris describes a similar concept, "reflexive anti-reflexivity":

> In the heavy metal scene, there is a strong tendency to ignore troubling or contradictory information using techniques that, while they seem may guileless and even stupid to those outside the scene, actually demonstrate a kind of reflexivity in choosing "what not to know." (Kahn-Harris 2016, 31)

Kahn-Harris illustrates this concept with a discussion of a picture of the Norwegian black metal band Immortal, a picture that is campy and cheesy and yet still "extreme" (2007, 146–47). He frames this dynamic as a matter of social and political knowledge: choosing to ignore a band's politically problematic statements or regrettable imagery, in order to enjoy their transgressive show.

But while Kahn-Harris's "reflexive anti-reflexivity" seems to describe a negative sense of "deciding not to know," heaviness sometimes seems to require an active buying in, a willingness to believe (or at least, to experience the music as if you did). Stephen King's description of the "suspension of disbelief" necessary to enjoy horror stories and films might be a better fit—especially since so much metal music is inspired by, and explicitly uses, imagery from the horror genre. King relates his first time watching *Creature from the Black Lagoon* (1954):

> I knew, watching, that the Creature had become my Creature; I had bought it. Even to a seven-year-old, it was not a terribly convincing Creature. I did not know then it was good old Ricou Browning, the famed underwater stuntman, in a molded latex suit, but I surely knew it was some guy in some kind of a monster suit....
>
> My reaction to the Creature on that night was perhaps the perfect reaction, the one every writer of horror fiction or director who has worked in the field hopes for

when he or she uncaps a pen or a lens: total emotional involvement, pretty much undiluted by any real thinking process—and you understand, don't you, that when it comes to horror movies, the only thought process really necessary to break the mood is for a friend to lean over and whisper, "See the zipper running down his back?" (King 2010, 103–4)

The suspension of disbelief that King describes involves knowing that an illusion is occurring, but choosing to experience horror as if the illusion were real. King argues that "it takes a sophisticated and muscular intellectual act to believe, even for a little while" in these monsters (King 2010, 104). Similarly, we might all know that the band members of Manowar are objectively silly, wearing anachronistic, fantastical outfits that are as unsuited to any real historical period as they are to the needs of present-day industrialized society; according to Kahn-Harris's concept of "reflexive anti-reflexivity," we might choose to ignore that fact and listen to them as a regular bar band. But to fully appreciate Manowar, to fully activate the illusion of heaviness, fans have to do something more: invest their imagination and intellectual energy to hear the music as if the band members symbolized or actually were powerful, legendary warriors.

This knowing-but-not-knowing involves a delicate balance. Mentioning the zipper running down the monster's back could break the illusion, but this is not because the audience believes the illusion is real; even seven-year-old Stephen King knew that the monster was an actor in a suit. Just like knowing how a power chord is played doesn't ruin the experience of heaviness, knowing that a monster is just an actor doesn't ruin the experience of horror. Instead, the reason the illusion might be dispelled is that mentioning the zipper could make you more aware of your suspension of disbelief, bring your attention to the fact that you do actually know an illusion is occurring, and highlight the artifice of your own buying in. Similarly, in metal music, what breaks the illusion of heaviness is not mere awareness of the fact that the musicians on stage are not actually demons or wizards or Viking warriors; everyone in the audience already knows this. What breaks the illusion of heaviness is aesthetic distaste, a revulsion that brings attention to the fickleness of our own participation.

This means that heaviness isn't just an illusion, it's also a fantasy, an *eagerness to be affected*. Power metal fans yearn to experience maximum heaviness from their favorite subgenre, power metal, but are just not that eager to be affected by death metal. Metal music is not really "tricking" the audience—that implies an illusion in which the audience is fooled. Metal audiences clearly recognize that the musicians are normal human beings playing mundane instruments, yet they often choose to experience the music *as if* it were scary, threatening, demonic, and so forth, in order to create heightened experiences of heaviness. This fantasy might be facilitated by the taboo topics, the loudness of the music, the legends or myths about the transgressive acts of the musicians and the scene—but the audience still has to "buy in," they have to accept the illusion's premises and suspend their disbelief in order to experience its effects.

This line of argument only applies to the imagined components of heaviness, though; one can still experience a band's actual loudness, pounding rhythm, and technical prowess as heavy without an act of suspending disbelief. (Although the metaphorical cognition of hearing sound as "heavy" seems to still involve hearing the sound as something more than it literally is.) But suspension of disbelief seems necessary to account for many metal fans' hyperbolic metaphorical language and extreme enthusiasm for bands that are, relative to the rest of the pop music industry, outlandishly dressed, peddling unreal fantasies, and barely sustaining a career.

The "zipper effect," or aesthetic distaste that calls of attention to the illusion's unreality, isn't the only way to ruin the basic illusion of heaviness. Another is if the danger or power of heaviness is *too* real. Winfried Menninghaus et al. (2017) have proposed an "art schema" by which we create psychological distance between ourselves and shocking or negative imagery, a mental schema which allows us to enjoy danger depicted in art without feeling like we are under a real threat. Framed in Berger's terms, this art schema would constitute part of our stance toward metal music, a fundamental precondition of our aesthetic or "valual" relationship with the music.

But some conditions can make this art schema difficult to maintain. In a review article which dissects Menninghaus's concept, Matthew Strohl proposes that there are "dealbreakers" which are each "an experiential element which is sufficient to render an experience overall aversive" (Strohl 2019, 3). For example, according to Strohl, "believing that one might actually die is usually a dealbreaker" (Strohl 2019, 3). The positive experience of heaviness in metal requires a sense of danger without dealbreakers.

This is one more flaw in the metaphor of heaviness as an illusion or simulation of danger: if the illusion is too real, it no longer creates a pleasurable aesthetic experience. This is the opposite of "tricking" the audience; if they really are fooled, if they believe the danger is real, then the illusion is too strong, and heaviness (the weighty impact of the music) becomes a negative or oppressive experience. I've only had this experience a handful of times, when I believed someone was actually harmed during a song's production, or when I believed the singer was genuinely advocating hate or violence.[4] That's a dealbreaker for me, and I stop buying in; the music no longer even feels like metal anymore— it loses the thrill of heaviness and becomes just a form of sickening violence.

Conclusion: Agency and Choice in Perceiving Heaviness

King's "suspension of disbelief" metaphor might be a better explanation than Kahn-Harris's "reflexive anti-reflexivity" or "deciding not to know," but I would argue that there is one detail of heaviness in metal that still works differently: agency and choice. King describes the suspension of disbelief as an action requiring effort: "Disbelief is not like a balloon, which may be suspended in air with a minimum of effort; it is like a lead weight, which has to be hoisted with a clean and a jerk and held up by main force" (2010, 104). His weightlifting metaphor seems to imply that audiences are making a conscious action, choosing to suspend disbelief. Similarly, Kahn-Harris describes "*choosing* what not to know." But the illusion of heaviness in metal is often a subconscious stance rather than a deliberate decision: heaviness can capture and entrance you, whether or not you've decided to experience it.

This is not true just of heaviness (which has been described as simulation of violence), but it is true of the sounds of violence, too; listeners have limited agency over sounds of violence. J. Martin Daughtry, in his study of wartime sounds, explains how listeners can have some very limited control over the impacts that sounds have upon them, but often only through preparation, not in the moment that the sound hits them.

> Our bodies are uniquely attuned to sounds; they are frequently driven by sounds into drastic states. Under normal circumstances, we listeners have access to a limited but significant amount of agency, however, and so we can train ourselves to react, or not react, to sounds in unique or culturally resonant ways. (Daughtry 2014, 32)

According to Daughtry, sounds have the power to compel us before our conscious self intervenes, but that doesn't mean sound entirely determines its own impact. We do have some agency to shape how sound affects us and to

---

[4] I once encountered a record by an underground metal band which claimed to have used recordings of patients in a mental asylum for their vocals. Given this understanding, I found the recording to be too sickening to enjoy as an aesthetic experience of heaviness. Ironically, I later discovered counter-allegations that the vocals were recorded by the band in their home studio. Whether the story is real or fake, I refuse to participate in this kind of exploitative notoriety by naming their project here.

shape how we respond. But as Daughtry describes, this agency manifests as training enacted over a long period of time, not as a free choice made in the moment of listening.

The kind of agency we have to shape our experience of wartime sounds is very different from the kind of agency we have when we view ambiguous (or "multistable") visual illusions like the Necker cube or the Rubin vase, in which one can switch perspectives at will to invert the image. Daughtry provides a concrete example of how training and imagination can shape the listening experience, through an analysis of some US Marines' encounter with a roadside explosion.

> Within this regime, exposure to the sensory evidence of violent acts presents service members with an opportunity to perform a kind of euphoric auditory hypermasculinity. Through a mixture of studied nonchalance, ... bravado, ... and expressions of imperturbability in the face of auditory trauma, ... the Marines seamlessly incorporated the explosion into their ongoing auto- (audio-) narratives of sangfroid and toughness. This experience obtains because the Marines have been trained to adopt this posture, because they have been equipped with headphones that mitigate the deleterious effects of loud sounds, and, importantly, because they reflect on the explosion from subject positions that are not fatally fractured. (Daughtry 2014, 36)

In Daughtry's example, it is only through well-established personal narratives of "sangfroid and toughness," cultivated through an institutional culture of obedience and endurance and reinforced by dependable protective equipment, that the Marines can experience violence as an exciting, euphoric sonic stimulus.

Trained or practiced listening shapes our experience of heaviness in a way that is analogous to the Marines' mental preparations for wartime sounds. Daughtry's "euphoric auditory hypermasculinity" resonates with Wallmark's account of death metal listening that I explored in Chapter 1; the Marines' "nonchalance," "bravado," and "imperturbability" remind me of Wallmark's arguments that death metal timbres "embody evil and chaos in order [for listeners] to demonstrate mastery over them" (Wallmark 2018, 66) and that "only the strong can withstand the ugliness and brutality" (Wallmark 2018, 72). As I argued in the previous chapter, this seems to me a limiting perspective on extreme metal, one which excludes a variety of other stances and experiences, including submission through listener collapse in its various forms, as well as more cooperative rather than combative types of empowerment. But Wallmark's account of death metal listening is a practiced form of listening, like the marines' listening practice that Daughtry described. It's a frame of perspective that involves long-term investment in a particular way of relating to and valuing the music. There are many kinds of stances one can take in listening to metal music, but many of these stances and listening experiences depend on factors beyond spur-of-the-moment choice: established listening practices, sedimented identities and cultural formations, and even equipment (a powerful PA system is required for a live metal show, and ear plugs are usually ubiquitous).

Personal listening history is one more component of listening stance which influences the illusion of heaviness, one more factor which lies outside our immediate control. Sheila Whitely reports that in the song "Purple Haze" by Jimi Hendrix, "sheer volume of noise works towards the drowning of personal consciousness" (Whitely 1992, 20). Theodore Gracyk criticizes Whitely's analysis, suggesting that any recording could be played loud enough to drown personal consciousness (Gracyk 1996, 100). Michael C. Heller responds, suggesting that Whitely's prior experiences listening to "Purple Haze" at high volume may have conditioned her to *always* associate it with experiences of listener collapse, highlighting how social context and training can impact one's propensity to imagine loudness.

> The conditioning process that links sounds with volumes is undoubtedly established through repeated exposure and learned expectations within a given culture.... Whitely's imagined loudness experience of "Purple Haze," for instance, might not resonate with a child of the 1990s whose musical upbringing affixed very different associations to the sound of Jimi Hendrix. For such a listener, the sound of Hendrix's guitar might evoke only the low-level playback of family car rides, not the overwhelming intensity of late 1960s rock bacchanalia. (Heller 2015, 47)

A major factor that is implicit in Heller's argument is a widely known tendency for the music of one's teenage years to play an outsized role in one's musical preferences and identity formation; Whitely would have been an impressionable teenager when "Purple Haze" came out, but for a "child of the 1990s," Jimi Hendrix would be dad rock. More generally, your ability or desire to buy into a metal song and experience heaviness is strongly shaped by your personal experiences with that song or songs like it—where you imagine this music to be played and heard, who you imagine listening to this music, and what you think of those people.[5]

---

[5] This factor of personal embodied listening history will be revisited in Chapter 9, which shows how metal music's conventions of song form create ritual spaces for reliving one's previous experiences of heaviness within the unfolding present of a song form.

3

Rock Is Dead, But Metal Will Live Forever

The Paradoxes of Metal's Progressionism

Whether Jimi Hendrix should be categorized as a heavy metal musician is one of the oldest debates in the genre, a paradoxical question which cuts to the heart of the genre's identity and ideology. In the 1970s and 1980s, his music was sometimes considered part of the genre. Robert Walser's field-defining book on heavy metal has an appendix featuring two "heavy metal canons" or best-albums lists, and Hendrix's album *Are You Experienced?* (1967) features in both: *Hit Parader*'s "Heavy Metal: The Hall of Fame" (1982) and "Top 100 Metal Albums" (1989).[1] Hendrix is often described as an architect of heavy metal lead guitar playing, having exaggerated and synthesized a variety of established and emerging guitar technologies and techniques—including fuzz distortion and wah pedals, deliberate use of feedback, new stylistic uses of whammy bar or tremolo bar, and Chuck-Berry-esque, rock'n'roll string-bending licks—into a new language that remains the basis for guitar soloing more than half a century later. A handful of his songs use the same musical building blocks that would come to define metal: the main riff to "Voodoo Child (slight return)," for example, features E power chords (the lowest open string on the guitar), and some of the lyrics anticipate power metal fantasies of later decades: "Well, I stand up next to a mountain / And I chop it down with the edge of my hand."

But when Hendrix's influence is discussed today, it's often with some distance to metal itself. Steve Waksman suggests that "heavy metal is understood as an extension of the music made by such performers as Cream, the Yardbirds, the Jimi Hendrix Experience" (2009, 150). Robert Walser argues that "Along with Jimi Hendrix, these British blues bands developed the sounds that would define metal: heavy drums and bass, virtuosic distorted guitar, and a powerful vocal style" (2014 [1993], 9). Ian Christe includes Hendrix in a list of "hard rock" bands who "contributed to the development of what would

---

[1] Alongside Hendrix's 1967 album, these two *Hit Parader* lists feature albums by several other artists who are usually located outside "metal" today, including Ted Nugent, Cream, and Grand Funk Railroad.

Heaviness in Metal Music. Stephen S. Hudson, Oxford University Press. © Oxford University Press 2026.
DOI: 10.1093/9780197774991.003.0005

later be considered heavy metal" (2003, 16). Hendrix played a pivotal role in the development of heavy metal, but since 1990 he has often been located outside of the genre.

Even if Hendrix is not part of heavy metal proper, he is part of an imaginary continuum of rock style which shapes how metal is understood. The existence of this imagined stylistic continuum ranging from "normal" rock to the most extreme metal is frequently invoked, alluded to, or implied by fans, critics, and outsiders alike. Those in the metal community often understand this "hard rock–heavy metal continuum" (Moore 1993) to be a chronological progression, mapping a music-historical trend of increasing heaviness and decreasing blues influence. As I'll explore over the next two chapters, these ways of thinking have an enormous influence on who gets to count as metal, and what it means to be included in or excluded from this category.

Leaving the Blues Behind: A Scenario of Oppositional Authenticity in Metal Discourse

Ian Christe's popular history *Sound of the Beast: The Complete Headbanging History of Heavy Metal* (2003) is bookended by two strikingly parallel passages from different eras in metal. The first one describes Black Sabbath's departure from blues-rock to create heavy metal.

> The first complete heavy metal work by the first heavy metal artists, Black Sabbath was an addictive musical suspension of time, informed by an ominous presence that crushed the bouncy rhythms of popular rock. [...] The entire ceremony sounded a death knell for the music known as rock and roll, which would forever after be merely the domesticated relative of heavy metal. (Christe 2003, 4–5)

This account resonates with the "relational approach to genre" described by some scholars (Brackett 2016, 7–8): Genres are defined not only through their own internal properties, but also in relation to other genres. A new genre may absorb works previously categorized in other genres, but it also reorients how genres are imagined to exist in relation to one another. In this case, Christe is giving metal a kind of oppositional authenticity: rock and roll became relatively domesticated by the sheer fact that an allegedly less-domesticated genre (heavy metal) came into being.

Much later in the book, after relating the history of the 1970s and 1980s, Christe describes the genesis of death metal in a striking parallel to Black

Sabbath's origin story. Again, an exciting new genre supersedes an older more established genre, by surpassing its heaviness and extremity, thereby moving further away from heavy metal's blues and rock roots.

> Once ignited by the furious, annihilating speed of grindcore in the late 1980s, the massive death metal conflagration pushed everything else into oblivion. The final traces of heavy metal that still resembled traditional rock and roll were utterly obliterated by the new masters—the triumvirate of Death, Morbid Angel, and Deicide. Born around the time of Black Sabbath's debut, these musicians lived nearly their entire lives in the era of heavy metal. They built their sound from the complex, high-speed explosions of Exodus and Kreator, not the rudimentary blues scales at the base of common rock. (Christe 2003, 238)

Christe outlines a whole chain of supersessions: just as Black Sabbath's heavy metal superseded "rudimentary blues" in the 1970s, the thrash metal style of Exodus and Kreator superseded earlier heavy metal in the 1980s; and in turn, the death metal of bands like Morbid Angel and Deicide supersedes thrash metal (see Figure 3.1).

Christe's accounts both invoke what I call metal's "scenario of oppositional authenticity"—his account of death metal's birth features the same dynamics of progression and authenticity as Black Sabbath's leaving the blues behind. The concept of a "scenario" comes from the work of the performance studies scholar Diana Taylor, who describes it as "a paradigm that is formulaic, portable, repeatable, and often banal because it leaves out complexity, reduces conflict to its stock elements, and encourages fantasies of participation" (Taylor 2003, 54). Unlike a narrative or script, a scenario is not exactly scripted, but a familiar framing which invokes previous similar actions, implying (and thus, to a certain degree, enacting) parallels in the setting and roles of the action. Many moments in metal history and culture draw on the setting and roles of Black Sabbath's "leaving the blues behind": a distinction is made between less-heavy music (which is by implication less authentic) and more-heavy music (which earns a sense of authenticity by surpassing the heaviness of previous styles). When this scenario is invoked in discourse about metal music, there is usually an implied partisanship—an unspoken invitation to take the side of the heavier music—casting the fans of less-heavy music as a vague and often faceless imagined "other." For example, Christe never names the artists or fans of "rudimentary blues" or "common rock"; the actual identities or beliefs of these people are unimportant to their status as a foil for the emergence and evolution of metal. In moments like these, metal fans and critics often allude to the genre's increasing distance from rock and/or the blues, so I've taken to thinking of the whole scenario and all its manifestations as "leaving the blues behind."

Metal culture is positioned in opposition to the mainstream: Deena Weinstein argues that "the core personal type cultivated by the [heavy metal] subculture is the proud pariah" (1991, 141), and Keith Kahn-Harris (2007) suggests that extreme metal culture is also based on transgression of mainstream tastes and a sense of abjection. This opposition is not entirely imagined: heavy metal has been subject to derision and moral panics over the years, although mainstream tolerance and acceptance of metal has grown over time and the genre is now relatively uncontroversial in many parts of the world (but not all). The opposition is mutual: metal culture has often held that mainstream music is commercial, formulaic, shallow, and inauthentic, so that metal fans and musicians must reject the mainstream to maintain their own authenticity (although the strength of this cultural norm has been waning in recent years). Musicians who attain any degree of mass appeal are treated with skepticism by metal fans, subjected to accusations of "selling out" and exclusion from the genre; unpopularity is so much a part of metal culture, that genuinely "popular" music must not be metal in the first place. This oppositional authenticity is, and has always been, a central determinant of metal culture and aesthetics. Each time the scenario of "leaving the blues behind" is invoked, it enacts the ideology of oppositional authenticity as a performative statement of partisan exclusion—casting previous, less-heavy music as "domesticated" or "inauthentic" and instead valorizing a vanguard of heavier music.[2]

The repetition of this scenario of oppositional authenticity throughout Christe's history resonates with Taylor's understanding that a scenario is "always in quotations, a copy of a lost copy" (Taylor 2003, 55). As I will explore in the next chapter, the scenario of oppositional authenticity actually predates heavy metal and was inherited from "White blues," a term which emerged as White American and British musicians tried to distance themselves from Black American "Traditional blues." As Andy Brown (2015) has shown, the term "heavy metal" initially emerged as a new name for the latest generation of "White blues," and at this moment the pointer to American Blackness became implicit and was soon forgotten. Black Sabbath's bassist

---

[2] This use of the word "performative" follows scholarship building on J. L. Austin's "performative sentences" (1975 [1962], 6). Unlike Austin's initial definition of "performatives" as sentences which "do not 'describe' or 'report' or constate anything at all, are not 'true or false'" (5), this term in subsequent scholarship is often taken to refer to the degree to which any sentence performs some kind of action, even if it is a sentence that does potentially carry some truth value, like the judgment "Black Sabbath is heavier than earlier blues styles."

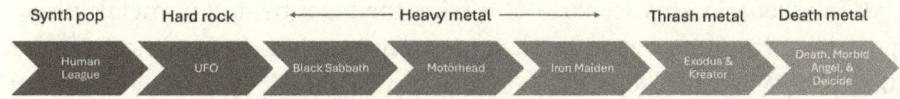

Figure 3.1 The hard rock–heavy metal continuum, expanded to feature bands mentioned by Christe and Dickenson.

Geezer Butler lamented later, "Most of our stuff goes back to 12-bar blues, really. Our younger fans sometimes find that surprising" (Sharpe-Young 2007, 14). As decades have gone by, invocations of the scenario of "leaving the blues behind" do not always explicitly reference the blues; but the same scenario becomes an echo of previous progressions within metal, with newer metal leaving older metal behind in the same way that older metal left behind the blues.

Oppositional Authenticity Across (and Beyond) the Hard Rock–Heavy Metal Continuum

The "setting" or "space" of this scenario of leaving the blues behind is a particular genre topology called the "Hard Rock–Heavy Metal continuum" (which I abbreviate below as "the HR-HM continuum"). Allan F. Moore posits that "the labels 'hard rock' and 'heavy metal' be thought of as points on a style continuum" (Moore 1993, 130), which can be expanded to map the whole chain of departures described by Christe in his account of death metal's origins (Figure 3.1). Christe's account shows how the scenario of leaving the blues behind can be (and has been) invoked at any point on this continuum—to distinguish classic heavy metal from blues-rock, or to distinguish death metal from thrash metal.

Moore describes the HR-HM continuum an inert style taxonomy, but I argue it also functions as a scenario which invites participation—an active field of meaning-making, identification, and distinction. Any genre classification or judgment of taste locates whoever is making that judgment within this continuum. Bruce Dickenson, the lead singer from Iron Maiden, explains this clearly.

> What is your viewpoint? I wouldn't call UFO a heavy metal band, but if you happen to be a fan of Human League, they probably are. And if you're a fan of Motörhead, UFO aren't heavy metal. If [Iron Maiden] said we are heavy metal, it wouldn't matter much in the way we sound. It's a category. (Walser 2014 [1993], 6–7)

Like any scenario, this scenario of leaving the blues behind in metal "places spectators within its frame, implicating us in its ethics and politics" (Taylor 2003, 33). When this scenario is invoked in writing, it is never abstract but always situated around a particular niche in this continuum. Readers are invited to imagine and embody a particular perspective on what music counts as metal, whether or not this is the perspective they might have chosen themselves.

When the scenario of leaving the blues behind is invoked in metal, readers are also are invited to pose in particular relationships with imagined fans of other bands. To paraphrase Bruce Dickenson, if you are passionate about the Human League, you might think of a UFO fan as a metal devotee; but if you're a Motörhead enthusiast, the fans of UFO are not really metalheads and are outside of the group you identify with—and fans of Human League might as well be aliens. Metal's scenario of oppositional authenticity (like the "scenario of discovery" Taylor observes recurring throughout the European conquest of the Americas) produces "a 'we' and an 'our' as it produces a 'them' " (Taylor 2003, 54). In metal, this "them" is usually the unwitting mainstream, often imagined as docile drones blindly consuming mass-produced drivel delivered by soulless corporate megalomaniacs.

Another aspect of these stories which evoke Taylor's concept of a scenario is the implied roles of mainstream and opposition. As in a stage drama, Taylor's concept of a scenario includes a setting, familiar roles, and preconceived actions and outcomes associated with those roles. Like all scenarios, once this scenario of oppositional authenticity is invoked, it sets up actors and actions without determining them entirely; as Taylor suggests, "The body in the scenario […] has space to maneuver because it is not scripted" (Taylor 2003, 55). If a band is accused of being too mainstream, their supporters may argue against this accusation by highlighting their originality or showing how they can be perceived as heavy—but this resistance usually unfolds within the scenario's preconditioning frame, as an attempt to valorize the band based on the same foundational assumptions rather than break out of the scenario's box.

It is of utmost importance to clarify that the HR-HM continuum, the concept of oppositional authenticity, and the scenario of leaving the blues behind are ideas about how genre works rather than fixed scripts or natural laws. One way in which the HR-HM continuum fails as a veridical model of reality is that the topology of genre is not actually as simple as a linear continuum implies. For example, while Motörhead uses more blues- and rock-'n'-roll-influenced riffs and song structures than Iron Maiden (Hudson 2021a, 5.3), Motörhead also uses much rougher and dirtier timbres than Iron Maiden, so there's space for reasonable disagreement about the relative heaviness or metal-ness of these bands. The concept of oppositional authenticity fails to represent reality as well, because heaviness is not always actually equated with authenticity. One female metal scholar told me that when she was younger, male metal fans were skeptical of her authenticity even though she listened to heavier music than they did, in part because she did not listen to the canonical bands they worshipped. But, as with the left-right continuum of American politics, the fact that the HR-HM continuum is a reductive and inaccurate model of reality does not seem to dampen anyone's enthusiasm for invoking this kind of thinking and rhetoric.

Teleological Treadmill of Increasing Brutality

This HR-HM continuum is often imagined as a chronological progression of metal styles away from rock and the blues, mapping the evolution of the metal genre through the decades. This perspective has some amount of truth, in that more extreme metal styles were often pioneered later. But each style has continued to be played and developed up to the present, so many individual bands in different regions of the continuum are exact contemporaries. However convenient it might be to think of the HR-HM continuum as a linear map of history, reality is much more complex.

By framing the genre's history as a progression toward increased heaviness, and framing this heaviness as one of the primary dimensions of distinction between metal and the blues, metal discourse often seems to frame increasing heaviness as an imperative or inevitability. The consequences of this framing are fleshed out in Zachary Wallmark's discussion of death metal timbre as a simulation of violence (I explore this metaphor in Chapter 2). Wallmark argues that we are "tricked" into hearing the high-tension timbres of the guitar and the voice as instantiations of actual physical danger, when in fact these sounds are carefully controlled and regulated. These extreme death metal timbres "are able to radically tear the listener out of 'music-listening' mode, forcing him or her to actually feel the horror" (Wallmark 2018, 75). Wallmark claims that the most extreme, bleeding-edge metal timbres are necessary to "force" this illusion of impact.

For example, "Into the Soil" by the German brutal death metal band Defeated Sanity (after a chaotic introduction) features verses with gurgled, growled vocals that sound like the grunting of some kind of massive beast instead of human singing. Alongside these vocals, the guitarists play palm-muted, down-tuned power chords whose harsh high-range distortion and guttural depth combine to give the kind of brain–body impact that one might normally associate with a nearby explosion or collision. But, of course, nothing is actually breaking; the physical consequences of the musicians' actions are no greater than any other highly amplified popular music performance. The timbres which Defeated Sanity uses are more extreme than those used by most of their peers and predecessors, and this gives their music a special edge, a sense of novelty and strangeness, an unfamiliarity bordering on discomfort, that goes beyond the experiences I have with older, more established metal sounds.

In Wallmark's theory of death metal aesthetics, death metal timbre has to be an abject sound, pushing at the limits of the familiar and the comprehensible, in order to create its simulation of violence. This creates what he calls a "teleological treadmill of increasing brutality," in which bands are always trying to outdo one another's heaviness and intensity.

> Since the genre's birth, groups have had to continually up the ante of "extreme" on a teleological treadmill of increasing brutality simply to stay in the same phenomenological place. There was a time when, as Lester Bangs reminds us, Ozzy Osbourne's keening and Tony Iommi's plodding riffs horrified rock critics with their unrelenting morbidity. [... But] The sacrificial scope of the genre has shifted, and new liminal timbres have been created to fill the void. In other words, the "extreme" as a timbral simulacrum of sacrifice loses its power over time, requiring sounds with a higher and higher brutality quotient just to get the same effect. (Wallmark 2018, 79)

This "teleological treadmill of increasing brutality" is not unique to death metal—it's a version of the same progressionism that has been characteristic of metal aesthetics and discourse since the 1970s. Defeated Sanity is a contemporary band, so its innovations may today feel more vital or current than previous bands, but it is just another instantiation of the same progressionism of Death surpassing Exodus in extremity, or Black Sabbath leaving the blues behind.

The logical consequence of this theory of extremity is that once a sound becomes familiar or established, it loses its power. Wallmark puts it this way:

> The sound of a heavily distorted electric guitar has long been leached of the power to transgress. Gradually metabolized into the bloodstream of mainstream popular music, pronounced metal-like distortion can be found in a wide range of music today; it is featured in the background to more than one Chevy truck commercial and plays a prominent role in both *The Daily Show* and Fox News intros and transitions. In short, this timbre has been tamed and naturalized to serve a variety of functions in the popular music economy. (Wallmark 2018, 71–72)

This is essentially the same way of thinking that framed metal's precursors in blues as "domesticated" once Black Sabbath entered the scene: a way of thinking which brackets off prior styles as "tamed," "dead," and thus no longer relevant. And it has some truth to it. As I discussed at the end of Chapter 2, Jimi Hendrix's sound, which was once among the loudest, noisiest, most transgressive guitar tones in the late 1960s, was literally domesticated a few decades later as it became the soundtrack to family road trips. Is it possible that all metal will endure the same fate, that even today's most inhospitable distortion might slowly neutralize with time and use?

Conclusion: The Paradox of Old Metal

But there is a common trope in metal discourse which contradicts this theory of domestication: beloved older recordings are said, decades after their first release, to have lost none of their heaviness or intensity. Chuck Schuldiner, the founder, guitarist, and lead singer of a seminal death metal band called Death, is a perfect example. Schuldiner pioneered a kind of extreme vocal style called the "death growl," which was beyond anything anyone else was doing when his band's debut album came out in 1987. Wallmark argues that a few years later, once many other vocalists had started using similar techniques, Schuldiner's sound lost its power:

> When Schuldiner was the only person singing with the gravelly death tone, it was appropriately liminal; when dozens were all singing the same way, the sound lost sacrificial power. (Wallmark 2018, 79)

But a recent retrospective review marking the album's 30th anniversary claims the opposite, although it focuses on Schuldiner's guitar playing instead of his vocals:

> Schuldiner's forward thinking approach to the guitar allowed cult classics [from Death's debut album] like "Evil Dead" and the timeless "Zombie Ritual" a frenetic barbarism that remains as effective today as it was thirty years ago. (Ferrous Bueller 2017)

I also think Chuck Schuldiner's riffs and vocals are still pretty unsettling, even 35 years after the album's original release. While I admit (and virtually everyone would agree) that "Into the Soil" by Defeated Sanity sounds heavier or more brutal than "Evil Dead," that doesn't mean that Death is no longer heavy.

I don't believe old metal loses its heaviness, its power to impact and affect listeners—at least, not completely. It's true that as a particular distorted timbre becomes less unique and more normalized, it loses a bit of its capacity to be truly surprising or shocking. But it can still be heavy. To return to the horror film analogy from Chapter 2, even if we've seen a horror film a hundred times, it can still feel chilling and suspenseful; we can still jump in our seats and feel our hearts racing when the monster jumps out of the dark, even if we know it's coming. All that it takes to create an experience of heaviness is (1) sonic features that allow for metaphorical perceptions of weight, intensity, and impact; and (2) a listener being open to that impact, suspending their disbelief or self-critique enough to experience the music as a fantasy of power and impact, through metaphorical cognition and embodied listening practices like headbanging. Novel extreme timbres are not required, although their overwhelming (imagined or real) loudness can certainly help one suspend one's disbelief. Listeners are able to hear distorted guitar or rough vocal timbres as a simulation of threat or violence throughout the metal genre, including in older or more mainstream metal, through the power of imagined loudness.

Older metal's continuing heaviness may seem paradoxical. Virtually everyone will agree that each band further to the right on the HR-HM continuum is heavier than all the bands to its left—but this doesn't mean bands on the left end are necessarily "not heavy." Heaviness is often understood in relative terms, but it doesn't need to be.

To summarize, within the warrior-like listening stance that Wallmark describes, it might seem like there's a perpetual genre crisis in death metal—"horror is a moving target" (Wallmark 2018, 75), and the genre is always running out of options to create freshly horrific experiences. But I think this crisis is artificial, created by an aesthetic ideology that mandates progression. Old metal still has plenty of heaviness and horror, if we choose to hear it that way. And metal does not need to leave the blues behind to create that heaviness—even though its fans have often believed that it does.

One more wrinkle that troubles the simple-seeming narrative of progressionism is that metal music periodically returns to its roots to achieve greater heaviness. For example, Ian Reyes describes the emergence of black metal as a "fundamentalist solution to a crisis of metal heaviness" (Reyes 2013, 241). In this moment in the early 1990s, a set of (mostly Norwegian) musicians felt that contemporary death metal was becoming too trendy, formulaic, and highly produced, and they instead created a new Norwegian black metal sound inspired by a loose collection of earlier low-budget underground demos that had circulated through a mail-based network of fans and musicians (see Harris 2000). None of that would make sense if the older underground demos had lost their heaviness in the passage of time; instead, in this moment as in many others (see Chapter 4 and the Epilogue), metal artists past and present have often drawn on past styles to create new kinds of heaviness for the future.

* * *

Afterthought: Narratives of Progression in Personal Listening Histories

This perpetual progression toward increasing brutality is not only a historical narrative for the genre; the same narrative of progression characterizes many metal fans' own narratives of their listening history. In other words, fans describe their own listening getting heavier over time, and describe themselves always seeking out new, even heavier, experiences. This tendency has been previously reported by Harris Berger:

> Both earlier fieldwork in Bloomington, Indiana, and my Ohio research uncovered a surprisingly robust genre of personal experience narratives that describe the local musician's participation in the history of metal. [. . .] The pivotal moment comes when an older sibling, friend, or a lucky accident introduces the would-be metal-head to his or her first metal album. More powerful than any music he or she has ever heard, the music is interpreted as an epiphany, a complete break from the pablum of commercial radio. [. . .] Like a drug addiction, numerous participants joked, they start out with the lighter stuff, and keep searching for heavier and heavier music. Unlike drug use, however, the highs do not diminish; they increase. The vast majority of people I talked with explained that just when they thought that metal was as heavy as it possibly could be, a new variety emerged that was even heavier than the last. (Berger 1999, 59)

In these narratives, metal fans are not only progressing deeper into metal, but increasing their distance from the "pablum of commercial radio"—or, in other words, the mainstream.

When a fan first discovers metal, it is often an "epiphany" of not only connoisseurship but identity. Berger's account also (although somewhat implicitly) describes metal fans increasing their distance from mainstream culture, but also from their past selves—the childhoods in which they listened to more mainstream music. When they discover metal, they discover a culture which they feel resonates with them more strongly, whether or not they consciously thought their life was missing something earlier. As fans subsequently dig deeper into metal, they are also strengthening their identity as metalheads, and acting out a personal version of the artistic scenario of a new heavy band superseding less-heavy music.

But for many metal fans, these accounts are selectively incomplete. Many of us continue to listen to mainstream music, and continue listening to less-heavy metal even after we've discovered more-heavy subgenres. I've had AC/DC's *Highway to Hell* (1979) in my car ever since I first learned to drive, and I don't plan to stop listening to it any time soon. Mercyful Fate's nightmarish visions on *Don't Break the Oath* (1983) continue to haunt me, Machine Head's bellicose shouting and bludgeoning riffs on *Burn My Eyes* (1994) continue to push me out of my seat, and Evanescence's *Fallen* (2003) continues to rock as hard as it ever did—all long after these albums' sounds stopped sounding current and started to signify a particular time in the past. Old metal's heaviness can live on in our continued listening; its sound continues to signify heaviness even if it no longer carries the same transgressive shock it had when it was new.

Those of us who were born after metal began have all had the experience of discovering for the first time an older metal album that we'd never known about before, that while not as extreme or brutal as the metal of today, is still dark, unnerving, powerful, and heavy. My favorite old-metal discoveries include Heart's *Little Queen* (1977), Angel Witch's 1980 self-titled debut album, and *Court in the Act* (1983) by the little-known NWOBHM band Satan. We can still get into less-heavy bands, even after we get into more-heavy bands. Our taste in heaviness does not have to grow in a single linear direction, but will branch off and bear fruit anywhere we allow it to spread.

Living on the teleological treadmill of increasing brutality is, and always has been, ultimately antisocial and unsustainable. To truly live out metal's progressionist mandate requires perennially rejecting one's own favorite bands in favor of new avenues of heaviness. It requires writing off "lighter" metal as not-serious, and writing off the people who listen to it as rubes, plebes, and dweebs, who are either out-of-the-know and unaware that heavier music exists, or not authentic or committed enough to actually listen to it. Such partisan progressionism also obligates one to continually discard the genre's past and keep the genre's present in a rootless vacuum. In my experience, few, if any, metal fans are actually so partisan in their listening or social practices. Instead, while we might get farther into metal over time when we first encounter the genre, we often explore sideways and backwards at the same time—and most of us continue to listen to some mainstream rock and pop, too.

PART II

WHERE DID HEAVINESS COME FROM?

4

Leaving the Blues Behind

The Racialized Origins of Metal and Its Progression Toward Heaviness

The Problem at the Root of Metal's Origin Story

While there is perpetually debate about which early bands count as heavy metal, histories of the genre (e.g., Walser 2014 [1993]; Christe 2003; Cope 2010) often focus on three British bands circa 1970: Black Sabbath, Led Zeppelin, and Deep Purple. But in his pioneering musicological study, Robert Walser criticizes this obsession with identifying a definitive first band or first album, and the tendency to treat any prior history as mostly irrelevant to what happened from that point forward. To counter this dynamic, Walser identifies many Black American antecedents who contributed to heavy metal style, including Howlin' Wolf, Jimi Hendrix, and Chuck Berry (Walser 2014 [1993], 8–9). But in this act of identifying Black artists as precursors to heavy metal, Walser and other writers have continued to place them (and Blackness more generally) "outside the frame" of the genre's duration and present. Instead, I argue that heavy metal emerged in highly racialized conditions, and that ideas about Blackness have continued to shape the genre despite the near absence of Black musicians and fans in some scenes at some times (Swiniartzki 2023, 180–81), and the erasure of race-coded terminology from the genre's discourses when compared with the 1960s blues scenes (Adelt 2010, 57–77).

Walser makes an analogy between heavy metal's origin story and the history of North America, which traditionally often began with European colonization rather than with the preceding centuries of Indigenous American societies.

> Just as histories of North America begin with the European invasion, the histories of musical genres such as rock and heavy metal commonly begin at the point of White dominance. But to emphasize Black Sabbath's contribution of occult concerns to rock is to forget Robert Johnson's struggles with the Devil and Howlin' Wolf's meditations on the problem of evil. (Walser 2014 [1993], 8)

Heaviness in Metal Music. Stephen S. Hudson, Oxford University Press. © Oxford University Press 2026. DOI: 10.1093/9780197774991.003.0007

It's not a perfect analogy, not least because (as Walser admits) White musicians and businessmen were already a dominant, controlling presence in rock music before 1970. But it's an analogy which I'd like to take one step further, to make a broader reappraisal of the neglected foundational and continuing influence of Black American music culture (and White stereotypes about Blackness) in the practices and ideologies of the metal genre community.

The exclusion of Black Americans from the history of metal, like the underrepresentation of Indigenous Americans in many histories of the United States, is an ideological blind spot which results from the basic framing of history. In histories of the United States, as in the genre of the Western that is so deeply woven into the fabric of American culture, Indigenous Americans are always cast as already in retreat, slowly being driven from their ancestral homelands by an inevitable tide of European settlers. In this way, Indigenous Americans are written out of the present and automatically relegated to the past. For example, images depicting early Chicago often show Indigenous people on the periphery, and they are often in transit, departing as refugees or visiting as traders. Figure 4.1 shows a map produced by the *Chicago Tribune* for the 100th anniversary of the city's founding, which depicts Indigenous Americans in two insets: one showing two Indigenous people witnessing the arrival of a boat full of Europeans, and the other showing Indigenous people in canoes passing by Fort Dearborn, pointed North as if they were headed away from the new town, escaping into the relative wilderness of Wisconsin. These two images are inset overlays, placed outside the map's veridical topology. This representation omits the ugly realities of how Indigenous Americans were physically and economically driven out, and presents them instead as abstract figures, an obligatory historical allusion which is always already outside the architecture and community of the city itself.[1]

The same framing issue affects the representation of Indigenous Americans in written histories as well. In his history of Chicago, William Cronon writes about the area's Indigenous cultures:

The proof of their tragedy is that the history of Chicago can be written from 1833 forward as if they had never lived there. [...] At precisely the moment that Charles Butler imagined the little village to be "a great commercial point," he averted his eyes and the Indians disappeared. The dream would not contain them. (Cronon 1991, 54)

---

[1] Readers might imagine these figures to be members of the Potawatomi or Illinois tribes who lived in the Chicago area prior to colonization, but their decontextualized framing suggests that they are "natives" in the abstract rather than any specific or actual local Indigenous people.

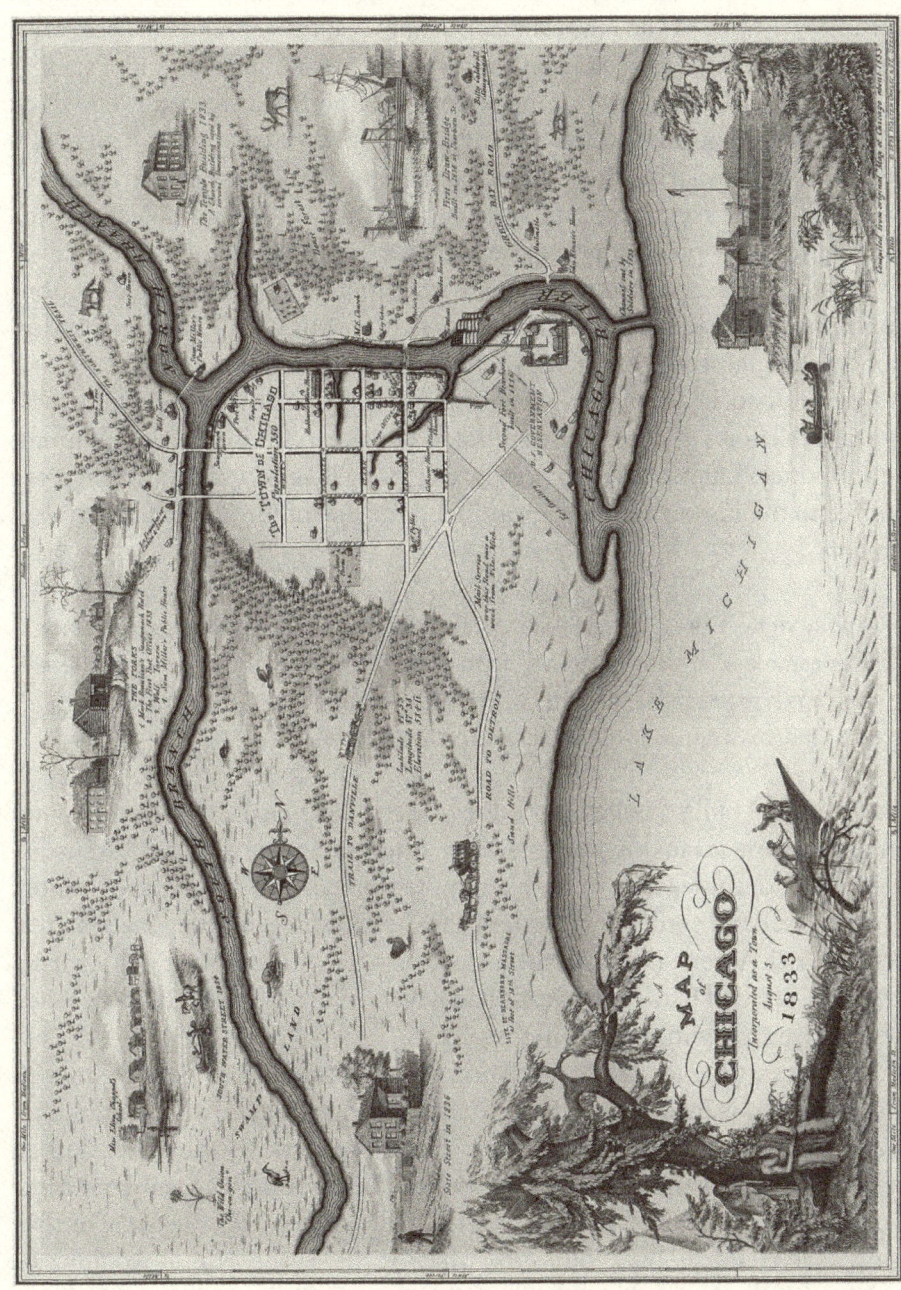

Figure 4.1 Map of early Chicago from the *Chicago Tribune*, printed in 1933.

It's not just that Indigenous Americans are not given enough airtime; it's that this scenario casts them as precursors with little relevance to the present, kept outside the frame of the main subject. As in Chapter 3, my use of "scenario" here is intended to invoke Diana Taylor's theorization of "scenarios" such as the "scenario of discovery" in the Americas, a performative framing which "transfers the not-ours to the ours, [...] translates past enactments (earlier discovery scenarios) into future outcomes (usually loss of native lands). In doing so, the scenario simultaneously constructs the wild object and the viewing subject—producing a 'we' and an 'our' as it produces a 'them'" (Taylor 2003, 54). Such scenarios do not necessarily limit Indigenous people's actions directly, but instead pre-determine how their actions will be seen and understood, seemingly scripting an inevitable colonial outcome.

The history of heavy metal suffers from a similar origin story problem. Even in Walser's efforts to correct the omission of Black Americans' contributions, he reproduces much of the problem by confining Black artists to an obligatory preface to the history of metal, positioned outside of the genre itself. Walser laments,

> To deify White rock guitarists like Eric Clapton or Jimmy Page is to forget the Black American musicians they were trying to copy; to dwell on the prowess of these guitarists is to relegate Jimi Hendrix, the most virtuosic rock guitarist of the 1960s, to the fringes of music history. (Walser 2014 [1993]: 8–9)

But in the rest of his book, Walser does exactly what he decries: Hendrix and other Black musicians are hardly ever mentioned, and he does not discuss issues of race or the legacies of the blues more generally. To paraphrase Cronon, while Walser and some other writers have acknowledged heavy metal's great debt to Black American artists, the history of metal music is often written from 1970 forward as if Black Americans had never lived there—as if Blackness had never played a significant role in the genre.

This framing has fostered a widespread assumption in Europe and America that the genre is by default a community of White people, which has sometimes made Black musicians and fans feel unwelcome. Kevin Fellezs, in an article about race and metal, interviews the Black American guitarist Mike Coffey from the band Stone Vengeance, who argues, "People act like they really love Hendrix. But, you know what? If that is the case, it wouldn't be so hard for Black people to get *in* to this music" (Fellezs 2011, 184). Other scholars have documented how Black artists and fans often are made to feel unwelcome in the metal scene, in part through acts of overt or covert racism (Creek 2024), but in part through a continual framing of metal as a White space in which Black people are exceptions, memorably captured by Laina Dawes' book title *What Are You Doing Here?* (Dawes 2012). Elsewhere, Dawes argues that despite this unwelcoming framing, metal genres can still offer "a space for Black listeners and musicians to assert their individuality through its aggressive musical properties, which temporarily liberates those Black listeners from anti-Black racism, racial violence, and racialized misogyny in their everyday experiences" (Dawes 2022, 1). But it would probably help if we could find a way to tell the history of metal music that didn't imply that Black musicians and Blackness had no relevance after 1970.

In this chapter, I argue for the opposite: Heavy metal slowly and gradually emerged from highly racialized understandings of blues music, and ideologies about Blackness within rock and blues from the 1960s shaped this emergence and have had lasting consequences. I will show how metal's mandate of ever-increasing heaviness, which I explored in the Chapter 3, emerged from and remains intertwined with the racial politics of leaving the blues behind. But it doesn't have to be this way: metal doesn't have to be constantly getting more extreme to be heavy and authentic, and it can be heavy and authentic while embracing the blues and Blackness.

From "Traditional Blues" to "White Blues": Race and the Ideology of Progression

Heavy metal gradually coalesced into a distinct style on both sides of the Atlantic, even though the origin story is often told as if the genre emerged in the United Kingdom. While I will return to the American context soon, I want to begin by placing early British heavy metal in a longer historical context. This history reveals that the British emergence of heavy metal was more racialized than metal histories have usually acknowledged. The broader picture, encompassing both sides of the Atlantic, shows how some ideas about artistic progression, oppositionality, extremity, and authenticity that lie at the core of the heavy metal genre were inherited from highly racialized ways of thinking in 1960s blues and blues-rock scenes.

Rebecca Schwartz relates in her book *How Britain Got the Blues* (2007) that blues music originally came to Britain via recordings of Black musicians imported from America. These imports were expensive, and it was nearly impossible for Black American artists to tour Britain with any frequency, so British musicians began trying to recreate the style on their own by imitating records. In this initial period, the dominating criterion of authenticity in British blues was fidelity to Black American styles as they appeared on record.

The critical language of this period often articulates a kind of racial authenticity; for example, an October 1952 issue of *Jazz Journal* about the then-new "rhythm and blues" style appreciated the "rocking, rolling beat which only a coloured band can generate" (quoted in Schwartz 2007, 50).[2]

In the 1960s, as British blues musicians began to be more successful at imitating Black American recordings, a new kind of authenticity (and a new kind of blues) became ascendant. Jimi Hendrix's 1966 arrival in Britain was not necessarily the only catalyst for this shift, but illustrates why this shift may have been inevitable. Hendrix had struggled to make it in the United States, where Jim Crow laws and racial prejudice stifled his career. But in London, according to Hendrix's biographer Charles R. Cross, "Rather than a liability, his race offered him a huge advantage [. . .]: There were so few musicians who were Black on the scene, and so many fans of American blues, that he was afforded instant credibility" (Cross 2005, 161). The color of Hendrix's skin, and his curriculum vitae backing up the Isley Brothers and Little Richard, caused White Brits to see him as a personification of the Black American tradition—a racial authenticity that the Brits themselves could never achieve.

Beyond his racial authenticity, Hendrix's playing also revealed the limitations of a scene built on imitating records. A small number of Black American musicians made it to Britain in the postwar years, but the expense of trans-Atlantic touring made such trips rare. British blues guitarists (Clapton, Beck, etc.) had mostly learned blues style from the same finite set of imported recordings, a small sample which was filtered through the American recording industry's limited perspective on what constituted authentic Black music (see Hagstrom-Miller 2010). But Hendrix had mastered blues styles through countless hours of in-person collaboration and live improvisation, a far more diverse and interactive exposure than the British bluesmen—and he had blended these influences organically into his own unique style. The British blues-rock keyboardist Brian Auger recalled, "There were a lot of B.B. King, Albert King, and Freddie King followers around in England. But Jimi wasn't following anyone—he was playing something new" (Cross 2005, 161). Hendrix's rendition of the "Star Spangled Banner," for example, expanded beyond traditional blues and rock'n'roll by using fuzz box and wah effects, chaotic variations, dive-bomb and ambulance sound effects, and an interpolation of the military elegy "Taps"—all of which cast his lead guitar playing as an anti-war political statement and radical psychedelic experience. For the British blues scene, Hendrix was paradoxically both an embodiment of Black

[2] Ronald Radano provides a deeper exploration of stereotypes about rhythm and Blackness in twentieth-century American popular music (Radano 2003, Chapter 5).

American tradition and, simultaneously, a champion of innovation and departure from that tradition.

Hendrix's presence revealed how in a scene built on the racial authenticity of Black American styles, White British artists would ultimately always be only secondhand imitations of "the real thing"; but Hendrix's playing championed another form of authenticity which focused more on personal expression and innovation. Schwartz observes that even before Hendrix's arrival, British bands had begun departing from their Black American sources, and calling the resulting styles "White blues."

> Some critics—even those who accepted Black and White blues as different entities—felt the British blues could not be viewed as a new stylistic approach until it abandoned wholesale copying of American artists. [...] One contributor to *Melody Maker* argued, "the derivative British Bluesmen come close to parody of a unique musical idiom. They have achieved nothing which has not been done with less contrivance and self-consciousness by countless authentic bluesmen." (quoted in Schwartz 2007, 237)[3]

According to this perspective, British musicians were "contrived" and "self-conscious" when they copied Black Americans, so they had to innovate to make music they could authentically claim as their own. This originality-based authenticity, and the music it led to, separated "White blues" from the "traditional blues" community; the latter continued for decades to be characterized by the earlier ideologies of racial authenticity and fidelity to pre-1960 Black American sources, and mostly patronized by White audiences (Adelt 2010).

Unfortunately, the contrast between tradition and innovation was often understood to correlate with race—despite how clear of a counterexample Hendrix posed. Eric Clapton, for example, understood blues in this racialized way, which Ulrich Adelt argues was similar to other European and White American rock musicians of that time period (Adelt 2010, 58).

> In Clapton's thinking, moving away from the blues was directly linked to racial categories. In a revealing statement from 1966, he commented: "I'm no longer trying to play anything but like a White man. The time is overdue when people should play like they are and what colour they are." (Adelt 2010, 66; quoting from Pidgeon 1985 [1976], 43)

---

[3] Schwarz's reference for this quotation is "S. B. Terry, Letter to the Editor, *Melody Maker*, 2 November 1968, 32."

Under the previous rubric of racial authenticity, departures from the Black American tradition were viewed as a White failure to accurately reproduce Black sounds. But Clapton and his contemporaries recast these departures as "first-person authentic" (Moore 2002, 211) expression, arguing that White artists were finally producing their own style rather than imitating Black Americans.

How White Artists Understood the Blues They Were Trying to Leave Behind

The racial dynamic of White Blues was not limited to the British context, but reflected changing attitudes on both sides of the Atlantic about White appropriations of Black musical styles. Deena Weinstein argues that for 1960s "White blues rock" bands in both the United States and the United Kingdom, cover songs often served as evidence of a band's fidelity to (Black American) "real blues" (Weinstein 1998, 142). However, later in that decade, "The modern Romantic notion of authenticity—creating out of one's own resources—became dominant over the idea that authenticity constituted a relationship, through creative repertoire, to an authentic source" (Weinstein 1998, 143). Evan Rapport observes the same shift, in a study which focuses on early punk rock or proto-punk in America:

> As the stakes intensified for White people using blues resources, some musicians who were previously deeply committed to the blues, such as Iggy Pop, altered their style. Iggy Pop "needed to go back [from Chicago to Michigan] and create his own blues," as Wayne Kramer put it. (Rapport 2020, 41)

Throughout the 1960s, on both sides of the Atlantic, White performers increasingly sought authenticity by deviating from Black American blues to create a style of their own.

When Iggy Pop "created his own blues," he was working in the same direction as several other heavy late-1960s blues-rock bands including the MC5, Velvet Underground, and the Kinks. Rapport groups these bands together under the label "raw power" music, named after the Stooges' 1973 album. He explains that raw power musicians "drew on approaches to the blues that they heard as the most powerful and the most unrestrained" (Rapport 2020, 35): specifically, they combined and exaggerated the distorted guitar sounds of urban electric blues, and the riff-based paradigms from country blues.

By the 1960s, approaches to the blues had come to loosely signify difference interpretations of African American experiences [. . .] the twelve-bar blues had become
a primary resource for communicating an urbane sound of African American life
in the northern cities. On the other hand, riff-based performances and three-part
structures with unequal phrase lengths [. . .] signaled the South and the rural back-
drop of the Great Migration. (Rapport 2020, 42–43)

Raw power bands' musical structures were aligned with the less-polished riff-
based blues of the South, focusing on short riffs that often featured only one
chord or shuttled between two chords in an open-ended vamp (rather than
the longer, more disciplined and regular, twelve-bar blues harmonic schemes
of urban blues artists).[4] On the other hand, the distorted guitar tones of raw
power aligned with the electric blues associated with Northern cities rather
than the acoustic instrumentation of Delta blues, but ventured into even
louder and noisier territory.

When Rapport describes how "the stakes intensified for White people
using blues resources," authenticity was only part of these stakes. Another was
an increasing sensitivity toward the crudity and inappropriateness of previous
White appropriations of Black musicality. The tradition of "blackface minstrelsy," in which a White artist put on black face paint and performed gro-
tesque and demeaning parodies of supposedly Black mannerisms, had been
a dominant force in American popular culture across much of the preceding
century. While blackface minstrelsy had begun to decline in popularity by
the beginning of the twentieth century, it had not entirely disappeared from
American culture; during the 1960s, some late but prominent examples
such as Al Jolson's film *The Jazz Singer* (1927) would have been within the
living memory of many blues fans and musicians. Some critics have seen direct parallels between White artists performing blues in the 1950s and 1960s,
and blackface performance of earlier decades: both involved White artists
performing an imitation of Blackness, and while these mid-century White
performances of the blues were more respectful than minstrelsy's derogatory
humor, they still often stereotyped Black people and culture as simple, crude,
violent, and highly sexualized.[5] Part of what motivated some White artists to

---

[4] Rapport offers the following examples of raw power vamps based on shuttling between two chords
rather than a proper twelve-bar blues form: the Stooges' "No Fun" (1969) vamp section from 1:45 to 3:30;
and the bridge of Patti Smith's "Gloria" (1975).

[5] For example, Steve Waksman observes, "The MC5 and the many legions of other white musicians who
drew from African-American culture no longer literalized the putting on of blackness through the application of blackface, but did adopt other signifiers to mark the exchange (especially hair, in the case of the
Five). However, I would argue that it was primarily by strapping on electric guitars, and in their use of technology more generally, that groups like the Five most clearly reproduced the logic of blackface" (2011, 34).

develop "their own blues," then, may have been a desire to escape this context of appropriation and ugly racial stereotypes.

This understanding of the blues as crude, simple, and highly sexualized is evident in several of the few metal songs which use twelve-bar blues forms, which often have lyrics that reference sex explicitly or implicitly. "Teacher's Pet" by Venom (1982) saddles their rendition of twelve-bar blues with raunchy, deliberately distasteful lyrics about a boy having sex with his school teacher. "Ice Cream Man" by Van Halen (1978) might appear to be more innocent, but their opening line "dedicate one to the ladies" confirms that the song's lyrics about an ice cream man whose "flavors are guaranteed to satisfy" is a not-so-subtle double entendre. Van Halen's seemingly good-natured lyrics also have a layer of nostalgia, which makes sense as the twelve-bar blues form was already old-fashioned and nostalgic at the beginning of the decade in Led Zeppelin's "Rock and Roll" (1971). While neither "Teacher's Pet" nor "Ice Cream Man" explicitly references Blackness, they both perpetuate a pairing of blues form with hypersexual content—a pairing which originated within the Black American blues of earlier decades (Hamilton 2016) but by the 1960s had been filtered through some White artists' and audiences' racist fantasies about Black sexuality and masculinity (Adelt 2010, 62).

Some metal bands have found other ways to read the blues, but they also tend to cast the blues as crude or simple. Megadeth's 1986 cover of Willie Dixon's song "I Ain't Superstitious" (first made famous by a Howlin' Wolf recording from 1961) might be described as a parody of the original. Howlin' Wolf's version portrays a character who exclaims "I ain't superstitious," but (ironically) immediately worries about a series of bad omens: "Whoa, the dogs are howlin', all over the neighborhood / That is true sign of death, baby, that ain't no good." Wolf's character is beset by troubles, born under a bad sign—a classic blues trope which implies a strength of character and persistence in the face of troubles—but the lyrics can also be read as a wry satire of over-confidence. In Megadeth's cover, their band leader Dave Mustaine has adjusted the lyrics to express a radically different meaning: "I ain't superstitious, under the ladder I go / And I ain't superstitious, it's all bullshit you know? / Ain't afraid of the shadows, I like the dark anyway." These new lyrics can be read as a naive send up of Howlin' Wolf, mocking his superstition—suggesting that Mustaine is reading Dixon's original lyrics too literally, and, ironically, inhabiting the same over-confidence which Dixon subtly lampooned. Megadeth's lyrics resonate with a tendency in metal to question religious and moral authority, often constructed (as in this song) as first-person, rebellious, free-thinking individualism. By implication, the blues that heavy metal is trying to leave behind is cast as backwards, superstitious, and afraid to question conventional wisdom.

"Parchment Farm Blues": Early Heavy Metal as a Transformation of Blues Materials

A song which demonstrates how raw power bands transformed blues materials to attempt to escape the racial stereotypes of previous genera-tions' blues, and which demonstrates how this context shaped the emerging style of heavy metal, is Blue Cheer's "Parchment Farm" (1968). Blue Cheer's liner notes identify this song as a cover of Mose Allison's "Parchman Farm" (1957), which itself was a cover of "Parchman Farm Blues" (1940) by the Delta bluesman Bukka White. This series of covers shows a shift from the 1950s to the late 1960s in how White artists synthesized and revised older Black blues, and shows how this newer raw power rock perspective eventually led toward heavy metal—and they also illustrate how many of metal's core values and genre dynamics emerged from the blues' racial politics.

White's "Parchman Farm Blues" was an autobiographical song, testifying on his own experience of forced labor while jailed at the Mississippi State Penitentiary (a prison whose nickname provides the title for his song), and warning others to avoid his fate. He sings earnestly and regretfully, over lan-guorous twelve-bar Delta blues with variable phrase lengths and uneven meter, "I wouldn't hate it so bad / But I left my wife in mourn / Oh goodbye wife / […] / I hope some day / You will hear my lonesome song." White audiences often imagined that this kind of autobiographical despair and suffering was the predominant theme of Black experience and the sole sentiment of the blues. The popular Black theologian James H. Cone, as part of his argument that the blues represent a secular spiritual, corrects this misunderstanding:

> It is a commonly held opinion that there is no hope in the blues. […] But it is impor-tant to point out that despair is not the whole picture. For underneath the despair there is also a firm hope in the possibility of Black people's survival despite their extreme situation of oppression. (Cone 1972, 138–39)

Cone then identifies how blues lyrics illustrate positive values of perspective, endurance, and resourcefulness. But if Cone is right that in 1972, right around the emergence of heavy metal, the "commonly held opinion" was that blues is all about despair, this way of hearing attributes to blues a kind of "heav-iness"—at least, in the 1960s Hippie sense of the term, meaning "serious, scary, ominous, or affecting." Indeed, it is easy to hear this kind of heaviness in Bukka White's slow tempo and sorrowful delivery. This sense of "heaviness" is surely a precursor to the heaviness of heavy metal, even though (or, perhaps, especially because) it is based on an incomplete understanding of the full meaning of the blues.

Allison's version of "Parchman Farm" couldn't be more different than White's original. Allison's recording was part of a broader trend in 1950s America of racial cover songs, in which a White artist would record a version of a Black artist's song, but remove sonic markers of Blackness; this literally White-washed, vanilla cover would then be marketed to mainstream audiences, while the Black artist's original song was only available on segregated "race records" catalogs and radio stations (Weinstein 1998, 139–40; Hamilton 2016, Chapter 2). In this case, the blandness of Allison's cover is not only superficial whitewashing, but also helps to effect a broader revision of the song's attitude and meaning. His piano arrangement sets an up-tempo and gentle stride rhythm, as if forced labor doesn't bother him too much. His polished blues form is tightly measured in exactly-repeating twelve-bar units, giving an impression of lighthearted sophistication rather than passion or sorrow, and the lyrics are much less self-reflective.[6] Then in his breezy, Sinatra-like tenor, Allison casually adds a chilling, psychopathic twist to the song's final verse: "All I did was shoot my wife."

Blue Cheer's "Parchment Farm" (1968) rejects the smooth polish of Allison's version and, like other raw power and White blues of the late 1960s, doubles down on heaviness instead. Blue Cheer has misheard Allison's cover, both in the misspelled title ("Parchment" instead of "Parchman") and nonsensical lyrics (Allison's "puttin' that cotton in a 'leven-foot sack" becomes "a leather foot sack"). Despite using a riff that resembles Allison's, and broadly similar lyrics, Blue Cheer's rendition is much heavier, noisier, and angrier. First, they add what in 1968 would have been relatively intense guitar distortion, and heavy, pounding drums. Then they add an exasperated explanation to Allison's confession: "All I did was shoot my wife. / She was no good!" In subsequent verses, the crime of homicide is replaced with drunkenness and drug use ("All I did was shoot my arm"), transforming the song from a chillingly cool confession by a psychopathic murder to a fervent complaint against extreme punishment for a range of crimes. These new lyrics might be heard to resonate with the increasing distrust of police and military during the civil

---

[6] Dave Headlam (1997) describes a similar "straightening out" of uneven or asymmetrical phrasing from Delta blues into regular, exact repetition in Cream's covers of Robert Johnson and other Black American artists.

rights and anti-war movements of the late 1960s and early 1970s, and antici-
pated heavy metal's enduring anti-authority stances. Blue Cheer's version also
anticipates later trends in metal by abstracting away from the autobiographical and geographical specificity of Bukka White's "Parchman Farm Blues" to
create a more generalized horror-fantasy of severe carceral punishment.

One might say that Blue Cheer, in creating a heavier cover of Mose Allison's
"Parchman Farm," was undoing Allison's whitewashing of the blues and returning to the spirit of Bukka White's original—except that Blue Cheer does
not return to White's sound or lyrics, but arrives at a different kind of heaviness. Blue Cheer and other raw power bands embraced rawer aspects of earlier blues, but exaggerated and recombined them. The album this cover song
was released on, *Vincebus Eruptum* (1968), is often described as early heavy
metal or an immediate precursor. This sense of returning to roots in order to
reach new heights of heaviness has continued to echo throughout the rhetoric
of many metal subgenres, including the emergence of so-called second wave
black metal in Norway in the early 1990s (Reyes 2013). As I mentioned in
Chapter 3, these Norwegian musicians felt that contemporary Swedish death
metal was becoming too trendy, formulaic, and highly produced, and they instead created a new sound inspired by a loose collection of earlier low-budget
underground demos that had circulated through a mail-based network of fans
and musicians. This "fundamentalism" restages the same going-back-to-go-
forwards approach which created raw power rock; in that sense, black metal's
fundamentalist rejection of death metal (and other metal styles) echoes the
racial politics of 1960s blues.

Primitivism, Race, and Oppositional Authenticity

Like other raw power songs, "Parchment Farm" is louder and noisier than
the Black American blues styles it inherits from. Rapport argues that the raw
power style was not simply an imitation or appropriation of elements from
country blues and urban blues, but a "transformation of blues resources"
(Rapport 2020, 55) into a new "primitive aesthetic [that] favored riff-based
music with looser frameworks and less harmonic movement" (Rapport
2020, 43). In addition to their developments of riff-based style, these raw
power bands pushed beyond the power and heaviness of earlier blues and
rock'n'roll by using faster tempos and straighter subdivisions of the beat,
and ever-increasing intensities of guitar distortion. These exaggerations created a new primitivist take on the blues that was simpler, noisier, louder, and
more physical. This raw power primitivism inherited from an ugly history

of racial primitivism in earlier White appraisals of blues music—and it also provided the foundations for how heaviness was created and understood in metal.

One parameter in which this dynamic is clear is in the noisiness of guitar and vocal timbres, which was in earlier decades thought on both sides of the Atlantic to embody an essential racial difference between Black and White sound. An early example was the American critic Carl Van Vechten's praise of the "wild, rough, Ethiopian voice, harsh and volcanic" on Bessie Smith's records (quoted in Davis 1998, 147). The term "Ethiopian" in Van Vechten's description has a long history in blackface minstrelsy, where it was used to conjure a sense of authenticity for the caricatures onstage in order to increase the impact of the performance—when in fact there was never any real connection to Ethiopia, nor any attempt to make one. Van Vechten's use of this word may or may not have been meant as a direct reference to blackface, but it clearly channels similar primitivist stereotypes, especially alongside his other descriptors like "wild" and "rough."

Writers in the United Kingdom argued that the rougher vocal styles of some Black artists transgressed British conceptions of propriety, establishing a link between noisiness and opposition to the mainstream that became a central tenet of metal. For example, Schwartz observes of the reviewer "Mike" Spike Hughes: "Though he believed that 'most of Bessie's discs have been a little too strong meat for the somewhat squeamish British public' he proclaimed her 'the Queen of the Blues if ever there was one'" (Schwartz 2007, 22; quoting from *Melody Maker*, April 14, 1934, 7). This same term "strong meat" was used by the blues historian Paul Oliver: "When Muddy Waters came to England [in 1958], his rocking blues and electric guitar was meat that proved too strong for many stomachs" (quoted in Narváez 2001, 31). These descriptions echoed old racist conceits (on both sides of the Atlantic) that Black singers were more intense and expressive because they were closer to a natural human state, uninhibited by the civilized conventions of White society. Sonic harshness was perceived as proof of direct, unmediated expression, and it resulted in a perceived oppositionality between blues and proper mainstream White society; this sound was too much for mainstream White listeners, but valorized by blues fans.

The same construction of oppositional authenticity expressed through unmediated harsh sound was inherited by heavy metal and has remained a central tenet of metal culture. This ideology is especially pronounced in black metal, as Khalil Boughali comments in his meditative short book *Thoughts on Black Metal* (2022):

Instruments and vocals are amongst the means used by artists to keep the unde-
sirable followers at bay. Bérenger Hainaut mentions "the idea of a 'bestial' vocality
used as a means to create a self-segregation, to build sonic barriers between the
common world and the world of extreme metal." (Boughali 2022, 59–60; quoting
Hainaut 2020)

There are uncanny and uncomfortable parallels between this description of
black metal and primitivist, explicitly racial descriptions of rough timbre
in the blues from the previous century. And while this connection between
harsh sound and anti-mainstream hostility may be expressed by black metal
musicians more directly than in other metal subgenres, it's hard not to hear
similar connotations behind other descriptions of metal's intense timbres.
For example, Natalie Purcell's pioneering study *Death Metal Music* (2003)
quotes the vocalist of the death metal band Necrophagia, who goes by the
name "Killjoy": "For me personally, Death Metal is raw, hideous, sick music
with blood curdling vocals" (Purcell 2003, 12), and Kyle Severn (drummer
for Incantation): "True Death Metal to me is metal that is played from your
fuckin' soul" (Purcell 2003, 13).

Primitivism also lurks behind the idea that the rhythm of the blues (and,
later, metal) was primal and unrestrained—or in other words, that this music's
rhythm was authentic, raw expression, unmediated by mainstream White
propriety. The musicologist Christopher Small reported, "I still remember
from my teens the impact made by [Jump Blues songs like] 'Caldonia' and
'Is You Is or Is You Ain't My Baby.' Neither I nor my contemporaries had the
slightest idea of the provenance of all that vigour, excitement, and sheer fun,
but we loved it...." (Small 1987, 209; quoted in Schwartz 2007, 50). The same
aspects of vigorous rhythm were cast in more negative terms by the music's
critics:

Derrick Stewart-Baxter also condemned the music as "blasting," "blaring," "banal,"
and "uninspired riffing." He decided that rhythm and blues meant: "smart lyrics....
funny enough to get by at one of those bottle parties where the wine is in and the
wit is out. The accompanying band is about as subtle as a pile driver, and just about
as attractive." (Schwartz 2007, 51; quoting from Baxter 1953)

This negative description resonates strongly with later descriptions of metal
music, especially with the writings of Lester Bangs, who essentially invented
the tradition of positive heavy metal criticism. In a review of *Psychotic
Reactions* (1967) by Count Five, Bangs reflects on the same constellation of

values as Derrick Stewart-Baxter, but valorizes them as positive instead of negative: "A poorboy of Port or Tokay, 'Psychotic Reactions' blasting off the walls and I would burn with pointless joy as I hopped and stomped around the turntable and couldn't have sat down if I'd tried" (Bangs 1987 [1971], 15). Count Five would never have been considered heavy metal, but Bangs' coverage of this and other White blues bands created a rhetorical template that was adapted by metal's advocates. Consider the following excerpt from the same piece:

> [...] the eternal promise that this time the guitars will jell like TNT and set off galvanic sizzles in your brain "KABLOOIE!!!" and this time at least at last blow your fucking lid sky-high. Brains gleaming on the ceiling, sticking like putty stalactites, while yer berserk body runs around and slams outside hollering subhuman gibberish, jigging in erratic circles [...] But that's only the fantasy. (Bangs 1987 [1971], 11)

Descriptions of death metal guitars' "skull-splitting tone" (see Chapter 1), a brutal deathcore band's "cave man guitar riffs," or a prog metal band's guitar solos that will "melt your face off" are clearly mining the same vein. Metal criticism throughout the decades has often continued to valorize simplicity, unpretentiousness, and brute force in language that clearly inherits from Bangs' early expression of the primitivist aesthetics of raw power rock.

Heavy metal inherited this ideological and musical constellation of primitivism and oppositional authenticity from White blues, a constellation that was previously associated with Blackness in the racialized (and often explicitly racist) understandings of White listeners earlier in the twentieth century. But as White blues became heavy metal, and these sounds' references to Blackness were disconnected or forgotten, the same musical parameters began to reference another disadvantaged group: lower-class young White men. This connection has been suggested before by Deena Weinstein:

> [... C]entral to heavy metal culture is the figure of the proud pariah [...] Perhaps the native homeland to the proud pariah is the blues. [...] Heavy metal is another home of proud pariahs. Indeed, it might be usefully thought of as White-boy blues, a music appealing to the ethos of the marginalized group of male, White, blue-collar youth. (Weinstein 1991, 271–72).

Raw power music embodied an aesthetic of primitivism which drew on longstanding racist stereotypes about Blackness and synthesized them into a new countercultural construction of Whiteness. This particular flavor of primitivism has been a central pillar of metal aesthetics ever since. Primitivism's ugly racial history was mostly forgotten or buried during the de-racialization that turned "White blues" into "heavy metal," but its ghost continues to haunt the genre today.

The Myth of Heavy Metal Leaving the Blues Behind

Metal's progressionism, primitivism, and oppositional authenticity all have clear precedents in White blues, and these precedents were all driven by the racial dynamics of blues in the 1950s and 1960s—a fact which complicates the genre's founding myth of "leaving the blues behind." Black Sabbath's departure from traditional blues is an indispensable part of the narrative that they invented heavy metal music, an article of faith recited by the band members themselves as often as anyone else. The band's bassist Geezer Butler describes how the first generation of British heavy metal bands were paradoxically both blues-based and also no longer blues.

> All our early gigs were blues songs and that is what we were—a blues band. I suppose the transition to heavy metal was through Tony and I developing these very simple three-chord blues riffs into something of our own. [....] It's the same for Led Zeppelin, Jethro Tull and Deep Purple too, all those bands of that period just expressed the blues differently. (Sharpe-Young 2007, 14)

He continues the well-rehearsed legend, "Somehow what we came up with was no longer blues. [...] That's why we changed the band name [from 'The Polka Tulk Blues Band' to 'Black Sabbath'], because we weren't a blues band anymore" (Sharpe-Young 2007, 14).[7] The message is clear: Black Sabbath's music was no longer blues, so it became something new—something that would eventually be called "heavy metal."

This origin myth relies on the idea that Black Sabbath's music was "a completely new thing," but Andy Brown's review of terminology in rock magazines tells a different story: "heavy metal" was nothing new, but the latest generation of an existing genre known as "White blues."

> The first known usage of the term by Gifford seems to refer to something—"heavy metal rock"—that is already in existence! This idea, that heavy metal already

---

[7] At the same time as Black Sabbath's name change was intended to separate their music from the blues (and from the blues' Black American identity), their name change also heralded a new meaning for the word "Black" in the context of blues-rock: using "Black" to mean evil or occult magic in a non-racial sense, which is later used in the genre term "black metal." This shift in usage seems significant, but unraveling these dual meanings of the word "Black" and thinking about their continuing significance for the metal genre deserves more space and consideration than I can afford to give here.

precedes it naming, is also to be found in the "wake of all the heavy metal robots of the year past" in Bangs' definitive naming review. But also, more tellingly, it is to be found in Mike Saunders' description "Third Generation heavy-metal groups" (Rolling Stone, April 27, 1972), ... (Brown 2015, 236)

Brown then cites several reviews from the 1970s which describe heavy metal as the "third generation" of a music that already existed, and Brown demonstrates that before 1974, the prior dominant term for this music was "White blues."[8] Among these bands, Black Sabbath was the most radical, and the only one that (in retrospect) seems to directly anticipate later heavy metal. Many of the other early bands to be labeled "heavy metal" would never be categorized that way today: Mountain, Grand Funk Railroad, and Cream. "Heavy metal," including Black Sabbath, was initially understood by critics as a type of White blues, rather than a new genre.

And, in fact, many of metal's musical foundations and central genre ideologies were either inherited from Black American music or shaped by the racial dynamics of late-1960s blues. The backbeat (which I explain in Chapter 5) originated in gospel music, and was widespread in many Black American genres before metal (including rock'n'roll, blues, and early soul). Elements of blues lead guitar style, including pentatonic patterns and string bends, formed the foundation for heavy metal guitar solos and remain in the repertoire. Melodic motions in metal riffs can be heard to echo the blues, even in progressive and extreme metal subgenres (Hudson 2025). Metal's dance practice of headbanging is also closely connected to ideas about Blackness within the context of the White blues scene, as I explore next in Chapter 5. And then there's the genre ideologies of progressionism, oppositional authenticity, and primitivism, which I've explored in this chapter and in Chapter 3. In other words, metal has never really left the blues behind; it emerged from the blues, and brought many elements of the blues with it.

In addition to these musical foundations, many themes in metal lyrics and imagery have continuities with prior Black American music, as Kevin Fellezs explores through interviews with Mike Coffey, the guitarist from the Bay Area underground thrash metal band Stone Vengeance.

---

[8] In this way of thinking, the "first generation" of rock was the early explosion of rock'n'roll (Chuck Berry, Elvis, Little Richard, etc.), the "second generation" was the British Invasion (the Beatles, the Rolling Stones, etc.), and the heavy blues-rock styles circa 1970 (Led Zeppelin, Grand Funk Railroad, the MC5, etc., which Rapport calls "raw power rock") was the "third generation"; the term "heavy metal" as a music genre label originated as a synonym for this "third generation" rock.

[...] Coffey maintains that Black American music has always dealt with the themes identified with heavy metal: individualism, anti-authoritarianism, anti-bourgeois sentiments connected to a working-class alienation and a morbid fascination with death and apocalyptic imagery that is often drawn from anti-, or, perhaps more accurately, pre- or non-Christian beliefs. Stone Vengeance treats these themes *as a fundamentally Black aesthetic*, thereby presenting thrash metal as part of a larger Black music tradition. (Fellezs 2011, 186)

Fellezs presents Coffey's viewpoint as a speculative or radical reading of the genre, but it is historically a mundane truth. To this day, metal's sounds, lyrical themes, images, and ideologies retain many characteristics which had in previous decades been associated with Black music, ranging from the imagery and attitudes Coffey describes to basic musical structures such as the backbeat, blues pentatonic scale patterns, and guitar distortion.

In summary, while metal discourse is often framed in terms of this scenario of "leaving the blues behind," it never succeeds in escaping the blues. The same stances of looking for extremity and rejecting less extreme music are often assumed, no matter where the fan or critic's perspective is located on the hard rock–heavy metal continuum. Metal fans and critics continued to reference the genre leaving the vestiges of the blues behind through the extreme music boom at the end of the millennium. Somehow, no matter how extreme metal got—or in other words, no matter how far to the right one extended the HR-HM continuum, no matter how far metal got from the blues—metal was still trying to leave the blues behind. So much of metal's story is framed as a reaction to the blues, so much of metal's progressionist and oppositional ideology depends on having the blues as a predecessor and foil, that the blues will always be shadowing metal wherever it goes.

In short, trying to leave the blues behind is futile—and it contributes to some of the genre's problematic aspects, like the belief that the genre is originally White and that Black artists or fans are exceptions who don't belong, or the unsustainable partisan elitism described in Chapter 3. Instead, we should describe metal as an extension or transformation of the blues and write historical narratives that draw more continuities across its alleged original boundary, that do not separate metal from Blackness or Black music, and that recognize how aspects of metal's heaviness and musical style extend before Black Sabbath—and, vice versa, that recognize how many legacies of blues music and culture remain in metal today.

5
Headbanging as a Legacy of Black Dance

Headbanging is sometimes associated with rock more broadly, but metal fans claim ownership over this dance form and take it to unique physical extremes.[1] Metal fans refer to themselves as "headbangers," and bands often reference headbanging in songs about the genre, such as Metallica's "Whiplash" (1983) or Quiet Riot's "Metal Health" (1983). During metal's commercial golden age in the 1980s, MTV's *Headbanger's Ball* was on televisions across the world. Twenty years later, Ian Christe titled his blockbuster history of the genre *Sound of the Beast: The Complete Headbanging History of Heavy Metal*. Other extreme dance practices described in Chapter 9, especially moshing, can share some of headbanging's purposes and effects which I explore in this chapter. However, moshing is not universal across all metal genres and communities, as evidenced by the slogan "No fun / No core / No mosh / No trends" for the infamous early 1990s Norwegian black metal label Deathlike Silence Productions, or the relative absence of moshing in slower metal styles like stoner metal. Headbanging unifies the many subcommunities of metal, while many other codes and practices have provoked genre boundary disputes throughout metal's history, including singing styles, dress, flamboyant theatricality, moshing, blues influences, occult or satanic iconography, and technical virtuosity.

Headbanging is woven into the genre's origin myths. Something recognizable as headbanging, although it is less stylized than later incarnations of the practice, is visible in live video of the three bands most frequently mentioned in metal's origin story (Deep Purple, Led Zeppelin, and Black Sabbath); one especially clear example is Black Sabbath's 1970 live performance recorded at the Théâtre 140 in Brussels (often mislabeled as "Live in Paris 1970").[2] There are several stories about the origin of the name "headbanging" or the

---

[1] In my experience, headbanging is rarely described as a type of "dance" by metal fans, so some readers may be surprised by this term. But as I show below, headbanging resonates deeply with scholarship on dance in popular music, so this is the context I have chosen to frame my study of headbanging in this and other publications.

[2] I have been unable to find much information about the original live video recording, which I've encountered through an online copy that seems to have been bootlegged from a Yorkshire Television rebroadcast in the 1980s.

Heaviness in Metal Music. Stephen S. Hudson, Oxford University Press. © Oxford University Press 2026.
DOI: 10.1093/9780197774991.003.0008

practice itself, each crediting a different iconic band. The phrase "Bang your head against the stage," which opens the second verse to Metallica's song "Whiplash," invokes a famous tall tale that fans invented headbanging in the front row at a Led Zeppelin concert when they started hitting their heads against the stage. But that story seems too improbable to be true; in my years of headbanging I've never seen anyone hit their head against anything—at least, not on purpose. Hitting your head against a stage even once with any kind of force would probably cut your forehead open and give you a concussion. On the other hand, it's hard to imagine a row of metal fans gingerly tapping their heads on the side of a stage, and even if this careful dance were to occur, such caution could never be identified with headbanging's essential character of reckless, wild abandon.

But while this origin story may not be factually true, it is true to the spirit of the dance: the purpose of headbanging is to experience heavy physical impacts. Headbanging is not merely nodding, but a wild head-shaking that involves the whole body; headbangers often move their shoulders and back, not just their head, and they often stand with their legs apart and bent for balance, leaning forward for greater depth of movement. They may even grab onto their knees or a nearby piece of furniture for support. This visceral whole-body motion gets your blood thundering in your ears, blocks out your awareness of your surroundings as your brain gets pushed to the front of your skull, and disorients you as your visual and vestibular systems are thrust wildly back and forth. Headbanging can also put extreme stress on your neck and shoulders—which is why the term "neckwrecker" is used for especially good metal music that really gets you moving.[3]

Headbanging is also deeply entangled with the racial politics of the White blues scene out of which heavy metal emerged, although this might be a surprise to some readers, given the widespread assumption that metal is essentially White. Several studies have documented metal dance practices ethnographically and explored issues of gender and simulation of violence (e.g., Riches 2011; Dodds 2011), but none have explored headbanging's history, especially its emergence from and relation to dance practices in earlier blues-rock. Several other dance practices are also endemic across many metal subgenres (including moshing, raising the devil's horns, and throwing fists in the air), but while I will occasionally reference metal dance more generally,

---

[3] The term "neckwrecker" is intended as hyperbole, but a few musicians have, in fact, wrecked their necks after years of headbanging abuse. The most famous is Tom Araya, the vocalist and bassist of the American thrash metal band Slayer, who underwent a surgery in 2010 which fused his neck vertebrae together with a titanium plate to treat his persistent cervical radiculopathy. This surgery has left him unable to headbang for the rest of his life.

I focus on headbanging. My arguments rely on understanding nodding to blues and rock'n'roll as a precedent for headbanging, so they do not apply as clearly or directly to moshing and other dance practices. Specifically, I argue that headbanging emerged as an exaggeration of nodding to the blues which valorized bodily excess rather than avoiding it, eventually resulting in a distinct novel dance practice that was no longer understood as a response to Black music.

An early review of a live performance by the Rolling Stones at the Crawdaddy Club in Richmond, England resonates with future heavy metal, but also invokes a Black musical past:

> ... In the half darkness, the guitars and drums twang and bang. Pulsating R&B. Shoulder to shoulder on the floor are 500 youngsters in black leather and sweaters. You could boil an egg in the atmosphere. Heads shake violently, and feet stamp in tribal style with hands above heads, clapped in rhythm. Shaking figures above the rest, held aloft by their colleagues, thrashing and yelling, like a revivalist meeting in America's deep south ... (Strausbaugh 2001, 43 [quoting a 1963 *Daily Mirror* article by Patrick Doncaster])

Andrew Cope observes that head-shaking is not an isolated element here, but already part of a constellation of practices and signifiers that remained in tight formation throughout the emergence of heavy metal: black leather, loudness, darkness, distorted guitar, head-shaking, and crowd surfing (Cope 2010, 24). But several other keywords clearly evoke a Black American past, including the reference to "a revivalist meeting in America's deep south" and the term "R&B"—short for "rhythm and blues"—which usually implies Blackness (whereas "rock" often implies Whiteness).

My investigation of these origins lies at the edge of a larger scholarly discourse on Black dance. The term "Black dance" has been used to describe a wide range of cultural traditions, ranging as widely as the traditional Guinean dance Kuku which was at one time taught so widely in the United States it became synonymous with West African dance (Johnson 2012, 75), the Alvin Ailey ballet company's fusions of ballet technique with contemporary and traditional Black movement (Dixon 1990), the "eccentric" tap dance team Brown and McGraw who influenced Louis Armstrong's development of jazz in the 1920s (Harker 2008, 69), and contemporary vernacular / popular styles including breakdancing and hip-hop (Johnson 2023). Scholars studying the vernacular dance styles of Black Americans, including Imani Kai Johnson, have observed a set of common stylistic traits as an "Africanist" inheritance or continuity (see Johnson 2023, 17), while arguing that Black American dance styles are new creations in America which have been shaped by (and hybridized with) European or Euro-American contexts and styles. For this reason, following the lead of Hall (1993) and Johnson (2023), I have used the term "Black" rather than "African American." When I describe Black dance as a precedent for headbanging, I am thinking primarily of live performances of blues, soul, and rock'n'roll; but some of the authors I cite discuss a much wider range of styles to reinforce their claims for Africanist continuities within Black dance.

Theorizing Appropriation and Transformation in Dance

It's long been recognized that rock and metal *music* contains transformations of blues materials (Headlam 1997), including pentatonic riffing, backbeats, gruff vocals, and string-bending techniques. But the potential existence of continuities or transformations from Black American music to other metal genre practices (including dance, aesthetics, lyrics, and social dynamics) has remained mostly unexplored—although studies of punk have explored such transformations (Hebdige 1979, 62–70; Rapport 2014, 2020).

The dance scholar Jane C. Desmond (1997) provides a valuable model for thinking through what it means to recognize some transfer or continuity from Black dance to headbanging. Desmond points out that transfer of a dance practice from one culture to another represents more than a simple "cultural appropriation."

> While the notion of "appropriation" may signal the transfer of source material from one group to another, it doesn't account for the changes in performance style and ideological meaning that accompany the transfer. Concepts of hybridity or syncretism more adequately describe the complex interactions among ideology, cultural forms, and power differentials that are manifest in such transfers. (Desmond 1997, 35)

Similarly, Eric Rapport describes the "raw power" blues-rock musical style of bands like the Stooges, Led Zeppelin, and Black Sabbath as more than a mere imitation or appropriation of Black practices, but a "transformation of blues resources" (Rapport 2020, 55 and 62) in which the musical performance style and ideological meaning changes substantially. If headbanging has any precedent in blues or White blues, like the musical dimensions of heavy metal, then it is not enough to simply observe some kind of continuity; we must understand how the movements and their meaning have changed during this transfer.

The clearest precursor for headbanging is a practice of nodding that can often be observed in video recordings of White audiences watching Black performers from the 1950s and 1960s, such as a broadcast of Chuck Berry which aired on Belgian television in 1965.[4] Nodding represents a compromise between White audiences' desire to demonstrate their knowledge of Black cultural conventions of active audience participation, and White society's norms of comportment. In such footage, White audiences nod repetitively, but the Black performers such as Berry are a lot more varied in their motion—with the exception of seated drummers and standing bass players, whose body motion is restricted by the bulkiness of their instruments. Black lead performers often moved their heads too, of course, but usually with more side-to-side motion, rather than just forwards and back. For example, James Brown performing "Get it Together" live at the Boston Gardens in 1968 briefly engages in head-shaking during a dance break between vocal phrases, but is moving his arms from side to side at the same time, and the motion of his head is more syncopated; and while performing "Voodoo Child (Slight Return)" at the 1969 Woodstock festival, Jimi Hendrix emphatically moves his head downwards in a way which resembles headbanging, but only for isolated moments, rather than on every beat. As I explore below, repetitively nodding on every beat might not be considered aesthetically successful in Black cultural contexts, but among White audiences, nodding was imagined as an appropriate response to Black music.

These differences between Black dance and White nodding—and those between nodding and headbanging—are not incidental, but reflect and reveal racial ideologies and power disparities. Desmond argues,

> In cases where a cultural form migrates from a subordinate to a dominant group, the meanings attached to that adoption (and remodeling) are generated within the parameters of the current and historical relations between the two groups, and their constitution of each as "other" and as different in particular ways. For example, the linkage in North American White culture of Blacks with sexuality, sensuality, and an alternately celebrated or denigrated presumedly "natural" propensity for physical ability, expressivity, or bodily excess tinges the adoption of Black dances. (Desmond 1997, 37)

[4] Chuck Berry's performance was recorded live on February 6, 1965, at Universal Studios in Waterloo, Belgium, and broadcast on May 11 of the same year.

Among White audiences for Black music before 1970, nodding was a way to participate without engaging in full-body motions that White culture would have viewed as inappropriate bodily excess. But it was also a performance of assent, of "I dig this," which in addition to its time-keeping function signaled that the nodder approved of Black music—a gesture of approval indelibly marked by power disparities between mid-century White artists, audiences, and businessmen, and the Black artists whose culture they appropriated and consumed.

Nodding itself was not necessarily imported from Black dance culture. White audiences may have engaged in nodding to other musics. But, crucially, nodding was imagined to be an appropriate response to blues, rock'n'roll, and blues-rock—at a time when these genres would often have been understood either as Black music, or a White version of Black music. As White blues gradually came to be called heavy metal, the practice of nodding continued to be paired with it. But unlike blackface minstrelsy, nodding was never understood as an imitation of Black dance, but to the contrary as a way for White fans to appreciate and participate in Black music while remaining within White acceptable comportment.

Headbanging, as I've said, emerged as a physical exaggeration of White audiences' nodding to Black music, and the consequences and meaning of this transformation of movement deserve further reflection. Desmond laments that research in her era is more focused "on representation of the body and/ or its discursive policing than with its actions/movements as a 'text' themselves" (Desmond 1997, 30), and suggests that "An analysis of appropriation must include not only the transmission pathway and the mediating effects of the media, immigration patterns, and the like, but also an analysis *at the level of the body* of what changes in the transmission" (Desmond 1997, 34). At the level of the body, headbanging is a primitivist version of nodding in the same way that raw power music was a primitivist version of the blues: exaggerating physicality and intensity, doubling down on certain negative racist stereotypes about Black culture and valorizing them as positive traits, while gradually removing their connection with race. During the era of White blues and raw power rock, the physical intensity of dance in these genres was often associated with Blackness, such the excerpt from Strausbaugh quoted above: "Heads shake violently, and feet stamp in tribal style ..." This connotation is even more explicit in the words of John Sinclair, member of the raw power group the MC5: "The actions of the Black Panthers in America have inspired us and given us strength, as has the music of Black America [...] our music contains and extends the power and feeling of the Black magic music that originally informed our bodies and told us we could be free" (quoted in Waksman 2011, 31). After the rise of the term "heavy metal" circa 1974, headbanging was not associated with Black music, but it was still understood as a liberating force along the lines that Sinclair implied—a performative expression of bodily freedom from more restrictive White norms of comportment.

Despite the fact that nodding was filtered through underinformed White stereotypes about Black Americans, it still resonated with some of the cultural values highlighted by Black dance scholars. As an exaggeration of this nodding practice, headbanging might be said to reflect some degree of understanding of Black dance by White artists and audiences—however partial, distorted, or secondhand that understanding might have been. Many similarities between the cultural values of Black dance (as described by previous scholars) and of headbanging suggest some substantial, though attenuated, continuity—even while they illuminate important differences, too.

Headbanging and Black Dance Are Both . . .

. . . Spontaneous, Unchoreographed Individual Expression

The spontaneous, expressive nature of headbanging is not unique to this dance style, but represents a broader rock movement culture. Susan Fast writes that in rock communities, "It is the music that should always remain the central focus of attention, not the performer's body, and it is the music that determines, supposedly in an unpremeditated way, how the body should respond" (Fast 2001, 148). This applies to all metal dance practices including headbanging; dancing fans are rarely "mickey-mousing" the motions of onstage performers, or following any rehearsed choreography. Instead, they are spontaneously expressing their own excitement, and acting out their individual understanding of the music's rhythm and flow.

Metal fans and musicians sometimes synchronize their headbanging for spectacular effect, but this is by no means required within the genre. For example, the musicologist Glenn T. Pillsbury reports that Metallica's former bassist Cliff Burton frequently headbanged to a much freer rhythm than the other band members.

Unlike Hetfield and Mustaine, Burton's headbanging [during the song "Whiplash"] does not always coincide strictly with the beat [. . .] Burton engaged with the changing rhythmic intensities of Metallica's music in a very flowing manner. [. . .] his body motions were generally slower than the others, but also more fluid and large-scale. (Pillsbury 2006, 14)

This is not unique to Burton; Metallica's current lineup also headbangs to different rhythms within the same passage of music (Hudson 2022a, 129), and I believe this is common among metal bands, especially during passages in which guitarists play asymmetrical or irregular riff rhythms over a steady back-beat. While there is no moratorium against synchronized headbanging, there is also no requirement that band members or their fans headbang together, and it is common to see adjacent people simultaneously engaging in headbanging in different ways. (This issue is explored systematically in Chapter 8.)

The dance historian Jacqui Malone reports a similar criterion of individuality in Black dance culture, especially in vernacular dance traditions.

In this dance tradition, the idea of executing any dance exactly like someone else is usually not valued. When vocal groups perform choreographed dance movements, the audience expects each singer to bring his or her own personality to the overall movement style […] Black idiomatic dancers always improvise. (Malone 1996, 34)

This isn't to say that there aren't moments in which performers instruct audience members: in Black American music, there's a strong tradition of didactic "dance fad" songs whose lyrics consist of choreographic cues (the closest analogue in metal are performers' live exhortations to "go crazy" or "start those circle pits"). But even in moments when many people are moving in synchrony, the aesthetic goal is still individual expression of musical feeling, rather than synchrony for synchrony's sake.

… Audible and Visible Audience Participation, Meant to Demonstrate Appreciation

Scholars writing about Black dance have long posited that one of the characteristic differences between Black and European traditions is a blurred distinction between performers and audiences. Malone traces this difference back to traditional African societies.

Most European conceptions of art would separate music from dance and both music and dance from the social situations that produce them. Most traditional

African conceptions, on the other hand, couple music with one or more other art forms, including dance. And most Africans experience music as part of a multidimensional social event that may take place in a village square, a town plaza, a courtyard […] Invariably audience members participate verbally and through physical movement. (Malone 1996, 10)

Following an argument by the pioneering Africanist Melville Herskovits, Malone posits the existence of "African continuances in African American culture" (Malone 1996, 24) and argues that the expectation of active audience participation in Black vernacular music is one of these continuances.

Malone suggests that audience members' active participation in Black vernacular music is often a way to recognize aesthetic success. The ethnomusicologist Portia Maultsby observes,

When performers demonstrate their knowledge of the Black musical aesthetic, the responses of audiences can become so audible that they momentarily drown out the performer. The verbal responses of audiences are accompanied by handclapping; foot-stomping; head, shoulder, hand, and arm movement; and spontaneous dance. (Maultsby 2015, 18)

The audible and visible participation of the audience is considered a crucial part of the performance, to the extent that a concert without such participation feels incomplete or even uncomfortable. When the audience members "momentarily drown out the performer," they are adding to, rather than interrupting, the performance.

Active audience participation is also expected in metal music and serves the same purpose of recognizing aesthetic success and generating excitement (Dodds 2011, 145–47). Natalie J. Purcell observes that "While popular [death metal] bands are playing, fans show their appreciation by 'getting into' the music" (Purcell 2003, 33) in several ways, including headbanging and moshing. Metal bands often banter with audiences to inspire greater physical investment. The powerful amplification used for metal music means there is no chance of "momentarily drowning out the performer," but many metal audiences sing or shout in addition to dancing, becoming an audible and visible part of the performance. This participation is an investment which generates a significant return; headbanging adds to one's own experience of heaviness (see Chapter 8), as well as amplifying the physical energy of the spectacle and encouraging other audience members to respond in kind (Berger 1999, 156).

... Full-Body Motion That Departs from Upright Posture and Dispels Mind–Body Dualism

In his pioneering musicological monograph about heavy metal, Robert Walser writes in a footnote that headbanging is "a vigorous nodding to the beat of the music" (Walser 2014 [1993], 180), but it is arguably much more than mere nodding. The musicologist Jonathan N. Piper observes, "the head does not simply pivot on the neck; the entire body undulates back and forth, up and down, to propel the head (and often long hair) through space in a spectacular display" (Piper 2013, 59–60). Careful or restrained headbanging is hardly recognizable as headbanging at all. Headbangers describe their dance as "ferocious," "extreme" full-body motion (Dodds 2011, 141 and 163) which constantly displaces the headbanger's central organs of vision, balance, hearing, and cognition, making dispassionate contemplation impossible.

Headbanging's physical postures and intensity of engagement resonate with descriptions of Black dance aesthetics. Headbangers often bend their knees to enable a greater range of motion and may grab on to their knees for support; similarly, Malone reports a Kongo proverb which advises one to "Dance with bended knees, lest you be taken for a corpse" (Malone 1996, 9). The essential motion of headbanging is to depart from an upright posture, bending at the waist and bending the back to thrust the head forwards; similarly, Malone argues that departure from upright posture is characteristic of African differences from European dance, because "To many western and central Africans, [...] straightened hips, elbows, and knees epitomized rigidity and death" (Malone 1996, 11–12).[5] Among audiences in Black music cultures, "Restrained contemplative behavior is not expected, nor is it assigned any particular value [...]" (Malone 1996, 10)—unlike many European and Euro-American aesthetic philosophies and practices, in which restrained, contemplative behavior is assumed.

... A Flexible Expression of Shifting Rhythmic Feel, Coordinated with the Backbeat

Headbanging in metal music and audience participatory dance motion in Black American music are both meant to express the music's beat or rhythmic

---

[5] In contrast, the dance scholar Jane C. Desmond observes that "In dance traditions originating in Europe, both popular and theatrical, such as ballet, the torso tends toward quietude and verticality" (Desmond 1997, 38).

feel. Malone describes this as a tendency to "dance the song" in traditional African and Black American musical cultures (Malone 1996, 28), in that dance enacts the music's rhythmic shifts. The anthropologist, author, and choreographer Zora Neale Hurston (who wrote primarily in the first half of the twentieth century, when the word "Negro" was considered the politest term for African Americans) reports that in Black dance,

> there is always rhythm, but it is the rhythm of segments. Each unit has a rhythm of its own, but when the whole is assembled it is lacking in symmetry. But easily workable to a Negro who is accustomed to the break in going from one part to another, so that he adjusts himself to the new tempo. (Hurston 1995 [1934], quoted in Malone 1996, 35)

The Black American vernacular songs Hurston discusses (she mentions in this passage "the St. Louis Blues" and the tap dancers Earl "Snakehips" Tucker and Bill "Bojangles" Robinson) have multiple sections, each with their own type of rhythm (often grounded by a backbeat, as defined below), and the dancers are expected to reflect the rhythmic shifts between sections through changes in their own dancing motion. As I will explore in Chapter 8, shifting rhythms are also a central aesthetic dimension in metal music, and headbanging is expected to reflect these shifts (see Hannan 2024).

In many popular music genres, but especially those with roots in Black America, the backbeat drum pattern is the primary, predominant musical technique for structuring and cueing these rhythmic shifts. The backbeat is a type of drum pattern counted in 4, in which there are snare hits on beats two and four that serve as both strong characteristic accents, and reference points for the coordination of musical notes and body motion (Figure 5.1). The musicologist Steven Baur (2021) reports that the origin of the backbeat can be traced to recordings of early Black American gospel musicians in the 1930s such as Sister Rosetta Tharpe, whose backing ensemble can be heard

Figure 5.1 A simple backbeat with hand claps and footsteps, followed by an idiomatic hard rock or heavy metal backbeat.

clapping on beats two and four. A crucial, defining feature of this early back-beat is that these claps on beats two and four are matched by less audible footsteps on beats one and three. These footsteps are surely more important for coordination and balance than the handclaps, even though they are hard to hear in recordings. We can think of the backbeat as both a sounding pattern (handclaps or snare hits on beats two and four) and a strategy for matching motion to sound, and as a guide to coordinate spontaneous individual motion with the group. Malone quotes an observation by the jazz dancer James Berry about the relationship between body and beat: "The rhythmic motion on the beat with the music has something. You feel free to do what you want and you can't get lost, because you can always come in, you can dance with abandon but still you are encased within the beat" (Malone 1996, 33). As I show in Chapter 8, backbeats play the same role in metal music, helping dancers stay oriented to the band's shifting rhythms.

This particular strategy for matching sound and motion, in which sounding accents on beats two and four are heard to imply felt beats or centers of gravity on beats one and three, has persisted through all of the musical style and genre transformations that lie between early Black gospel music and metal, as well as many other popular styles. Unlike some rhythms, the backbeat is not very cul-turally exclusive. Kofi Agawu (2003, 73) explains that among scholars studying African musics, cultural insiders recognize the beat spontaneously and without conscious effort, but "those not familiar with the choreographic supplement, however, sometimes have trouble locating the main beats and expressing them in movement." But the ethnomusicologist and performance studies scholar Harris Berger clarifies that a piece of expressive culture can still be "culturally specific" even if it is not "exclusive to that culture."

> To say that [such modes of experience] are culturally specific is not to posit a world of discrete cultures, each with a fixed repertoire of ways of engaging with expressive forms... However varied, emergent, and subject to agency such practices are, though, they will always emerge in response to a particular cultural context, and in this sense are "culturally specific." (Berger 2009, 20)

The backbeat, then, is not exclusive to metal music, since it is shared among a wide range of popular genres and understood by a diverse range of audiences. But it is culturally specific to the context of metal music: when you hear metal, you expect a backbeat.[6]

---

[6] Extreme metal is the exception that proves the rule: to differentiate themselves from mainstream metal, some extreme metal bands avoid regular-time backbeats, and instead only use double-time backbeats or blast beats (see Chapter 8).

In this context, these patterns are heard to have unique, heavy qualities. The hierarchies between strong and weak beats conventionally evoked by the term "meter" are often flattened out by the maximal aesthetics and practices of metal (headbanging, fist-pumping, overdriven guitars, pummeling drums, etc.). This is perhaps what Robert Walser meant when he said that "although most metal is in 4/4 time, the rhythmic framework is organized more basically around a pulse than a meter" (Walser 2014 [1993], 49). A backbeat in rock'n'roll or jazz has substantial differences in feeling between even and odd beats, evoking a side-to-side motion, but in metal, every beat feels superlatively, viscerally emphatic.

Headbanging as a Transformation of Black Dance

Walser argues that there is a strong contrast in physical style between metal and Black dance: "Metal's relatively rigid sense of the body [...] reflect[s] European-American transformation of African-American musical materials and cultural values" (Walser 2014 [1993], 17). This is true: one of Malone's signal arguments about Black dance is to observe an "aesthetic of cool" and "idiomatic effortlessness"—and headbanging certainly diverges from this aesthetic. Malone observes that in Black dance, "practitioners of this style do not throw their bodies around, they do not cut completely loose. When the musical break comes, it is not a matter of 'letting it all hang out' [...] A loss of control and a loss of coolness places one *squarely* outside of the tradition" (Malone 1996, 34). In metal culture, on the other hand, dance practices often simulate a loss of control and coolness, although unspoken ground rules prevent the chaos of actual violence (Riches 2011; Dodds 2011, 157–61).

Headbanging's effortfulness or "uncoolness" can also be read as a departure from Black cultural values. While headbanging's rigidity might signify death or reservedness within the Africanist perspective of Black dance, in metal culture it signifies the opposite—unrestrained intensity. Headbanging, like moshing, is an experience of recklessness, simulated violence, and play with transgression (Kahn-Harris 2007), reflecting metal culture's broader aesthetics of heaviness, power, and force (Walser 2014 [1993]; Weinstein 1991). From this perspective, headbanging embodies an earnestness and total commitment which makes White blues seem reserved by comparison—part of a broader, common narrative that heavy metal made earlier rock seem "domesticated" and less authentic (e.g., Christe 2003, 4–5).

While nodding represented a compromise between Black participatory movement and White norms of comportment, headbanging rudely transgresses those norms in a way that is paradoxically both collinear and orthogonal with White blues' transformation of Black dance. White blues required more physicality than previous White popular music styles like skiffle, but heavy metal's dance style of headbanging required yet more physical commitment. This transformation reaches back toward Black dance in its full-body motion and sense of direct expression, yet careens away from Black dance in its effortfulness and emphatic repetition.

Conclusion: Toward a More Continuous, Integrated History of Heavy Metal

Each step in this trajectory—from the coolness of Black dance and White audiences' hypersexual, racist stereotypes of Black Americans, to the effortfulness and heaviness and transgression of headbanging—represents a performative distinction, not just an incidental variation. The pioneering Africanist Melville Herskovits wrote,

> Whether Negroes borrowed from Whites or Whites from Negroes, in this or any other aspect of culture, it must always be remembered that the borrowing was never achieved without resultant change in whatever was borrowed, and, in addition, without incorporating elements which originated in the new habitat that, as much as anything else, give the new form its distinctive quality. (Herskovitz 1941, 225; quoted in Desmond 1997, 36)

Following Herskovits and Desmond, the aspects of headbanging which depart from Black dance and the nodding of White audiences in the 1960s are an essential part of what defines metal music and gives the genre its distinct character.

Paradoxically, however, headbanging will always connect the genre to Blackness. Headbanging is an exaggeration of nodding, which is in turn based on White audiences' observations of and desire to participate in Black music and dance; and as the metal genre has doubled down on headbanging over the decades, it is to a certain degree fetishizing certain dynamics derived from Black music culture (or, at least, White audiences' misunderstandings of Black culture). So long as metal retains headbanging, it cannot completely leave the blues behind, but carries with it the aftereffects of the genre's racialized past.

In this sense, headbanging reflects larger issues of the legacies of Black American music and musicians within the metal genre. Metal music did not emerge from nothing in 1970, but in many aspects and to an extent that is only beginning to be understood, it built on blues materials and White listeners' ideas about blues and Blackness. Deena Weinstein has argued that metal style didn't "crystallize" until the 1980s (Weinstein 1991, 44–45), and I would add that both the initial conditions of the style's emergence and the direction of its crystallization were shaped by the highly racialized ideologies of "White blues" and the subsequent erasure of race from metal discourses when the genre was renamed "heavy metal." Fellezs states that "Stone Vengeance makes a strong case for considering thrash metal as a Black musical tradition by remembering the links between the blues and rock" (Fellezs 2011, 135), but this is not as speculative as it might sound—it is a hidden truth lying in plain sight, whose ramifications must be explored further if we are to fully understand the nature and meaning of metal music and its dance practices today.

6

Angels and Demons

Hearing Gender and Heaviness in Metal's Fantastical Vocals

During the winter before the Ukrainian progressive metal band Jinjer released their second full-length album *King of Everything* (2016), they traveled to the city of Kiev to record a live version of the album's penultimate track "Pisces," which has since become the band's biggest hit to date. Discussions of Jinjer often highlight the striking vocal performances of the band's lead singer Tatiana Shmayluk, who alternates between blisteringly intense growls in a death metal style, and a melancholy melodic style more reminiscent of jazz cabaret (Burns 2023, 3.3). The two highest-voted comments on the YouTube video release of "Pisces (Live Session)" are no exception, and they map out some of the extraordinary ways in which vocals are heard in the metal genre:

> @davidacus956 3 years ago [as of August 2024]
> I heard this on Spotify and was like "I like the distinction between the two vocalists" and then I watched this

> @18spara 5 years ago [as of August 2024]
> She looks like an egyptian goddess and has the vocal range from demon to angel. This is so good.

Metal vocals are extraordinary—vocalists in this genre often transcend everyday uses of the voice, instead developing fantastical vocals that are heard to invoke or incarnate aspects of the otherworldly, supernatural, inhuman, and more-than-human. The longtime 'zine auteur Bill Zebub has said, "When you hear a death metal vocalist, you should be under the impression that you are hearing a demon" (quoted in Purcell 2003, 11), and while death metal represents the extreme end of screamed or growled vocal techniques, it illustrates key issues that are more broadly relevant. Metal vocalists in every subgenre often use a variety of specialized techniques for rough vocal timbres (screams, growls, etc.) that portray or convey an extraordinary sense of power,

Heaviness in Metal Music. Stephen S. Hudson, Oxford University Press. © Oxford University Press 2026.
DOI: 10.1093/9780197774991.003.0009

whose impact can be felt in a number of different ways depending on the listener's stance toward the music (this framework of stance and impact was outlined in Chapter 1). As with the concepts of heaviness and progressionism (Chapter 4) and the practice of headbanging (Chapter 5), these rough-timbered vocal techniques emerged from the complex racial (and, as we will see, gendered) ideology of previous blues and rock. Additionally, many metal bands incorporate more conventional classical and popular music singing styles, which in a metal context are referred to as "clean singing"—but with the exception of a few subgenres (power metal and symphonic metal), these clean-singing styles have often been controversial in metal (as illustrated by the title of the popular blog *No Clean Singing*).

The musicologist Nina Eidsheim (2019) has argued that throughout the history of popular music, a singer's voice has often been heard as a reflection of their biography and identity—a hearing which often blends authentic truth with essentializing (if not blatantly racist or sexist) assumptions and imaginative mythologizing—and metal's fantastical vocals distort and refract this listening process in fascinating ways. To say that metal vocalists are "depicting a character" is a bit too literal, with the exception of a few bands like Lordi and GWAR who actually dress as demons or aliens onstage. But most metal fans recognize that the voices of their favorite metal singers are, at least to some extent, costumes that are put on—not the singers' natural, mundane, everyday voices, but extraordinary registers used just for metal (whose roughness is often augmented with additional distortion in post-production). Metal fans often describe metal vocals as inhuman or greater-than-human, holding this discourse in paradoxical but productive tension with the universally acknowledged reality that the singers are, in fact, merely human (this dynamic was theorized in Chapter 2 as a "suspension of disbelief" forming the "basic illusion of heaviness"). In other words, there is often some tension between "what the singer sounds like" and "who the singer actually is" in metal music—and one might even say that the basic illusion of heaviness depends on this productive tension.

Some of the greatest consequences of this dynamic of mishearing are revealed in the metal community's discourse about non-male vocalists, whose performances are often either misidentified as male vocalizations, interpreted as gender-crossing or -betraying performances of masculinity, or associated with femininity and cast to the margins (or outside) of the metal genre. Heaviness in metal has often been understood in highly gendered terms that have excluded femininity, feminine performers, and female fans. With several notable exceptions (such as Clifford-Napoleone 2016; Hill 2016; Heesch and Scott 2016), metal scholarship has often failed to disrupt these assumptions. For example, Robert Walser argues,

Since the language and traditions of heavy metal have been developed by and are still dominated by men, my discussion of gender in metal will initially be an investigation of masculinity; I will return later to issues of the reception of these male spectacles by female fans. (Walser 2014 [1993], 110)

In Walser's formulation (and in too much other writing on the genre), men make metal music and therefore anything that is characteristic of metal is interpreted as inherently masculine—creating a closed loop of masculinity which might seem to lock out gendered Others, offering them only the role of passive observers of a musical masculinity that they cannot claim as their own. But women, trans, and non-gender-binary singers in metal have torn an ever-growing hole through this tautological gender bias, appropriating vocal techniques often heard as masculine to create feminine or gender-flexible spectacles. In this chapter, I build on Eidsheim's conception of voice and identity to study what musicians and fans say about vocals, accomplishing three goals: (1) reveal the racialized historical origins of metal's fantastical vocals and explain why they are so often heard as male, (2) recuperate the reputation of clean vocals (whether masculine or feminine) as a central part of the metal genre which contributes to heaviness, and (3) argue that women in metal today are creating new expressions of femininity (or, even, new kinds of femininity) and challenging the genre's masculinist framing at an unprecedented rate.

A Brief History of Rough-Timbered Vocals: From Blues and Black Feminism to White Rock Masculinity

There are a range of techniques for producing rough-timbered vocal sounds, but they usually involve the vestibular folds or "false cords" that are located above the vocal fold used in conventional speaking and singing (Heidemann 2016, 3.10). The false cords are sometimes activated at the same time as the regular vocal cords, which can produce rough or raspy vocals with definite pitch (common throughout blues, gospel, rock, and metal styles), or even special illusions of multiple pitches or notes an octave below the voice's ordinary range (as in the Tuvan throat singing tradition, recently championed by the Mongolian folk metal band The Hu). But the false cords can also be activated without using the regular vocal cords at all, to produce unpitched rough vocal sounds, like the guttural growls of death metal or the piercing screams of black metal. In any of these cases, while conventional vocal cords produce a resonant sound with a regular harmonic series that emphasizes the fundamental and its lowest harmonics, the use of false cords produces more inharmonic noise and strengthens higher harmonics, leading to perceptions of "rougher" timbre that listeners often associate with heightened effort or intensity of feeling.

Since the late 1960s, rough-timbered vocal styles have often been understood as a construction of White rock masculinity—but this was not the case in earlier American popular music. In the 1930s and 1940s, many of the most prominent rough-timbered singers were Black women—recall descriptions of Bessie Smith's "wild, rough, Ethiopian, harsh, volcanic" voice that I quoted in Chapter 4. Black female singers from this period (including blues singers like Bessie Smith, Billie Holiday, as well as gospel stars like Mahalia Jackson) were some of the most impactful models for vocal styles in early rock'n'roll. In an article about the pioneering singer and electric guitarist Sister Rosetta Tharpe, the American Studies scholar Gayle Wald reports:

> At some point during my research, I came upon this startling discovery: in the early 1970s, a British observer, writing about a Tharpe concert in England, had compared Rosetta to Elvis Presley. While this would not, on the surface, seem surprising (Elvis was, in fact, deeply influenced by Rosetta [...]), this observer had gone on to write that Rosetta Tharpe looked and sounded like a "blacked-up Elvis in drag," thereby not merely causing offense but getting the narrative of musical influence completely and utterly wrong. (Wald 2009, 158)

Histories of rock today widely acknowledge that White rock artists of the 1960s inherited their screams and shouts from Black performers of the 1950s, but as the scholar and activist Angela Y. Davis (1998) has argued, the prominence (or even preeminence) of female singers in the blues before 1950 is often still forgotten.

By the mid-1950s, rough-timbered vocals were associated more strictly with masculinity.[1] The long history of Black women singing rough vocals in the blues and gospel has often conflicted with constructions of femininity as delicate and demure (arguably imposed by middle- and upper-class White American culture). Tina Turner, for example, once said, "[W]hen I say I can sing, I know that I don't have a 'pretty' voice. My voice is not the voice of a woman, so to speak." (Fast 2010, 214; quoted from Turner and Loder 1986,

---

[1] Drawing on research about transgender voices, Nina Eidsheim argues that while range has classically been defined as the primary distinguishing parameter of vocal gender, mens' and womens' ranges overlap significantly, and other cues like timbre, word choice, and intonation often have more of an impact on what gender listeners think they are hearing in a voice (Eidsheim 2019, 104–6).

204). But also, throughout the 1950s, leading Black male singers like Bo Diddley, Little Richard, James Brown, and Howlin' Wolf often prominently associated their screams and growls with male sexuality and hypermasculinity (Little Richard's gender-bending costumes aside). The small temporal distance between the prominent female rough vocals of the 1930s, and the strong association of rough vocals with masculinity only twenty years later, led to some gendered statements that seem contradictory out of context: for example, Tina Turner's contemporary Gene Washington said, "A woman doing that type of thing then was kind of a no-no. She was like Bessie Smith and some of those other great singers ..." (Fast 2010, 214; quoted from Turner and Loder 1986, 65). Paradoxically, while Washington identifies earlier leading blues women as the primary referential context for Tina Turner's voice, he simultaneously labels her vocal techniques as unwomanly.

Rough timbres have often been heard to carry a kind of authenticity, with the presumption that they reflect intense feelings, traumas, or other difficult life experiences. According to Rudolph Fisher, a Black physician who wrote a famous essay about the Harlem jazz scene of the 1920s, many early female blues singers working before the widespread availability of cheap amplification "yelled themselves hoarse [...] and acquired that throaty roughness which is so frequent among blues singers, and which, though admired as characteristically African, is as a matter of fact nothing but a form of chronic laryngitis" (Fisher 1999, 62; quoted in Stras 2006, 179). Nina Sun Eidsheim (2019, 151–56) discusses how Billie Holiday's rough vocal timbre has often been described as audible evidence of her sensationalized biography of poverty, fast living, and drug abuse, but notes that Holiday's sound has been accurately simulated by vocalists who share none of those experiences (including a seven-year-old contestant on *Norway's Got Talent*). Laurie Stras, framing rough timbres as "disrupted voice" indicative of "vocal damage," argues that in popular music, "Many singers have learned to simulate or manipulate damage in the voice," and this damage "seems to be linked with concepts of authority, authenticity, and integrity" (Stras 2006, 174).

In the late 1960s, White rock singers began drawing on these techniques in ways that activated similar ideas about authenticity, including the Beatles (on John Lennon's heavier songs), Steppenwolf, Cream, the Rolling Stones, and Led Zeppelin. These singers were often quite willing to admit that they were channeling Black artists in their performances, and sometimes looked like they were putting on an unfamiliar character (I'm thinking of early performances by Steppenwolf), including stiff imitations of Black dialect or trying awkwardly to move in a less inhibited manner. Throughout the 1960s, White artists began to copy these kinds of vocal stylings from other White artists instead of from Black artists—a dynamic which Hamilton (2016) calls the "White Atlantic." Rough vocal timbres gradually lost their close association with Blackness by the mid-1970s, and became an established part of White male rock vocality (paralleling my arguments in Chapter 4). But they retained a sense of authenticity derived from opposition to the (less-rough-timbered) mainstream (paralleling my arguments in Chapter 3).

Metal Inherited (Vocal) Constructions of White Rock Masculinity

Heavy metal began as an intensification of rock and blues musical materials, and this is true of voice types and vocal techniques as much as any other dimension. The paradigmatic classic heavy metal voice type is a high-tension tenor ranging over a wide range of textures, including Ozzy Osbourne's eerie high-pitched screel (Black Sabbath, Ozzy Osbourne); Bruce Dickinson's semi-operatic shout (Iron Maiden); Ronnie James Dio's scratchy, electric belting (Rainbow, Black Sabbath, Dio); the swaggering falsetto of Axl Rose (Guns 'n Roses); and the two voice types of Rob Halford (Judas Priest)—his tough-guy shout (which can be heard in hits before 1990, such as "Breaking the Law") and barely-tuneful, banshee-like scream (which he began using on 1990's *Painkiller*). Doro Pesch (Warlock), whose slightly hoarse singing tone and powerful screams fit right into classic heavy metal vocality, was one of the only female metal vocalists before the millennium to become famous for this voice type and launch her own solo career. Each of these singers bears some family resemblance to the preceding generation of White rock vocalists, such as Led Zeppelin's Robert Plant, or the Rolling Stones' Mick Jagger—but often with greater intensity.

As an exaggeration of the rougher end of rock vocals, the classic heavy metal style inherited a close association with masculinity, but as the genre developed, its singing styles deviated further and further from the mainstream popular music vocals of previous decades. In a chapter on the jazz singer Jimmy Scott (who never went through puberty because of a medical condition called Kallmann syndrome), Eidsheim describes falsetto as a normative feature of masculine vocality in the 1960s that Jimmy Scott did not share, although the pitch range he used was similar to many of his contemporaries.

> However, one differentiating factor is the use of what I call timbral scare quotes— the use of a portion of the voice that is set apart timbrally from what the singer deems to be the normative part of his or her voice. [...] By enlisting falsetto, a

vocal technique and recognizable timbral shift, male performers can utilize larger portions of their voices while maintaining an image of masculinity. Indeed, the most recognized and recognizable African American male vocalists of the 1960s, the decade that could have included Scott's mainstream breakthrough, made liberal use of falsetto technique [to signal] hypermasculinity. (Eidsheim 2019, 107)

But falsetto is rarely, if ever, used in the classic heavy metal vocal style. Instead of falsetto (which has a soft, breathy timbre and relatively low maximum volume), metal singers often use a technique called "head voice" in their high range—a technique which produces more intensely bright timbre (Heidemann 2016, 3.24).[2] When head voice is used with strong breath support and high volume, the singer is working with the same basic techniques as an operatic tenor, conveying an impression of force and power.

The 1980s saw two big new trends in metal vocals, moving in opposite directions.[3] One was an exaggeration of the classic heavy metal style, developing into something more tuneful, heroic, and sometimes androgynous by the glam metal scene centered around Los Angeles (Mötley Crüe, Poison, Nitro, Dokken). Glam metal bands paired highly produced music and pretty, accessible singing with "beautiful" appearances—building on a long tradition of blended hypermasculine and feminine costuming in rock, carrying forward the transgressive sartorial experiments of rock stars like Little Richard, Jimi Hendrix, David Bowie, and Sweet. Walser claims that in heavy metal, "[a]ndrogynous musicians and fans appropriate the visual signs of feminine identity in order to claim the powers of spectacularity for themselves" (Walser 2014 [1993], 128–29), providing men transgressive power and some release (even if only temporarily) from the suffocating rigidities of normative masculinity in everyday life.

At the same time as glam metal vocalists pursued prettier melodic singing, many underground metal musicians were moving toward increasingly extreme and unmelodic styles. While the glam metal vocal style was closely related to classic heavy metal style, and thus retained a family resemblance with conventional rock vocals, the increasingly "rabid vocalisations" (Cope 2010, 98) of underground and extreme metal grew increasingly distinct from

---

[2] Ozzy Osbourne is the rare exception who sings in a head voice timbre but without the impression of operatic power that it normally takes for a man to sing in this range without falsetto; this gives his voice an eerie quality that is especially well suited to the spooky lyrics he often sings. In centuries past, the now-extinct castrato voice type was often used to represent exceptionally heroic or supernatural characters; Ozzy's uncannily high voice (without falsetto) seems to index a comparable range of expression.

[3] The classic heavy metal style vocalists, of course, didn't go anywhere during the 1980s, and in fact continued to be featured on what some consider to be the style's most iconic records, including *Blizzard of Ozz* (1980), *The Number of the Beast* (1982), *Appetite for Destruction* (1987), and *Painkiller* (1990).

mainstream aesthetics, and inaccessible to (or at least, distasteful to) mainstream audiences. Underground extreme metal vocal techniques were less normal and "more metal" than those of glam metal, and vocals became a key field in the oppositional authenticity and progressionism which I discussed in Chapter 3. Within metal discourses, clean vocal styles became increasingly associated with alignment against metal, perceived inauthenticity, commercial viability, and the mainstream.

Extreme metal's growling and screaming styles developed gradually over time, part of the "teleological treadmill of increasing brutality" (Wallmark 2018) which I discussed in Chapter 3. At the beginning of the 1980s, a few bands like Motörhead and Venom experimented with gruff, shouting styles that still had some similarity with previous rock vocal styles, especially punk rock. But as the 1980s progressed, bands experimented with increasingly unsettling vocal sounds. The bone-chilling high-pitched scream descending into a tortured howl at the beginning of Slayer's "Angel of Death" (1986) is a memorable moment that opened up a new world of vocal expression in metal, and Tom Araya's gruff shouting in the rest of the song was another prominent point on the journey toward the unmelodic growling and screaming that characterized the extreme genres that developed over the next decade. In the next year, *Scream Bloody Gore* (1987) by the Florida-based band Death coalesced an even more guttural growling style that was refined by a generation of "death metal" bands into a distinct aesthetic of "death growls." While one can trace an unbroken, continuous, gradual development from classic rock vocals to death growls, the destination is so radically different from the origin that it is, to many, unrecognizable as "singing."

Since growled vocals are produced by the false cords, not conventional vocal cords, the association between growled vocals and masculinity does not reflect any gendered difference in physiological ability. Conventional voices are often lower in men than women, because vocal cords in men are on average 60% longer—but this has no direct effect on growled vocal techniques since growls use the false folds (Heesch 2018, 18). Biological tendencies for men to have greater body size, strength, and aggression may correlate with widespread cultural or cognitive associations of growled vocals with men, but these are differences in how we hear and think about the voice, rather than how we can use it. In short, metal listeners are often pre-conditioned to hear growled vocals as male-gendered, not because of basic biological differences in vocal capability, but because of (1) cultural constructions of vocal masculinity reified during the rock era, and (2) cultural or personal prejudices about femininity that cast rough vocal timbres as unnatural or improper expression for women.

Women Performing Death Growls: Misogyny, Disbelief, and Mishearing

Angela Gossow is the first female vocalist to become well-known within metal for performing death growls, and her case illustrates the consequences of this construction of rough-timbered masculinity which metal inherited from rock. The gender studies scholar Florian Heesch (2018) points out that there have been female vocalists performing death growls on record since almost the beginning of the death metal subgenre—specifically, he mentions the Dutch band Acrostichon, whose female vocalist Corinne van der Brand recorded death growls on demos as early as 1989. But it seems that Gossow became the first woman widely known for performing death growls when she auditioned in the year 2000 to become the lead singer for the Swedish melodic death metal band Arch Enemy. She remained the most prominent woman performing death growls for over a decade, until she stepped back from that role to become the band's manager in 2014.

Gossow is hardly ever discussed without mentioning her status as a woman in a field dominated by men—like many other people in other areas of society who are viewed as the "first" person from an under-represented demographic category to have some particular role. Early responses to her work with Arch Enemy included disbelief, such as the following fan review posted on the popular metal website *Encyclopedia Metallum*: "[…] the new vocalist really has some growling talent! I was kind of shocked by the fact that it is a she! A female growler by the name of Angela. And she growls just as good as any male in this genre!" (HawkMoon 2002). By performing death growls, Gossow has continually disproven the assumption that growl styles are inherently male, or that female vocal anatomy is incapable of producing such rough timbres. When listeners have misrecognized her voice on recordings as the performance of a male vocalist, her unambiguously female name and appearance challenge that interpretation, claiming a space for women in those listeners' understanding of extreme metal vocals.

Another symptom of this disbelief is that Gossow has been subjected to disproportionate scrutiny about her vocal technique over the years (Chaker and Heesch 2016). Even sympathetic journalists constantly asked questions about her techniques, her warm-ups, and after-concert vocal care—questions which are rarely posed to male singers in the same genre. (This is true even when the interviewer is also female, and clearly a fan; the longtime 'zine auteur Lady Enslain asked Gossow in 2009, "So how do you keep your voice from destroying itself? [… and later …] So you just have naturally thick vocal chords [sic]?") Gossow reports getting fewer of these questions as the years went on, perhaps indicating an increase in acceptance. But these questions suggest that there was initially widespread skepticism about women's ability to perform death growls and other extreme vocal techniques.

These phenomena of mishearing and disbelief highlight how, like heaviness, vocal gender is not an essential characteristic of the sound itself, or solely determined by the artist's choices, but something which is coproduced by listeners. Eidsheim (2019, 178) provocatively argues that "Voice's source is not the singer; it is the listener." There are many different ways to hear Angela Gossow's voice: as a woman performing a type of masculinity, a performance of a distinct type of "female masculinity" (Halberstam 1998), a woman reclaiming vocal modes that had been forbidden to her as masculine territory, or an "alternative femininity" (Burns 2023; Schippers 2002, 2007) which integrates aspects of masculine vocality into a new configuration or expression of femininity. But each of these hearings is an interpretive act by listeners: while Gossow selects her own vocal techniques, curates her dress and physical behavior on stage, Eidsheim would argue that it is listeners who categorize Gossow's sounds, assign a perceived gender, and imagine connections between this perception and their previous experiences of gendered voice.

Beauty and the Beast: Femininity Cast in Opposition to Metal

Angela Gossow became the first woman widely known for singing death growls in the early 2000s, but this does not mean she was the only woman singing in underground or extreme metal styles at that time. Several others became famous for clean-timbre singing within symphonic metal, melodic death metal, and other styles around or just after the turn of the millennium. But unlike Gossow's growls, these women's performances were often caught up in an existing discourse about clean- and rough-timbre, shaped by the opposition between melodic vocals in glam metal and rough-timbre vocals in early extreme metal. Clean-timbre singing in metal was, and is, often marginalized in the genre, in ways that are entangled with gender.

A common arrangement of female clean vocals which seems to reinforce this opposition between clean singing and metal is one often called the "Beauty and the Beast" archetype (Burns 2025), which is especially prominent in symphonic metal and melodic death metal. Several prominent bands in these styles feature women with various forms of clean-tone technique listed as "lead singers" or "clean lead vocals," contrasted with a growling male vocalist whose role is listed as "unclean vocals," "harsh vocals," or "male vocals." The most iconic example might be Nightwish, whose founding lead singer Tarja Turunen performs with an operatic tone that clearly reflects her classical training at the prestigious Sibelius Academy in Helsinki. In many songs, Turunen's voice is contrasted against the rough-timbre sung vocals of Marko Hietala, the band's bassist, who uses a melodic growling technique that retains some sense of pitch. For example, in the band's famous dance-metal hit "Wish I Had an Angel," Turunen sings the verses (starting at 0:21 and 1:23), while Hietala growls the choruses (0:57, 1:45, and 3:14—although Turunen joins this final chorus) as well as the bridge (2:25). The same opposition between clean female vocals and growled male vocals repeats throughout Nightwish's discography, including after Turunen was ejected from the band in 2005 and replaced by Anette Olzon (2007–2012) and Floor Jansen (2013–present), each of whom had less classical background and technique than Turunen.

This alternation and contrast between a clean-toned female lead and male growling often seems to center the male singer in the metal style, but separate the female singer from the rest of the band, as a foreign element imported from outside the metal genre (from classical music, hard rock, folk, or pop). In addition to Nightwish, other prominent bands who frequently use this dynamic include Epica (Simone Simons' clean female vocals vs. Mark Jansen's growls) and Within Temptation (Sharon den Adel vs. Robert Westerholt). In each of these cases, the male vocalist is also a guitarist, while the woman is only a vocalist; and the men often dress in black, denim, and leather, while the female vocalists often dresses differently than the rest of the band (e.g., Turunen often wore brightly colored, monochromatic, full-length formal dresses; in contrast, Jansen, the band's current female lead, wears black leather and headbangs with the rest of the band). These onstage roles and costumes can reinforce an alignment between the growling men and metal, while undermining the clean-toned women's alignment with the genre—sometimes giving the impression that these clean-tone female lead vocalists are not really part of the band, and perhaps not even part of metal culture at all. Ironically, while the clean-toned singers in Nightwish and Epica are among the most prominent women in metal, their roles within their respective bands simultaneously marginalize them within the genre.

In other bands where the rough-timbered male vocalist is the lead and the clean-singing women are labeled as "backing vocalists" or play "non-metal" instruments, this dynamic is even worse. For example, Netta Skog has provided accordion parts and backing vocals for the symphonic power metal band Turisas (2007–2011) and the symphonic black metal band Ensiferum (2017). Another example is the Swiss folk metal band Eluveitie, who have featured a number of women over the years on flute, harp, violin, or hurdy-gurdy (including Anna Murphy, Fabienne Erni, and Nicole Ansperger—all of whom have also provided clean vocals to accompany the band's growling lead male vocalist Chrigel Glanzmann); but Eluveitie has never had a female guitar player. These backing or non-metal roles for clean-tone female vocalists, and the oppositional positioning created by alternating their performances with a growled male vocalist, often seem to frame clean-tone female vocalists as a foreign element to metal, included to represent other musical traditions (folk, classical, etc.) imported to make a hybrid metal style.

The Feminization and Rejection of Clean Vocals in Metal

This is not a problem unique to female singers; clean-tone vocals by singers of any gender have often been often cast in opposition to the aesthetics of heaviness that are at the core of the metal genre. Gossow is no exception; when asked if she would ever do clean vocals on an Arch Enemy track, she responded:

> I am really not a big fan of clean vocals. I like the aggressive Dio or Halford type of voice, but the girls out there usually sound quite cute. And a cute voice and metal doesn't go well in my head. [. . .] I sound pretty when I sing clean. And Arch Enemy is not about sweet vocals. Its about throat cutting screams, hehe. (Gossow 2008; translated from Patacas 2008)

Gossow claims that clean singing by women, which she hears as "pretty," "sweet," and "cute," does not belong in metal, which is about "throat cutting screams."

Arch Enemy's guitarist, Michael Amott, makes a similar criticism of clean singing by men, implying that clean singing is not masculine enough, not serious enough, and contrary to the metal genre. Amott argues, "I don't feel like the melodies usually are metal; they sound more like a little boy singing in the chorus. It just doesn't fit. It's more like a pop sensibility to it, which is just not my taste at all, and it's not what we want to do" (Amott 2022). But like Gossow, he immediately suggests that classic heavy metal vocals are an exception: "[. . .] some of my favorite vocalists are who you would call 'clean vocalists,' like Rob Halford [Judas Priest], people like that, Ronnie James Dio [Black Sabbath, Rainbow, Dio]" (Amott 2022). This exception sounds like a contradiction, but follows from metal's combined values of progressionism and worship of "firsts" and predecessors: clean vocals may have seemed increasingly less metal in juxtaposition with the more extreme metal vocal techniques developing during the 1980s and 1990s, but comparatively clean-singing artists like Halford and Dio are unimpeachably "classic," and have thus been excluded from skepticism.[4]

Aside from specific clean-tone singers, clean vocal technique is itself disparaged in feminine or feminizing terms. The popular metal blog *No Clean Singing* (whose position is already clear from the site's title) states in a section about their "first principles":

> In our evolution as metal fans, the original founders of this site reached the point where we got upset when otherwise promising metal songs with good riffage and crushing drumwork were interrupted by an attack of clean crooning, particularly the breathy, whiny, upper-octave kind of excretions that used to characterize a lot of metalcore [...] If you know what we mean, then you've come to the right place. (*No Clean Singing*, n.d.)

The parameters of voice that the authors of *No Clean Singing* disparage ("breathy, whiny, upper-octave excretions") align with the terms that Eidsheim provides to define femininity in conventional singing: "increased breathiness, a limited dynamic range, a less dynamic variable, particular articulation, and vocal timbral manipulation" (Eidsheim 2019, 106). The blog's readers are invited to join an (implied) kind of boys' club imagined community, whose (presumably) homosocial bonds are formed through the rejection of clean singing in feminine (or at least, feminizing) terms.

Finally, genres and styles in which clean vocals are common are also disparaged in feminine or feminizing terms. Theresa Nink and Florian Heesch argue that ballads in metal are often derided in ways that associate these songs with femininity.

> In this context, it seems to be precisely the aesthetic and performative production of sentimentality that [...] is reflected in a discursive feminization in value judgments. This feminine connotations of ballads in hard rock and metal is accompanied by their devaluation as something low, often affirmed by their popularity, which is itself connoted and devalued as feminine. (Nink and Heesch 2023, 1–2)

Metal discourse often conflates masculinity, oppositional authenticity (see Chapter 3), and rough timbres—but it also often conflates their opposites: femininity (and/or lack of masculinity), inauthenticity, commerciality, mainstreamness, and clean timbre. As I will argue in Chapter 7, these

---

[4] A similar argument has been made by Kahn-Harris (2016).

softer sounds are not foreign to metal music, but are an established part of the genre's expressive palate. The rejection of clean vocals in metal (and, by extension, acoustic guitar and other softer timbres) often resonates with a history of misogynistic thinking and language that has plagued the genre for decades.

Recuperating Clean Vocals: They Contribute to Heaviness

But there are other ways to think about clean vocals that bring them into the center of the experience of heaviness, rather than casting them out of the metal genre. One is to focus on how contrasts between clean vocals and distorted sounds could heighten the heaviness of the distorted parts. The music psychologists Tzu-Han Cheng and Chen-Gia Tsai (2016, 9) have shown how moving between contrasting sections of distorted metal and more peaceful sounds leads to greater physiological impact, in the form of higher heart rates, than staying within one of those atmospheres. One might reasonably argue that the alternation between clean vocals and growled vocals can lead to more intense experiences of heaviness than sticking to only one vocal type.

Examples of this contrast between clean and rough vocals include the "Beauty and the Beast" bands mentioned earlier, but also bands like Opeth, who have become famous for contrasting sections featuring intense guitar distortion and guttural screams with more mellow, melancholy sections featuring clean-tone singing and gentle guitar parts with jazz-fusion and psychedelic rock influences—a part of their style which is especially evident in their quieter songs like "Windowpane" (2003). One of my favorite Opeth songs, "The Grand Conjuration" (2005), starts with a distorted power-chord-based buildup intro, but then winds down the instrumentation, starting the verse with only a soft vocal, bass, acoustic guitar, and hi-hat—before erupting into a chorus (at 2:00) featuring growled vocals and an intense, pummeling distorted power chord riff. During the quieter verse sections, I feel an anticipation for the louder chorus riff, which makes the chorus feel much heavier than the intro riff that has a similar rhythm (and it becomes even heavier when this bludgeoning chorus riff builds into a monstrous runaway breakdown with guitar solo, starting at 3:27).

Clean-tone vocals can also create experiences of heaviness on their own, without contrasting with harsh vocals. For example, between 2009 and 2020, the Dutch symphonic metal band Delain consistently centered their female vocalist Charlotte Wessels in both verses and choruses, with the male members of the band occasionally providing only clean-tone supporting vocal lines.[5] In the song "Masters of Destiny" (2019), Wessels' voice ranges from intimate, feminine opening lines to a belted, nearly operatic chorus backed by a huge synthesized orchestra. The cinematic range of expression in her vocals and in the instrumental parts invites me to hear her voice representing the cosmic power of fate and epic, life-spanning context described in the lyrics. Clean female vocals deliver a more abstract type of power in the work of the Florida-based progressive metal band Aghora, whose original vocalist Danishta Rivero sang clean-toned lyrics meditating on ideas from Buddhist philosophy. In their song "Atmas Heave" (2006), Rivero's reverberating voice seems to take on various qualities depending on the riffs underneath: mystical, contemplative, epic, and sublime. The pairing of her vocals with the band's complex, frenetic, progressive riffing evocatively match the heaviness of the lyrics' encounters with sublime truths that transcend the ego and self. These two singers' clean-tone vocals seem to be ideal for types of heaviness heard with a listening stance in which the music represents awesome wonder and transcendent power, and the listener imagines themselves to be encountering this power, joining it, or mastering it for their own ends.

Clean-toned vocals also seem to be ideally suited to invite another stance toward heaviness: the experience of being overwhelmed by heaviness's power. The California-based doom metal band King Woman features strained, tormented, but clean-toned vocals by Kris Esfandiari. On many of the band's songs, like "Celestial Blues" (2021), Esfandiari's anguished lyrics are perpetually on the edge of being overwhelmed by the band's desolate, crushingly loud guitars. This arrangement seems to iconically suggest a stance toward heaviness where one imagines oneself to be subjected to the power of the guitars, being blown away by their force. Male vocalists can play the same role, but female vocalists do not need belting techniques in order to reach a high register, so they may have an easier time finding the delicate ensemble balance required to represent this stance in sound: the paradoxical balance between carrying over the guitars and being buried by them.

---

[5] Delain's debut album *Lucidity* (2006) and their most recent album *Dark Waters* (2023) both credit men with "harsh vocals," which are alternated with female vocals in the "Beauty and the Beast" tradition—unlike the band's intervening releases.

Mixed Vocals and Split Identities

When singers alternate between different registers, the productive tension that is maintained between the imagined characters of metal's fantastic vocals and the mundane realities of its human singers (in combination with the fact that these registers are so far from normal human song and speech) makes it especially easy for listeners to misrecognize a singer's identity in yet another way: to hear two vocalists taking turns when, in fact, only one is singing. This phenomenon is especially consequential for female singers who growl, who are already often misrecognized due to the widespread assumption by many listeners that growled vocals are inherently masculine.

When a singer switches between two highly contrasting styles that are kept completely separate, like Jinjer's lead singer Tatiana Shmayluk, this two-singer illusion is more likely to occur.[6] As I said at the chapter's opening, Shmayluk effectively has two voices: an intense pitchless death growl, and a melodic singing voice that has been compared to jazz, cabaret, and R&B. Lori Burns (2023) argues that in addition to these vocal switches, Jinjer draws on, but reconfigures, the musical styles and thematic materials used by male-fronted metal bands to create new "alternative femininities." But when listening to Jinjer's albums (without video), some listeners assume that they are hearing two separate singers—a male growling vocalist and a female clean-tone singer, in the "Beauty and the Beast" style—and only realize when they see a video or live performance that both voices belong to Shmayluk. This is a result of the common assumption that a voice is a direct representation of the singer's essential identity and biography (Eidsheim 2019). Even those who are aware that these voices belong to the same singer describe them as two separate voices with two personalities, like "angel" and "demon."

Many metal singers use dramatic shifts in vocal technique in this way to clearly delineate separate characters, theatrical registers, or song sections. The Finnish symphonic/folk metal band Turisas uses shifts between sung and growled vocals in their song "Cursed Be Iron" (2007) to distinguish between two characters from the Finnish epic poem *The Kalevala*, one of whom (the clean-tone voice) relates the myth of the origin of iron, and the other (the growled voice) angrily curses iron for the evil and violence it has brought onto the world (Schaller 2025). Analogous disjunctions of voice and character can be made without extreme metal vocal techniques: Van Halen's "Ice Cream

---

[6] Another prominent and notable example of switches between vocal styles resulting in a two-singer illusion is the metal/art-pop solo artist Poppy—especially her performance on "Suffocate" by the metallic hardcore punk band Knocked Loose, which was nominated for the 2025 Grammy for Best Metal Performance.

Man" (1978) shifts from low-key clean singing in an acoustic blues verse, but transforms the same riff and lyrics into a transcendent hard rock verse with raspy vocals, extreme falsetto leaps, and virtuosic guitar soloing. These vocal shifts create a heightened sense of theatricality or epic scope in each of these songs, in addition to distinguishing separate characters or registers of expression.

Some female metal singers who use contrasting styles are able to avoid the two-singer mishearing by blending more smoothly between these vocal types or registers. Noora Louhimo, the lead singer of the Finnish power metal band Battle Beast, ranges from breathy feminine tone to a blood-curdling scream reminiscent of (but arguably even more intense than) classic heavy metal screamers like Rob Halford of Judas Priest. But in many songs, she moves gradually between these techniques rather than switching directly between extremes, such as in Louhimo's first single with the band "Black Ninja" (2013), in which she starts the verse singing in a soft and airy tone (0:11), steps up to a slightly raspy hard rock tone for the prechorus (0:33), then breaks out a full-throated heavy metal scream for the chorus (0:44). In an early interview (Rossi 2013), Louhimo describes these as "feminine" and "masculine" sides to her voice, consistent with the gendered hearings of metal vocal techniques discussed throughout this chapter. But unlike Jinjer's lead singer, it's impossible to hear Louhimo's performance as anything but the work of a single singer, because she blends smoothly between these extremes. This creates a stronger continuity of character throughout each individual song. Since the gradual transitions make it harder to hear Louhimo's intense screams as a separate voice, she is arguably more effective than Shmayluk or Gossow at reclaiming rough vocal timbres from their masculine associations and integrating them into a single vocality that can be heard as feminine or female.

Conclusion: "Someone's Daughter"

The distance between the specialized vocal techniques of metal and the mundane registers of ordinary human speech and singing allows singers to speak in the unreal voices of gods, legends, myths, and horror stories—but it also allows them to give voice to the most heightened, intense, and urgent human emotions. On Iron Maiden's "Run to the Hills" (1982), their singer Bruce Dickinson uses a relatively soft voice and clean-tone guitars to relate the perspective of Indigenous Americans in the song's intro, and a gruff voice and heavy metal stylings in the verses to embody the perspective of the invading colonial soldiers (Hudson 2023b, 22). Like many metal songs, this song presents multiple viewpoints without taking a side (Phillipov 2012, 97–99), and invokes conflicting sets of symbols and imagery (Walser 2014 [1993], 151–60), collapsing the historical distance between twentieth-century heavy metal and (a portrayal of) eighteenth-century American history and inviting listeners to "try out" different subjectivities within that story—to imagine and experience what it might be like to be both the victim and the perpetrator of a terrifying massacre. It is not clear whether the song's chorus lyrics "Run to the Hills" represents a command by the invading soldiers, or a call to escape by the remaining villagers. Many metal songs' urgency and impact depend on this kind of ambiguity of perspective. And it is much easier for listeners to suspend disbelief and accept a singer's portrayal of multiple perspectives (especially when they are legendary, mythical, or from the remote past) when the singer uses extraordinary techniques that create distance from the mundane, everyday vocalities with which we are more familiar.

Metal's fantastical vocals and the powers they invoke and confer (however imaginatively or illusorily) have in the past often been understood as belonging to men or masculinity, but the increasing prominence of female or otherwise non-male metal vocalists is a symptom of a broader cultural shift in gendered power. In 1993, Walser argued,

> Female fans identify with a kind of power that is usually understood in our culture as male—because physical power, dominance, rebellion, and flirting with the dark side of life are all culturally designated as male prerogatives. Yet women are able to access this power because it is channeled through a medium, music, that is intangible and difficult to police. (Walser 2014 [1993], 131–32)

Today, more and more people are questioning whether dominance, rebellion, etc. should be male prerogatives—or specific to masculinity at all. Women around the world are ascending to the highest levels of political and corporate power, and popular media (including the metal genre) is full of images of powerful, forceful female warriors and heroes. The gradual proliferation of female metal vocalists is not an isolated phenomenon, but resonates with a more general expansion of the roles women are allowed and encouraged to play in stories and society, which is to say, an imagination of new possibilities for the constitution of femininity and feminine power.

But metal's fantastical vocals are still heard through the lens of gender, so this gradual expansion of women's vocal range within metal has created some gender anxieties. User comments I collected from several of Arch Enemy's YouTube videos (some dating back years, others added quite recently) represent an array of uneasinesses sparked by Gossow's growled vocals.

- "imagine if she was your mom yelling at you like that lol"
- "Rip any husband or son who tries to argue with this woman"
- "Husband: Angela, make me a sandwich
  Angela: WHAAAAAAT??
  Husband: Nothing dear, nothing."
- "I'm a guy and I wish I had the voice of this woman."

These comments are triggered by listeners' gendered hearings of Gossow's vocals as masculine: speculated incongruity between Gossow's aggressive vocals and the role of motherhood, satirical commentary on a presumed inversion of traditional gender roles within marriage, and male admiration and envy (and fear?) of the strength and intensity of Gossow's voice. While it may no longer be controversial or even unexpected for a woman to sing growls or other extreme techniques, this does not mean that sexism is over.

Jinjer's blistering, brutal new single "Someone's Daughter" (2024) seems to speak directly to the misogyny, mishearing, and gender anxieties that surround female metal vocalists. Shmayluk begins the song in a soft, clean-timbered, melodic voice lamenting the unfair obstacles and prejudice which pioneering, pathbreaking women have often had to face: "Though I am someone's daughter / The path of warrior was set for me / And I had to try on the armour / No, it doesn't suit me." Throughout the song, the character she portrays is gradually forced to become a different person to overcome these challenges ("So my gentleness is turned into rigidity," etc.). Metal news outlets widely reported that Shmayluk said in a press statement: " 'Someone's Daughter' is an artistic attempt to cast the light on the inner world of women, who in various scenarios and circumstances have had to choose a path that was historically made by men" (Blabbermouth 2024). Although this stated scope includes innumerable pioneering women throughout history, it seems especially resonant to interpret the song as a meditation about pathbreaking female vocalists in metal, including Shmayluk herself.

Shmayluk's character is empowered by the transformation she endures across the song, singing "I've found talents beyond comprehension / All my battles are a sight to behold." This can easily be heard as a reference to the fantastical vocals which Shmayluk performs herself. In her growled voice, Shmayluk expresses an anxiety that this expansion of her character's (diegetic, but also vocal?) powers has come only at substantial cost to her femininity. In the second half of the song (starting at 2:30), she breaks into cataclysmic death growls to lament the cruelty of her path and its obstacles, accompanied by increasingly brutal riffs with stomach-churning chromaticism. After a chaotic breakdown, she growls ominously, "If a woman's wings are trimmed / and her radiance is dimmed / [...] You will see her ride a broom" (2:40–2:55). After another ground-splitting breakdown without vocals, she returns to sing the song's climax (3:15–3:35): "With a force to be reckoned / To be no longer the second / I am no longer the daughter / I throw the first punch." Her own voice growling beyond recognition seems to mirror this transformation, as if the trials her character faces have compelled her to leave ordinary womanhood behind and become something else.

There are many ways to hear the ending of the song, but one way is a defiant affirmation of femininity. After the growled chorus, Shmayluk repeats the climactic lines of the song in her clean-timbered style (3:40–4:00). One interpretation is that she may be "no longer the daughter" but has found a way to incorporate the challenges she has faced, and the new abilities she has developed to combat them, into a version of femininity. Burns argues that Shmayluk "Consistently [...] embodies—in the expressive channels of words, music, and images—representations of femininity that are salient within metal music cultures, but that *she* demonstrates to be deserving of critique and transformation" (Burns 2023, 8.1), and this song is no exception, representing anxieties about strength and femininity, and working through them. "Someone's Daughter" is a lament over the difficulty of the obstacles and alienation caused by misogyny and mishearing, but ultimately, by ending with clean-timbered vocals, it marks the survival and triumph of the protagonist's femininity in spite of these gendered biases and anxieties.

PART III

HOW IS HEAVINESS CREATED AND WHAT DOES IT FEEL LIKE?

7

How Metallica Created Extreme Metal

Active Listening, Connoisseurship, and Cover Songs

From the origins of heavy metal to the twenty-first century, the genre's story and values have been determined by a master narrative of "leaving the blues behind," which I investigated in Chapter 3, and which often manifests as an aesthetic imperative for constantly increasing heaviness. This chapter focuses in from that broad tapestry to a single historical moment, to tell a microhistory of the early career of a single band: Metallica. Metallica began as fans of the "New Wave of British Heavy Metal," but in their songwriting and performance, they shaped the evolution of the metal genre in an even heavier direction, leading to the emergence of a distinct new style that would eventually called "thrash metal."

This brief narrative will be familiar to most metal fans, but my account synthesizes the many different musical and non-musical roles Metallica played during this period, in a way that I think is unique. Metallica is already widely recognized as an early pioneer within the increasingly extreme metal styles of the 1980s, but I want to make an even stronger claim: While Metallica would not usually be labeled as "extreme metal" today, they (along with many other fans and bands in the early 1980s) helped create a paradigm that would later be known as "extreme metal"—a way of thinking about metal that has dominated how fans, musicians, and critics think and talk ever since.[1] This was accomplished not only through their own music but also through many other activities and roles. Metallica collected records as fans, shared bootleg copies as tastemakers, cited other bands as influences in interviews, learned to play other bands' songs and then made their cover versions faster and heavier, advertised a particular musical pantheon or pedigree through patches worn on their jackets during live concerts, and finally, made original compositions in a style which was inspired by their roots but surpassed them. Their actions as fans, connoisseurs, and tastemakers provided examples of new ways to be a

---

[1] All genre terms are somewhat subjective and always under dispute, but bands that are described as "extreme metal" today (such as Cannibal Corpse or Darkthrone) are usually sonically harsher than Metallica, often featuring blast beats and screamed or growled vocal techniques.

Heaviness in Metal Music. Stephen S. Hudson, Oxford University Press. © Oxford University Press 2026.
DOI: 10.1093/9780197774991.003.0011

metal fan and critic, just as much as their album releases provided examples of new ways to play metal music.

To understand how Metallica's actions as fans helped re-shape genre, it's worth revisiting what musical genre is in the first place. Robert Walser, exploring the nature of genre in heavy metal, draws on literary theory to describe metal songs as texts for semiotic analysis, but also as utterances in a discourse—the latter of which provides the foundation for Walser's argument that musical details are imbued with social and political meanings and reveal traces of social and institutional power structures (a central cause of the "new musicology" of the 1990s). My work in many other chapters of this book builds on Walser's perspective, showing how songs participate in and gradually define a set of norms for what happens in the genre, a "horizon of expectations" (Walser 2014 [1993], 27). But the songs and the norms or expectations for what happens inside them are only one half of the picture. Genre consists of not only music, but also what we might call "mundane" activities: talking about music, buying records and merchandise, attending shows, making social distinctions, wearing band shirts or dressing in particular styles, and creating and viewing imagery associated with the music.

An understanding of how genre works and evolves must synthesize these intertwined musical and social dimensions—but several scholars before me have argued that this is rare, both in metal music studies (Kahn-Harris 2007, 2010; Phillipov 2012) and in popular music studies more widely (Lena and Peterson 2008). Scholars writing about the music (and journalists or fan historians) tend to over-emphasize landmark recordings and legendary musical "firsts" by solitary genius artists (Lena 2012, 2–3). Sociologists have tried to correct this by focusing on the social structures of fan communities (Lena 2012; Kahn-Harris 2007; etc.), which some might be tempted to call "non-musical" dimensions of genre—but these fan actions often revolve around the music, so studying them without studying the music, too, is missing half the action.

Part of the problem is that the mundane and musical dimensions are usually defined separately: musicologists often understand genre primarily as a collection of pieces of music (or rules or expectations about those pieces of music), while anthropologists and sociologists primarily theorize genre as a social formation (a subculture, scene, or neotribe—with live ceremonies and material cultures). In this chapter, I theorize genre as a set of repertoires of ways of playing and thinking about music, drawing on the distinction between "repertoire" and "archive" by the performance studies scholar Diana Taylor. This allows me to weave together Metallica's musical utterances with their verbal discourse to give a multimodal account of genre—a synthesis

which shows how music, ideology, and discourse often develop together gradually, even though in retrospect we often describe them instead as if they were
discontinuous shifts to new categories, communities, and style labels. My goal
in this chapter is to focus on music without sacrificing genre's democratic nature, by showing how many kinds of actions that Metallica took to shape genre
(naming favorite bands, collecting and categorizing records, talking about
musical aesthetics, learning to play other artists' songs) are things that many
fans do, too.

Another goal is to trace where the idea of extreme metal came from in the
first place, how it emerged, and what kind of consequences it had on the trajectory of metal's artistic, ideological, and social dynamics. While heavy metal
was originally associated with the working class, it has for decades been driven
by a kind of self-actualizing connoisseurship that challenges lower-class
stereotypes and is often more compatible with upper-class values (Allet 2011;
Smialek and St.-Laurent 2018). Extremity in heaviness became the defining
ideological and aesthetic paradigm through which the genre was understood,
but while this paradigm was grounded in down-to-earth, enthusiastic physicality, I show how it led to a genre that has, in moments, become exclusive and
even snobby: despite Metallica's central pioneering role, extreme metal fans
have cast the band outside of their genre.

How Metallica Was Built on the New Wave of British Heavy Metal

In the late 1970s, a small scene coalesced around a club called The Heavy Metal
Soundhouse in the Kingsbury district of London, where a DJ named Neal
Kay played heavy metal records including demos and independent releases
collected from around the United Kingdom.[2] The intensity of the community that developed around this club attracted the attention of Geoff Barton,
a staff writer for the weekly British music paper *Sounds*. Barton wrote favor-
ably about The Heavy Metal Soundhouse, and invited Kay to compile a weekly
chart for *Sounds* of the most popular heavy metal records from his club. The
cohort of bands that emerged was dubbed the "New Wave of British Heavy
Metal" (NWOBHM) by Barton's editor. Between Barton's weekly charts,
regular feature articles about new heavy metal bands, and occasional live
concerts, a scene slowly developed. Major labels were slow to take notice, and
not many venues existed dedicated to the new scene, so most of the creativity

---

[2] My narrative is based on previous histories, especially Christe (2003) and Waksman (2009).

of these young bands was channeled into making rehearsal tapes, demos, and singles which were circulated in an informal manner or sold through small-time, relatively local independent record labels. A handful of NWOBHM bands (such as Iron Maiden, Def Leppard, Judas Priest, and Diamond Head) eventually made it to larger labels, but the vast majority relied on local venues and small-scale circulation of underground or alternative media to reach their audiences.

During the 1990s, this underground, independent mode of production developed into an international tape-trading culture that served as an incubator for subsequent, more extreme metal styles (see Harris 2000; Kahn-Harris 2007). A thriving community of underground metal fans in every corner of the globe produced 'zines and traded tape copies of demos and bootleg recordings through international mail. Scene members active during the 1980s describe having heard of bands in 'zines received via mail, but having no idea what the band actually sounded like because few underground or international metal releases were ever available in normal domestic record stores. Through this international mail network, more extreme styles of metal developed in many parts of the world simultaneously, forming a transnational extreme metal scene that is the focus of Kahn-Harris's 2007 book. This DIY material culture of bootlegs and paper 'zines has continued to exist well into the new millennium, years after it became much easier and more economical to discover bands and listen to their recordings through social media online.

Metallica's origin story is grounded in the NWOBHM, and occurred in the early years of the tape-trading culture that later fostered the development of extreme metal. At the beginning of the 1980s, Lars Ulrich, who would become Metallica's drummer, was "[b]arely a musician himself, owning just a few mismatched pieces of a drum set" (Christe 2003, 60)—he had no prior musical training or performance experience. Ulrich had grown up in Denmark as the son of a wealthy star tennis player, and while the family moved to California when he was a teenager, he traveled back to Europe frequently. These regular travels between America and Europe gave him access to the British scene beyond the limited imports available to most Americans, which positioned him as a taste-maker and evangelist for NWOBHM in the United States. In interviews and histories of metal music, Lars Ulrich is often described as being one of the most knowledgeable and committed collectors of NWOBHM records in the early 1980s, and in his own report he is not shy about claiming a certain status.

The scenes were all centered around stores that imported a lot of records and driven by word-of-mouth, grassroots movements, and tape trading. By the time you got a copy of a demo, it was like the fourteenth generation of it. You could barely make it out, but man, you knew it was the thing: "Hey, guess what, I got a demo you don't have, ha-ha. I'm super extra cool." It was sort of like the early version of the Internet. (Ulrich, quoted in Wiederhorn and Turman 2013, 196)

The difficulty of collecting recordings from this dispersed international scene during the 1980s restricted the exposure of NWOBHM music, and later of extreme metal, to fans committed to a high degree of involvement.

In the summer of 1981, Ulrich flew to England (apparently on a whim) to meet his favorite band, Diamond Head, and talked his way into staying with one of the band members for weeks while observing their rehearsals and traveling with them to gigs. This experience motivated him to form Metallica. After he got back to the United States, he listed a call for collaborators in a Southern California weekly classified ads publication called *The Recycler*, and one of the musicians who responded was the guitarist James Hetfield. Ulrich reports that nothing much came from their first jam session, but before the end of the year, he reached out to Hetfield again. Ulrich had managed to talk his friend Brian Slagel into giving him a slot on an upcoming compilation album of unsigned metal bands—even though Ulrich had no band.

I called up Hetfield and I said, "My friend's putting this [heavy metal compilation] record together. Do you want to take another shot at it?" He came down and we started hanging out pretty much every day. I started subjecting him to every single New Wave of British Heavy Metal thing, from Praying Mantis to Black Axe to Silverwing. Then we basically wrote a song together—"Hit the Lights." (Ulrich, quoted in Wiederhorn and Turman 2013, 200)

The compilation was eventually released as *Metal Massacre*, the first in a long-running series that Slagel published through his own label, Metal Blade Records, which became a scene institution. But the crucial point for my story is that Metallica was founded on mutual appreciation of NWOBHM recordings, driven by Ulrich's enthusiasm for, access to, and evangelism of this rare (in America, at least) commodity.

Theorizing Genre

Metallica's activities throughout their origin story are not inconsequential actions which have no effect on the genre in which they worked. Instead, in their roles as fans, connoisseurs, performers, and songwriters, Metallica participated in a re-shaping of existing NWOBHM styles that led to the emergence of a new genre: thrash metal. The earliest stages of Metallica's story involved curating a particular interpretation of, or selection from, the NWOBHM; then throughout the 1980s, their original compositions pioneered a new style that would eventually be called "thrash metal"; and, finally, the aesthetics and ways of thinking about genre which they embodied and promoted helped create the "extreme metal" paradigm which has dominated discourse about metal for decades. Exploring the concept of genre will help show how Metallica's everyday mundane and musical actions could become so consequential.

A genre is conventionally and colloquially described as a category to which particular pieces of music belong. When particular artists or songs are strongly and universally associated with a single style, this conventional way of understanding genre seems to make a lot of sense: Entombed's album *Left Hand Path* (1990) is death metal, and Darkthrone's album *A Blaze in the Northern Sky* (1990) is black metal, and it would be foolish to argue otherwise in either case. Of course, this is partly because these two albums have been reified by fans and critics as paradigmatic examples of their styles, what Robert Walser (following Frederic Jameson) calls "fixed stars" that orient our understanding of genre (Walser 2014 [1993], 27) and Joti Rockwell (following Lawrence Zbikowski and Lawrence Barsalou) might call the "models for prototype-based categories representing these genres" (Rockwell 2012). In other words, it might be more accurate to say that black metal is music that sounds like *A Blaze in the Northern Sky*, than to say *A Blaze in the Northern Sky* is music that sounds like black metal.

But when things get more complicated, this model of genre-as-a-category seems less clear and more reductive. Evanescence's breakout hit "Bring Me to Life" is often described as a hybrid between metal and rap, but most metal fans and most rap fans would place it outside their respective genres. Meshuggah is a band whose many imitators have populated the "djent" subgenre, but they are rarely labeled as djent themselves; none of the imitators sound quite like Meshuggah, and as a result Meshuggah is often described as genre-defying, or categorized in vaguer terms like "progressive extreme metal." In their early years, Metallica was often described as "speed metal," one of the most common terms in metal discourse in the 1980s. But this label has been associated with songs as disparate in style as "Angeldust" by Venom and "I Want Out" by Helloween. If you can find a "speed metal" category at any record shops today, let me know—in most contexts, the bands formerly known as "speed metal" have been recategorized using terms that seem to contrast strongly, like "power metal," "thrash metal," "first-wave black metal,"

"NWOBHM," or even (recently) "traditional heavy metal." From the perspective of today's genre classifications and style descriptions, then, it can be hard to understand what it meant to fans in the 1980s when they called Metallica "speed metal" (other than, obviously, that Metallica's music was relatively fast compared to their most immediate predecessors and contemporaries).

Theorists of genre have long argued that genre is more mercurial, subjective, and diffuse than how category membership usually works. As I explored in Chapter 3, genre classification depends on your viewpoint; what a hard rock fan considers "metal music" may include bands that an extreme metal fan would reject from the genre. Walser (2014 [1993], 4–7) points out that the boundaries between genres are always contested by fans, perpetually being argued over and redrawn. David Brackett builds on this insight, describing genres as categories which shift over time; "Rather than focusing on what constitutes the contents of a musical category, the emphasis here falls on how a particular idea of a category emerges and stabilizes momentarily (if at all)" (Brackett 2016, 5–6). Specifically, Brackett studies how genres are often imagined to represent racial, geographic, and/or socioeconomic communities or classes of people, although he is quick to point out that these range from genuinely homological relationships between categories of music and identity, to entirely fantasized correspondences (Brackett 2005, 2016). Finally, Jacques Derrida (1992) suggests that works of literature "participate" in genres, rather than belonging to them—allowing a single song to reference or invoke several (sometimes opposing or contrasting) genres without theoretical difficulty.

Also, a genre is more than just a category. Genres are also strongly associated with particular ways of thinking, aesthetics, ideologies, and identity formations that guide how we interpret the music in the genre, and are as much a part of the genre as any style norms or rules. For example, Walser describes genre as a "horizon of expectations" that guides listening (2014 [1993], 27), following the work of the Russian literary theorist and philosopher Mikhail Bakhtin. Others describe this aspect of genre as a "contract" between author and audience, governing which kinds of events normally happen within a genre's texts, and how those events are to be understood.

Genre as an Act of Grouping

Given this subjective, contested nature of genre, it's tempting to think of genre as the act of grouping rather than the group itself. The music theorist Eric Drott proposes exactly that in an article about genre in twentieth-century art

music (Drott 2013, 10). Like Walser and Kahn-Harris, Drott defines genre ho-
listically as involving both musical events and social ideas; genre includes

> a dynamic ensemble of correlations, linking together a variety of material, insti-
> tutional, social, and symbolic resources: repertories, performance practices, dis-
> tinctive formal and stylistic traits, aesthetic discourses, forms of self-presentation,
> institutions, specific modes of technological mediation, social identities, and so
> forth. (Drott 2013, 9)

Drott discusses how groupings can be articulated subjectively by individuals
or institutions, and argues that if these instances of grouping align or resonate closely enough with one another, then out of their gradual aggregation, a
broader intersubjective edifice of genre can emerge.

Many of the mundane and musical actions Metallica took in their
early years are acts of grouping which contributed to the eventual emergence of thrash metal. At the beginning of the 1980s, before the members
of Metallica had formed their band (and, even, before some of them were
making music at all), they were already contributing to the re-shaping of the
metal genre through the groupings they created as fans and connoisseurs.
Ulrich remembers,

> In the fall of 1981, after coming back from a trip in England, I wanted to put a band
> together. I put together an ad in *The Recycler* saying, "Heavy metal drummer
> looking for other musicians. Influences: Tygers of Pan Tang, Angel Witch, Saxon."
> Most people would call up and be like, "I'm into heavy metal but I've never heard of
> any of those bands. But I like Journey and I like REO Speedwagon. Does that work?"
> (Wiederhorn and Turman 2013, 199).

In this advertisement, Ulrich was creating a new grouping which advertised his own knowledgeable and extremely current musical taste. Two of
these three bands had only released music through independent European
labels by the time Ulrich mentioned them. Metallica's first full-time lead guitarist Dave Mustaine recalls joining the band in 1982 after answering a similar advertisement in *The Recycler* mentioning Iron Maiden, Motörhead, and
Budgie (Wiederhorn and Turman 2013, 120). While these three bands would
have been more available to American metal fans, two of them (Iron Maiden
and Motörhead) still represented the heaviest, fastest leading edge of metal
music at that time. Ulrich's groupings in these advertisements created a new
interpretation of the NWOBHM which trended in a heavier and heavier
direction—and through these groupings, Metallica was already contributing

to the re-shaping of the metal genre, before they recorded a single note of their own music.

Crafting their own selection from the NWOBHM continued to be an important part of Metallica's coalescing aesthetic vision and artistic identity. In an interview from early 1983, Metallica claims the following bands as influences: "Angel Witch, [Mercyful] Fate, Venom, Motörhead, Rush*, Diamond Head, Black Sabbath*, ZZ Top*" (Davis 1983). The bands marked with an asterisk are mentioned by Cliff Burton, the rest by Dave Mustaine and Lars Ulrich. Burton was in many ways an outlier within the band: he was a few years older, and by all accounts broadened the musical tastes of the other members of the band, introducing them to older rock and heavy metal, and teaching them to appreciate melody more.[3] Burton's contributions lie outside of the sphere of the NWOBHM, but the bands that are mentioned by Mustaine and Ulrich represent the fastest, heaviest reaches of the NWOBHM, including several of the same bands mentioned in their *Recycler* advertisements. Mustaine recited a similar list when asked decades later about his short tenure with the band: "When I was drinking and hanging out with [Metallica guitarist] James Hetfield, we would listen to Venom and Motörhead and Raven and Tank and Mercyful Fate and Diamond Head and Angel Witch and Witchfinder General and stuff like that" (Christe 2003, 44). These interview statements became one of the most wide-reaching and explicit ways in which Metallica projected their own selection of heavier NWOBHM bands out into the world, articulating new groupings to promote their own vision of genre.

Another way in which Metallica generated visibility for their own selection of especially heavy music from the broader NWOBHM scene was through what are often called "battle jackets," a metal scene tradition in which a fan plasters a denim or leather jacket with a collection of cloth patches featuring the names or album artwork of their favorite bands, which are usually only available at live shows. These garments serve as a visible track record of a fan's commitment to attending live shows, but also a carefully curated grouping of artists meant to represent that fan's ideals and tastes. The patches may be hard to read for outsiders, but to scene insiders who are intimately familiar with band logos and artwork, many patches are instantly recognizable from a distance based on color and shape, even when the letters are too small to see. James Hetfield has been seen wearing at least three battle jackets over the years, with patches representing every band mentioned in my quotes from

---

[3] According to Pillsbury, Burton "stands as the musical guide for the other members of the group during the first few albums, and many see the kind of complexity in Metallica's music, particularly the sections of lyrical diatonicism under discussion here, as coming from his quasi-mentorship of Hetfield and Ulrich as songwriters" (Pillsbury 2006, 67).

Ulrich and Mustaine—Angel Witch, Blitzkrieg, Diamond Head, Holocaust, Iron Maiden, Mercyful Fate, Motörhead, Raven, Saxon, Tank, the Tygers of Pan Tang, Venom, and Witchfinder General. Metallica repeatedly identifies themselves with these bands at the heavier end of the NWOBHM, choosing this group over and over as the frame or context for their own music.

Metallica, of course, were not the only ones creating groupings and shaping genre in this way. Virtually every metal musician and fan, then and now, creates their own groupings by citing favorite artists and albums, curating their own album collection, and wearing merchandise that advertises their tastes. Keith Kahn-Harris describes how avid collecting of records and merchandise accumulates "mundane subcultural capital" (2007, 122–27), a kind of status or notoriety within the scene, which resonates with Lars Ulrich's eagerness to find and brag about obscure demos—this is distinct from Pierre Bourdieu's conception of "cultural capital" that is a kind of elite status recognized by society at large, since "subcultural capital" is only recognized by others in the same subculture, which can represent an obsessiveness that is ignored or even laughed at by outside observers. But these capital-accruing activities are often also taste-making actions which shape genre, not a neutral accrual of status within a fixed scene. Nicola Allet describes these fans as "extreme metal connoisseurs," highlighting the resonance with high-culture constructions of prestige and discernment, but also arguing that "Unlike the connoisseur and flâneur, however, the extreme metal fan is active. S/he participates in the DIY culture of the scene" (Allett 2011, 177). Almost every scene activity that fans participate in creates groupings, associations, or distinctions which contribute to the maintenance and re-shaping of genres.

Given Metallica's centrality and ubiquity within the earliest years of the underground metal scene and their commercial dominance in later years, their groupings were especially prominent and influential. Drott says of genre groupings,

> their legitimacy depends on how many people recognize them, take them up, and thereby reproduce the specific configuration of texts and contexts that they establish. And this in turn depends upon the material, discursive, institutional, and symbolic resources enlisted to perpetuate a given grouping. (Drott 2013, 12)

While many bands were pursuing heavier styles in parallel with Metallica (especially Slayer, Exodus, Testament, and Megadeth), Metallica released their landmark recordings earlier than the others, giving the impression that Metallica was setting the latest trends in extremity in the early 1980s. Metallica's head start, luck, and determination to succeed at all costs propelled them to become the most visible and commercially successful band as thrash metal began to coalesce as a musical style.

Metallica's tireless touring and inescapable media presence helped to disseminate their generic groupings, and their immense subcultural capital as the foremost thrash metal band in the late 1980s made their perspective on metal music highly influential. For example, at the end of the 1980s, the pioneering British metal journalist Geoff Barton partnered with Lars Ulrich to produce the *New Wave of British Heavy Metal '79 Revisited* compilation, which was not only the capstone of Ulrich's NWOBHM connoisseurship, but also arguably a pioneering archival document of the NWOBHM scene. While this album represented a much wider, less partisan selection of the NWOBHM, it included virtually all of the bands Metallica cited as influences in their early days (except Motörhead, who as an established band were not part of the "new" wave of British bands, and Mercyful Fate, who were from Denmark). In other words, Metallica's groupings from the NWOBHM were not only perpetuated within their own performances and statements, but also fixed in one of the most prominent, authoritative, and enduring objects of institutional memory through which the scene has been commemorated.

Genre as a Repertoire, Genre Distinction as a Performative Act

To get the most vivid and accurate model of genre, we might understand these individual groupings of bands and songs as part of a genre's *repertoire of ways of playing and thinking* (as opposed to the "archive" of musical compositions and recordings), and the act of grouping as a performance of that repertoire. Genre is made up of a number of repertoires. When "thrash metal" is performed, this performance draws on (and contributes to) a musical repertoire of songs, timbres, techniques, and musical structures that are associated with this genre label. But it also draws on a repertoire of sartorial choices for listeners and band members, a repertoire of dance and embodied listening practices, a repertoire of ways of thinking about aesthetics, a repertoire of onstage comportment and theatrical gestures, a repertoire of familiar props and backdrops—as illustrated in genre commentary by thrash metal musicians Gary Holt and Dave Mustaine.

> Gary Holt (Exodus): I think the thrash bands and the hair metal bands needed each other. We were mutual enemies, and it gave us ammunition. They were the pretty boys in the makeup and we were the guys in the denim vests with Motörhead

patches on the back. But by the same token, we always went to the hair band shows because we knew that's where the girls were.

Dave Mustaine: The hair bands turned metal into a farce or a joke. You had the video [for Whitesnake's "Here I Go Again"] where Tawny Kitaen is trying to swallow a Jaguar with her vagina. That kind of stuff cheapened everything. You've got guys like us who live heavy metal. It's what we eat and breathe. Then there were bands like Warrant and Poison, and when people thought of metal, they thought of *them*, which did a terrible disservice to the music. But at the same time, there was a loyal following of thrash fans who hated that shit, and it made them want to be even heavier and less commercial. (Wiederhorn and Turman 2013, 192–93)

Holt and Mustaine's conceptions of thrash metal define the genre through a complex web of misogyny-laced social distinction: a symbiotic rivalry between thrash metal and hair metal, and in the background behind this localized opposition, an unmentioned joint rebellion against mainstream pop and rock. Each genre draws on its own musical repertoire, but also ideological, sartorial, social, gendered, and sexual repertoires, all intertwined in a game of mutual distinction. Performances of musical genre connote social distinctions, and social performances connote musical distinctions.

Considering genres as a set of repertoires brings to the foreground how each act of genre grouping is a *performance* of genre, a live enactment of genre ideology and aesthetics which (explicitly or implicitly) communicates and reinscribes many of these dimensions of distinction. The performance studies scholar Diana Taylor highlights how a repertoire requires the live enactment of knowledge, contrasted with the supposedly stable preservation of knowledge in an archive of fixed texts. While an archive preserves human knowledge in an external material medium to enable later access, "[t]he repertoire requires presence: people participate in the production and reproduction of knowledge by 'being there,' being a part of the transmission" (Taylor 2003, 20). Performances are "acts of transfer" (Taylor 2003, 2–3) which transfer (between participants, and to onlookers) the repertoires of knowledge and practice which they draw on, by enacting that knowledge and practice in real time.

By framing genre as a set of repertoires that are enacted in performances, we can analyze distinctions of genre as performative assertions of identity and belonging within the metal community. This is especially clear in a review of Van Halen's album *Women and Children First* (1980) by the *Creem* magazine journalist Rick Johnson, who praises the band's raucous heavy metal energy with some of the most memorably hyperbolic imagery of that time ("Combining as they do the most endearing musical aspects of helicopter decapitations, clothes dryers full of hunting knives, and your average hailstorm of frozen aluminum dinnerware sets striking a Pepsi-Cola bottling plant …"). But Johnson sours on the album's final tracks, including the ballads "Take Your Whiskey Home" and "Could This Be Magic?":

> Warning to Consumers: no one will be admitted during the last 10 minutes of this album, which are as shockingly distasteful as going to take a swig of Diet Pepsi and getting a mouthful of toenail clippings instead (this really happened). It sucks is what I'm getting at. Nothing but some acoustic guitar dribble and our friend wanglungs mewing through a tryout for Sopwith Camel. (Johnson 1980, 53)

This review not only pans Van Halen's performance of these ballads but also polices the genre community, literally forbidding readers (assumed to be heavy metal fans) from listening ("no one will be admitted"). The implication is clear: last few tracks on the album (compared by the reviewer to the cute and laughably un-metal psychedelic rock band Sopwith Camel) are not "our" music (heavy metal), and anyone who likes them does not belong in the tribe. Genre distinctions don't just imply social categories, they often actively police them, casting bands and listeners inside and outside of various genre communities. (For example, Mustaine's and Holt's genre distinctions quoted above cast femininity outside of thrash metal and position women as sexual objects, enacting misogynistic exclusion; see Hill 2016, Chapter 4.) Genre judgments are performative statements that create groupings, but also acts of transfer; they teach readers particular ways of thinking about musical and social distinctions, while also enacting those distinctions.

How a Newer Repertoire Emerges Through the Performance of an Older One

Metallica's own musical style—the characteristics of their songs as musical texts or utterances—emerged within this matrix of genre groupings that are social as much as musical distinctions. But by participating in these acts of grouping, Metallica inevitably changed the repertoires that constituted the genre they started with. Taylor explains that this is an inherent property of repertoires: "As opposed to the supposedly stable objects in the archive, the actions that are the repertoire do not remain the same. The repertoire both keeps and transforms choreographies of meaning" (Taylor 2003, 20).

Metallica's selection of which bands to listen to and which covers to play literally re-shaped the metal genre, not only because of the abstract correlations produced by associating them with other bands, but also because what they listen to, jam with, and perform on stage has a direct influence on how they think and play as musicians, and thus on what kinds of musical style are perpetuated and re-performed. As Metallica drew on and restaged the choreographies of meaning and musical style that constitute the repertoire of NWOBHM, these choreographies gradually evolved with each performance, eventually constituting their own new musical repertoire that became known as "thrash metal." This evolution of musical repertoire is especially clear in Metallica's audible transformations of NWOBHM musical style.

At the very beginning of their career, Metallica was basically a NWOBHM cover band; specifically, their earliest setlists had more covers of Diamond Head than original songs (Pillsbury 2006, 25). Two covers, of Diamond Head's "Am I Evil?" and Blitzkrieg's "Blitzkrieg," continued to remain nightly staples of Metallica's set list even after they released their second album *Ride the Lightning* (1984), and Metallica recorded these covers for the B-side of their "Creeping Death" single in the same year. In a 1983 interview for the prominent fanzine *Metal Forces*, Ulrich declared, "we're not a band who likes to submit our own songs solely for B-sides because we like to have them on albums, so we just went into the studio and knocked out a couple of cover songs. It's the only two cover songs that we still play at rehearsals, or live for the seventh encore!" (Doe 1984). By incorporating cover songs into their regular practice and performances, Metallica displayed this music as part of the image of their band, reinforcing the verbal references detailed above. Metallica continually reasserted their own conception of the metal genre through this cover song performance, grouping individual NWOBHM songs alongside their own original compositions.

Metallica's nightly repertoire was performative in two ways: they not only created and reinforced groupings of songs, they also literally re-enacted and developed the evolving genre's musical codes and aesthetics in real time through their onstage performance. Through their cover songs, Metallica internalized NWOBHM idioms and playing techniques into their own performance practice. These NWOBHM covers serve as the rungs of the ladder which Metallica climbed to grow from amateurs to professional musicians, and their musical materials and style became deeply integrated into Metallica's playing technique and musical cognition. These select NWOBHM songs were an active part of Metallica's repertoire as covers, but also, some of the cover songs' constituent elements became part of Metallica's original compositions. However, these core elements gradually and subtle evolved through Metallica's iterative reperformance.

Metallica selected some of the darkest, most musically complex songs from the NWOBHM, and then made these songs even heavier, faster, and more progressive. For example, Diamond Head's original version of "Am I Evil" (as released on their debut album in 1980) began with an ominous intro that is reminiscent of Gustav Holst's "Mars, Bringer of War." In their cover version, Metallica inserted a new contrasting phrase at the very beginning, and then played the Holst quote more percussively than Diamond Head, with less sustain and with more bass in the mix. Metallica's vocals in the first verse have less reverb and a rougher, more shout-like quality than Diamond Head's, and the guitar riffs in this section are again heavier and more percussive. After the second chorus, Metallica takes a faster tempo heading into the bridge (at 4:07, just before the phrase "On with the action now"). Metallica maintains this faster tempo throughout the guitar solo, which is otherwise note-for-note almost exactly the same as Diamond Head's, but with a clearer, colder, more piercing guitar tone. The most substantial alterations come after the guitar solo, when Diamond Head ends with a brief reprise of the chorus. Metallica adds a whole third verse (6:35), and then doubles the chorus (6:55), extending the length of the song and building more energy. Metallica (as in Diamond Head's original version) then brings back the ominously heavy verse riff for a re-intro (7:25), but the faster tempo Metallica has taken for the B section makes this return to the relatively slower verse riff seem even heavier than in Diamond Head's original. Even in a faithful cover, Metallica surpasses the extremity of the original composition.

Metallica's cover of Blitzkrieg's eponymous song "Blitzkrieg" is analogous— the notes played are often almost identical to the original, but faster and heavier—but also demonstrates how Metallica developed Blitzkrieg's playing techniques into their own nascent thrash metal style. The first riff of "Blitzkrieg" begins with a sliding-power-chord figure, and while Blitzkrieg's rendition is reminiscent of bluesy double-string bends and slides that had already been popular in previous decades of rock music, Metallica's increased speed makes this slide feel more like a percussive articulation and less like a slide. This transformed sliding-power-chord technique is used in some of Metallica's most iconic thrash riffs, such as the verse in "Master of Puppets" (0:52–1:27). In "Blitzkrieg," after this sliding figure, the first riff has several repeated notes on the bottom string, followed by an octave leap. Metallica's rendition of these notes is faster, and adds strong palm-muting that gives these notes a stronger attack and quick decay, making this technique more percussive and propulsive than Blitzkrieg's version. Metallica's rhythm guitarist James Hetfield gained a reputation for playing such palm-muted notes all picked in the same direction (down-picking) faster than most other guitarists were able to, and the resulting relentless rhythmic chugging is a driving force in the majority of their original compositions over the next decade, ranging from the first song they ever wrote "Hit the Lights" to their most famous barnstormers, "Enter Sandman," "Master of Puppets," and "For Whom The Bell Tolls." These transformed NWOBHM playing techniques also became staples of thrash metal style more broadly, hallmarks that separate the genre from previous metal music.

To summarize, Metallica selected particularly heavy, fast, and progressive NWOBHM music, and promoted this grouping as their own vision of darker, more extreme metal. They then performed covers of some of these NWOBHM bands, through which they internalized the musical materials of the NWOBHM, while transforming them slightly to make them even heavier and faster and more rhythmic. Through these kinds of transformations, Metallica's performances of NWOBHM repertoire pushed this heaviest version of NWOBHM style in an even more extreme direction, until it became a new style in its own right. In this way, thrash metal literally emerged from groupings of, interpretations of, and performances of the NWOBHM.

Conclusion: "Fade to Black"

In this chapter, I've sought to develop an understanding of genre that is radically participatory and democratic, and which equally includes mundane and musical actions. I specifically want to draw a contrast with the fawning, hagiographic histories of "great composers" that historically were the stock and trade of classical musicology. Metallica are certainly some of the most famous metal musicians, but they have deliberately cultivated a down-to-earth, everyman image. The activities they do to re-shape genre are no different from the actions that every scene member can, and does, perform in their own way—although I admit that Metallica's visibility and reputation give their actions greater reach and influence than anyone else. Genre thus emerges from the collective participation of a community, rather than solely through the innovations of solitary genius artists.

In fact, genre is so democratic that even iconic artists who pioneer a genre like Metallica can get pushed out of the genre through the distinctions and grouping actions of fans. Among extreme metal fans, Metallica's reputation as lions of the underground was upended within a decade, and the band was more or less cast out of the extreme metal scene even while they continued to reach higher and higher levels of commercial success during the 1990s. The most famous turning point in this narrative of Metallica "selling out" was the release of their 1991 self-titled album *Metallica*, more often known as the "Black Album," in which the band's style shifted substantially to more rock-oriented sounds and song structures (Smialek 2016b; see also Hudson 2021b). But there is an earlier moment in which Metallica's music was first cast in opposition to thrash metal: the release of their first ballad, "Fade to Black," in 1984. The manner in which this first rejection played out reveals some key consequences of the democratic nature of genre, and of the ideology of the emerging extreme metal paradigm.

The song "Fade to Black" was released on Metallica's second album, *Ride the Lightning* (1984), and was the first of a series of ballad-style Metallica songs that use acoustic guitars, quietly arpeggiated chords, moderate tempo, and a more reserved singing style—including "Welcome Home (Sanitarium)" (1986), "One" (1988), and "The Unforgiven" (1991). In his book about Metallica, Glenn T. Pillsbury describes these songs as the "Fade to Black Paradigm," and suggests that their quiet or subdued characteristics are the opposite of what usually defines thrash metal. Pillsbury argues that these songs were harshly rejected by many thrash metal fans, recollecting from his own childhood, "an older kid told me that I should listen to Megadeth rather than Metallica because, as he put it, 'Megadeth [was] like Metallica but without that "Fade to Black" shit'" (Pillsbury 2006, 33). A German fanzine printed right after the album's release corroborates this reaction, albeit in less strong terms:

> "Fade to Black" begins slow, and again an acoustic guitar is heard in the background, which complements the singing style. This song also appeals to me, although I had expected something more of a *Metalli-kill* [i.e. more intensely heavy/ aggressive]. [. . .] Hardcore thrashers will be somewhat disappointed, that it lacks in rawness; despite that, this masterwork is most warmly received. (Zohren 1984, 19; my translation from the original German)

This review reports that "Fade to Black" was surprisingly, disappointingly unaggressive. I think it's significant that the most negative criticism is displaced onto an imagined category of "hardcore thrashers" rather than stated in the author's own voice, giving it a hypothetical quality—this says a lot about how genre judgments and criticisms are shaped by our social imagination of the kind of listeners we imagine or associate with the music.

Why might "Fade to Black" be a disappointment? A common explanation, but one which I think is ultimately untrue, is Pillsbury's argument that these songs "appropriate musical codes from outside thrash metal" (2006, 34). He explains,

> For my schoolmate, "Fade to Black" stood outside of what he took to be several Truths about metal. [. . .] Downplaying the aggressive tempo and chromaticism

characteristic of thrash metal, they inject a dramatically diatonic element into Metallica's music, an element virtually nonexistent in music by other thrash metal bands like Slayer, Anthrax, or Megadeth. (Pillsbury 2006, 34–35)

But the problem with this explanation of why "Fade to Black" might be disappointing is that there were very few other thrash metal recordings which were released before Metallica's album. Judging from a traditional model of genre as a category, or genre as a set of expectations based on an existing corpus or repertoire, one might assume from the rejection of "Fade to Black" that Metallica was doing something entirely unprecedented in thrash metal. But in fact, in 1984, there wasn't much thrash metal to form any kind of precedent. Steve Waksman acknowledges this in his review of Pillsbury's book, where he argues that Metallica "served at once as one of the foremost architects of the genre (or subgenre) of thrash metal, and as a band that stretched the rules of thrash almost as soon as the genre assumed some sort of early definition" (Waksman 2008, 196). Metallica could not have violated the normative characteristics of thrash metal because, in 1984, there were hardly any recordings of thrash metal from which to extrapolate such a norm.

On the other hand, there's a long tradition of acoustic songs in metal, reaching back at least as early as Black Sabbath's "Orchid" or Led Zeppelin's "Stairway to Heaven." In addition to this ancient history, quiet sounds were an established presence during the development of thrash metal, including many bands which Metallica selected as part of their heavier grouping within the NWOBHM. Iron Maiden, Angel Witch, and the Tygers of Pan Tang each had at least one song on every album they released before 1984 that is comparable to "Fade to Black," with clean or acoustic guitar, softer singing, classical/ folk influences, and often with topics of introspection or vulnerability. The following is a representative but not exhaustive list:

- Motörhead "Capricorn" from *Overkill* (1979)
- Iron Maiden "Strange World" from *Iron Maiden* (1980)
- Angel Witch "Sorcerers" from *Angel Witch* (1980)
- Iron Maiden "Prodigal Son" from *Killers* (1981)
- Tygers of Pan Tang "Mirror" from *Spellbound* (1981)
- Venom "Mayhem with Mercy" from *Welcome to Hell* (1981)
- Diamond Head "Sucking My Love" from *Lightning to the Nations* (1981)
- Iron Maiden "Children of the Damned" from *The Number of the Beast* (1982)
- Witchfinder General "Invisible Hate" from *Witchfinder General* (1982)
- Mercyful Fate "Into the Coven" from *Melissa* (1983)

This list makes it clear that Metallica's "Fade to Black" was building on an established tradition of quiet songs in heavy metal music, rather than importing something foreign from another genre.

The reason that Metallica's "Fade to Black" was viewed as a disappointment was not because it strayed from tradition, but the opposite—it remained within the bounds of tradition, in a new extreme metal paradigm where artists were expected to exceed those bounds.[4] Extreme metal doubled down on heavy metal's master narrative of "leaving the blues behind," and the quest for more heaviness became an aesthetic imperative. Eric Smialek argues that "Fans for whom thrash metal represents an underground opposition to mass culture are more likely to associate Metallica's folk-rooted material with commercial success and thus compromise" (Smialek 2016b, 113)—and this clearly applies to "Fade to Black," not just Metallica's "Black album" which Smialek was writing about.[5] (Zohren, the reviewer I quote above, clearly holds the beliefs Smialek alludes to: when Zohren describes the song "Ride the Lightning" as "much too melodic for Metallica's position [within the scene]," he offers a preemptive defense, "… no, not too commercial!") Metallica's folk-influenced material perpetuates an established tradition of quiet music in heavy metal, but that tradition runs counter to the aesthetic mandate for ever-increasing heaviness through which Metallica brought thrash metal into being, a mandate which defined the emergence of extreme metal and its development for decades afterwards. In other words, "Fade to Black" struck some fans as a betrayal or breach of genre because of (rather than despite) its continuation of established musical repertoires.

Arguably, "Fade to Black" is an integral part of thrash metal, not outside of it. Contrary to Metallica's critics, I believe that "Fade to Black" and similar songs, if heard from a less partisan perspective, are quite heavy—they directly confront horrific situations and mental anguish, and through rage and frustration, they somehow transmute despair into catharsis during their thrashing bridge sections (Hudson 2023b, 16–19). Plenty of Metallica fans agree, and these ballads are some of the band's most beloved songs. Any critical view of thrash metal which casts Metallica's ballads outside the genre is missing a key component of thrash metal's history, success, and aesthetic universe. If there is a genre breach in this historical moment, then, it does not lie in Metallica's

---

[4] Florian Walch describes a concept called "metal-becoming-extreme" (Walch 2023, 35) which quite neatly theorizes many aspects of this paradigm.

[5] Smialek also "connects the negative reception of Metallica to racial tensions in metal discourses: one thinks of metal critics' eagerness to praise the elimination of blues elements in '80s metal" (Smialek 2016b, 117).

creating the song "Fade to Black": the breach of genre was that so many extreme metal fans rejected it.

This disparity between fans' embrace of "Fade to Black" and the song's rejection by extreme metal tastemakers is a side-effect of viewing genres too literally, as strict categories defined by specific musical qualities or aesthetic principles. Drott appropriately describes this kind of partisan genre policing as a kind of violence.

> Conceiving genre in such a prescriptive fashion transforms it into an instrument of symbolic violence, whose baleful effects may be seen in the sanctions that musicians incur when they stray from the norms promulgated by the genre with which they are affiliated or in the exclusions that result from the habitual identification of certain genres with certain social groups. (Drott 2013, 9)

On the one hand, the rejection of "Fade to Black" as a breach of genre was an extremely prescriptive and partisan stance. But on the other hand, Drott's reading of such rejections as a kind of violence is a perspective that many metal musician and fans might not find all that problematic. Metal discourse is full of hyperbolic rhetoric about killing posers and demolishing non-metal styles. It is through this kind of partisan grouping and violent rejection that Metallica shaped the NWOBHM in their own image, and then broke through to create a new style, reifying the ideology of ever-increasing heaviness as the guiding principle of the nascent extreme metal scene. So perhaps it is only fitting that Metallica eventually became the victim of the monster they had created, as the same ideologies which they used to distinguish themselves were turned against them to cast them out of the genre.

8
Headbanging to Drum Patterns to Create Heaviness

In Chapter 5, I argued that headbanging was "spontaneous, unchoreographed individual expression" and also "a flexible expression of shifting rhythmic feel." These dimensions of spontaneity and subjectivity distinguish headbanging from classical constructions of rhythm and meter. Music theorists, whose discipline is based in methods developed for the notated scores of classical music, often assume that a piece of music's meter or beat is an objective (or at least intersubjective) common ground available to all listeners and participants. This is somewhat true in classical music, when meter and beat are clearly dictated by time signatures, bar lines, and other notation elements in the score and visibly manifested by the motions of a conductor. But in metal, the body is less disciplined and the beat is less autocratically determined. Headbanging is a way for listeners to create their own subjective rhythmic understanding and their own experiences of heaviness—to create their own sensations of beat and impact.[1]

Headbanging's individualized physical motion (like all metal dance practices, including moshing and fist-pumping) adds a visceral, performative dimension to experiences of heaviness, augmenting and amplifying the real and imagined impacts of metal's sound described in Chapters 1 and 2. Metallica vividly describes how headbanging of their song "Whiplash" (1983):

Adrenaline starts to flow, you're thrashing all around
Acting like a maniac. —Whiplash!

---

[1] Elsewhere, I have engaged more with meter theory (especially Ito 2020) to develop this argument that headbanging is a construal of beat (Hudson 2022a).

Heaviness in Metal Music. Stephen S. Hudson, Oxford University Press. © Oxford University Press 2026.
DOI: 10.1093/9780197774991.003.0012

It would be fair to interpret the word "whiplash" as a reference to headbanging's potential for neck damage. But it also reflects the music's sudden change in rhythm at this exact moment—when, after a disarmingly quiet roll on the tom-toms, the singer shouts the word "whiplash" just as the chorus is about to end, after which the guitars immediately come crashing in with the blisteringly fast verse riff. These dramatic rhythmic shifts and changes in intensity are crucial dynamics in metal music, and headbanging is part of how listeners experience them.

While headbangers decide for themselves how to move, the musicians have a conscious influence, as testified by Harris Berger's observation that "death metal composers develop their forms to orchestrate the ebb and flow of the audience's interactions" (1999, 64). As I will explore in Chapter 9, all types of metal dancing create "cycles of energy" (Pillsbury 2006) across a song's form, and the interior of a metal song can be imagined as a ritual space for experiences of heaviness. Some forms of dance like moshing are deliberately chaotic and untimed, but headbangers' individual decisions are made in close coordination with the music—and especially the drum patterns. While I focus on headbanging in this chapter, my arguments about drum patterns and timing apply to other dance behaviors that coordinate with musical rhythm, including fist-pumping; and my broader arguments about motion, subjectivity, and togetherness apply even more broadly to all metal dance.

In rock and metal, guitar riffs are understood to imply visceral physical motion (see Fast 2001, Chapter 4), but drumming often provides the clearest, most conventionalized cues, an insight indicated by Jonathan Piper's observation that "if the last 4/4 measure in a four-bar phrase is accented in a 3+3+2 feel, the banging of heads will change to match it" (Piper 2013, 60). Subsequent research has systematically explored the rhythmic and motional cues that drum patterns offer to metal listeners (Gamble 2019; Garza 2021; Hudson 2022a; Kozak 2021). This chapter adds direct investigation of how headbangers create experiences of heaviness as they navigate these cues. Through a close analysis of Metallica's "Whiplash," I document how headbangers can coordinate with these common drum patterns, analyze how headbanging can increase one's perception of heaviness, and explore listeners' agency in creating their own experiences. Next, I consider how sequences of changes in drum patterns architectonically accumulate into large-scale cycles of energy across an entire song form in Sepultura's "Refuse/Resist," and then end by reflecting on headbanging's counterintuitive combination of individualism and community.

Figure 8.1 Headbanging to (a) every quarter note beat; (b) beats one and three, or (c) beats two and four. The arcs above the staff notation represent headbanging motion. The vertex at the lowest point represents the lowest point of the head's motion, which usually is felt as a beat organizing the time and motion around it (compare with notation in Hudson 2022a; see also Ito 2020).

How Backbeats in Metal Afford Headbanging and Heaviness

While headbanging is unchoreographed, it usually correlates with common drum patterns in predictable ways. The main drum pattern used in much of "Whiplash" is a type of backbeat (defined in Chapter 5), which is the default drum pattern in metal music. Although the backbeat does not force metal fans to headbang in a particular way, it does specify a particular set of affordances for motion (Kozak 2021).[2] In other words, the sonic cues of the most basic backbeat drum pattern are associated in the minds of metal fans with common strategies for headbanging along (Hudson 2022a), as shown in Figure 8.1.[3] One such strategy is to headbang on beats one and three, opposite to the snare accents on beats two and four; another common strategy is to headbang on every beat (one, two, three, and four). Finally, the backbeat

---

[2] The terms "affordance" and "specify" are today primarily associated with the ecological psychology of James J. Gibson (1966; 1978). I primarily cite Kozak (2020), who carefully redefines these terms for a musical context, building on and critiquing previous applications of ecological psychology to music (including Clarke 2005; see Hudson 2023a for a brief summary and explanation of Kozak's interventions).

[3] For simplicity's sake, I have chosen to use the most basic backbeat here. My reviewer Brad Osborn points out that there are additional motional possibilities for a compound-meter backbeat with a triplet subdivision of the beat, including 3:2 hemiola relationships between the head motion and the drums.

also affords headbanging on beats two and four; this is contraindicated by a century of rhythmic practice associating a backbeat with centers of gravity on beats one and three, so it will feel unnatural to many listeners, but this interpretation of the backbeat is occasionally used, as in the verses of Metallica's "Fight Fire with Fire" (1984).[4]

I argued in the previous chapter that metal inherits the basic logic of the backbeat from earlier blues, rock, gospel, and jazz; this means that metal's drum patterns are often accessible to listeners familiar with other popular music styles—but metal backbeats also have their own idiomatic norms. Metal backbeats are rarely played in their most prototypical form, but instead take widely varying manifestations, a sample of which are shown in Figure 8.2. Snare accents on beats two and four usually remain constant, identifying the backbeat pattern and defining the time feel. The kick drum can vary more widely, either reinforcing the riff's rhythms or playing constant notes to fill out the texture and add rhythmic intensity. Cymbals are often struck on every beat or on a subdivision, making them the most consistent time-keepers throughout a passage (Garza 2021, 19); but they may also be used for sporadic accents.

This logic of the backbeat also structures drum patterns across much of the substantial range of metal music that is not (or at least, not only) in 4/4. Progressive metal bands, like the prog rock genre they inherit from, are known for frequently incorporating odd or asymmetrical meters. These meters are also endemic, though somewhat less common, in other metal styles; odd meters like 5/4 and 7/4 can be found on a number of classic thrash metal songs, such as Metallica's "Blackened" (1988) and Anthrax's "Time" (1990), and frequent meter changes are a presence on some relatively mainstream alternative metal albums including *Believe* (2002) by Disturbed and *Dirt* (1992) by Alice in Chains. In a broader corpus of rock (including many metal examples), Scott Hanenberg found that most songs in most quintuple and septuple meters (excepting 5/16) used drum patterns that were variants of a backbeat (Hanenberg 2020, Example 4). This holds true for many metal songs in odd meters; for example, "Them Bones" by Alice in Chains begins with a 7/8 drum pattern (Figure 8.3a) that is essentially a shortened version

---

[4] "Fight Fire with Fire" features a continuous double-time backbeat drum pattern from 0:51 through 1:43. During the verse strophes (1:12–1:22 and 1:28–1:38), the main accents in the vocals and guitar (and their headbanging, in live videos) coincide with the snare hits of the backbeat, but during the inter-verse link sections (1:22–1:27 and 1:38–1:42) the band appears to switch to a normal interpretation of the backbeat, headbanging with the kick drum instead of the snare.

Figure 8.2 Representative examples of how different backbeat feels can manifest in varied and elaborate ways in metal music. (a) Queen "Bohemian Rhapsody" finale (4:55–5:07), normal-time backbeat; (b) Ningen Isu "Heartless Scat" verse (1:23–1:28), more elaborate normal-time backbeat; (c) Motörhead "Ace of Spades" verse (0:14–0:21), double-time backbeat; (d) King Woman "Celestial Blues" prechorus (0:46–0:59), half-time backbeat; (e) Meshuggah "Bleed" intro (0:00–0:16), more elaborate half-time backbeat; (f) Darkthrone "Transylvanian Hunger" Intro (0:00–0:29) blast beat.

of a conventional backbeat (Figure 8.3b), with the last four eighth notes compressed into the space of three. Brad Osborn's article on odd meters and time signature shifts in math rock contains a number of similar metal or metal-adjacent examples (Osborn 2010). A number of metal bands, most notably Meshuggah and their imitators in the djent subgenre, superimpose complex-meter riffs over 4/4 backbeats (see Figure 8.2e). In other words, while metal is notably (or perhaps even characteristically) welcoming of complex meter, much of this complex meter is also organized by the logic of the backbeat.

Figure 8.3 (a) The 7/8 drum pattern used for the opening of "Them Bones" by Alice in Chains; and (b) an imaginary 4/4 version of the same drum pattern, showing how the 7/8 drum pattern can be understood as a shortened version of a normal backbeat.

How Shifts and Variations in Backbeats Afford Additional Heaviness

One reason why the backbeat in metal music is heard to have such intense qualities of impact and heaviness is that, in this cultural and musical context, it is associated with such visceral physical movement styles.[5] As in many Black American music traditions, audience participation is an appreciative response to music which succeeds according to the community's values and aesthetics (see Chapter 5). In metal, of course, a foundational aesthetic value is heaviness. In short, there is a virtuous cycle in which louder, more rhythmically intense music invites more vigorous headbanging, which in turn amplifies the felt impact of the music.

But this only establishes a baseline association with heaviness, and beyond this baseline, the variations with which musicians deploy these patterns and the ways in which listeners interact with them can create more (and more varied) heaviness. There are a variety of culturally appropriate ways to move to a backbeat in metal, ranging from standing still to frenzied extremes of motion—so even given a single, repetitive, unchanging drum pattern, listeners can modulate or shape their experience of heaviness by changing between these different options. Remember back to Figure 8.1. One listener, nursing a sore neck from the night before, might nod gently at the slower rate of moving once every half note; another listener, feeling epic and theatrical, might choose the same speed of motion but invest more physicality, grabbing their knees and bending over to dig their head deep toward the floor. A third listener, young and full of manic energy, might headbang at twice the speed, thrashing their head forwards with every quarter-note beat. Listeners can also

---

[5] This association between backbeats and headbanging is theorized Kozak through the concept of "social affordances" (Kozak 2021).

change speed or increase the intensity of their physical motion at any moment for a variety of reasons; maybe they feel a shift in intensity in the music, or maybe they caught the eye of a friend and want to nonverbally communicate their excitement about the band onstage, or maybe someone in front of them moved out of the way and now there's finally enough space to let loose.

. But metal music rarely uses a single drum pattern for an entire song; it frequently changes between rhythm patterns, implying or encouraging shifts in headbanging and felt rhythmic intensity. Glenn T. Pillsbury's concept of "cycles of energy" provides a simple but powerful heuristic for understanding these shifts: more intense music invites more intense participation, structured in cycles of building energy. Pillsbury considers cycles at different levels of scale, from the insistent motion of a single recurring riff to verse-chorus sequences spanning an entire song form. For example, during the verse of "Whiplash" (see Figure 8.4 for a complete form chart), Pillsbury describes cycles of energy through metaphors from classical mechanics, arguing that "we could describe the Low E base in the guitars and the drum pattern as an expression of kinetic energy, or the energy of stable motion: nothing in the verse music itself points us toward the inevitability of a different riff or change of energy," but then in the chorus, "the new rhythmic pattern, pitch, and palm-muted timbre then reconstitute the energy as a build-up of potential energy, energy released as kinetic by another explosion back to C" (2006, 12). Pillsbury describes these cycles primarily in terms of rhythmic intensity, but Ciro Scotto has described analogous cycles in terms of changes in loudness and timbre (Scotto 2016). Pillsbury's concept of cycles of energy is evocative but rather vague. I'd like to add more specificity by exploring some of the idiomatic changes or variations in drum patterns in "Whiplash" (as well as some other common patterns), the possibilities for coordinating headbanging motion that these shifts afford to listeners, and the experiences of heaviness these ways of moving might create.

One of the common idioms of rhythmic change that shapes cycles of energy in metal is what Pillsbury identifies as "a doubling of the drum pattern against a rhythmically unchanging guitar riff, a hallmark of thrash metal's rhythmic language" (2006, 18). For example, this kind of doubling occurs at 2:54 in the B section of "Whiplash" (Figure 8.5a). Here the rate of alternation between snare and kick drum which defines the backbeat doubles, creating what is called a "double-time feel" (see de Clercq 2016). One might expect that a doubled drum pattern would imply that headbangers should headbang twice as fast, and in some songs this can happen. But in "Whiplash," at the beginning of Figure 8.5a, I am usually already headbanging at a quarter-note rate, and given the tempo of about 150 quarter-note beats per minute, it would be virtually impossible to double my speed of headbanging to an eighth-note pulse in excess of 300 headbangs per minute (five per second). Instead, the doubling in the drums invites me to add greater energy or range of motion to my headbanging, rather than specifying a new, faster rate of motion. The doubled drum pattern at 2:54 coincides with the start of the guitar solo, and it feels like this breaks through some sort of ceiling to bring the song to a higher level of power, with qualities of manic energy or a runaway chain reaction.

"Whiplash" also features the opposite shift during its chorus, when at 1:19 the double-time rate of alternation between snare and kick drum is halved to create a normal-time backbeat (Figure 8.5b). Like with the shift to double time, one might expect this halving of the pattern's speed of alternation to afford half-speed headbanging, and in some songs or to some listeners this might feel appropriate; but instead, in this moment, I usually continue with the same rate of headbanging to the quarter note. The halving of the drum pattern's speed does not necessarily translate into a drop in headbanging energy, either; I experience the slower frequency of snare hits as a broadening or opening of space, which feels like an invitation to increase my range of motion, building energy rather than losing it. This draws on familiar entailments of the cognitive metaphor of heaviness (explored in Chapter 1): slower objects in the real world are often bigger, and require or involve more weight or force. The drums alternate back and forth between double-time and normal-time feels before the dramatic climax at the end of the chorus, "... Whiplash!"—and to me, at least, both types of shift afford increased energy in my headbanging.

Normal backbeats and double-time feels are only two options out of a broad spectrum of "time feels" shown in Figure 8.6, which are theorized by Garza (2021). Metal drummers frequently change between these different backbeat feels in different song sections, which Smialek (2016a, 226) describes as an "idiomatic tendency [in metal] for the rate of the snare drum to determine the music's overall pulse," shaping large-scale cycles of energy levels across entire songs. Calder Hannan (2024, 183) suggests that cymbals are a more salient than the snare as a cue for felt pulse; it is more accurate to say, then, that the snare does not determine the music's "overall pulse," but rather a more abstract quality of pacing that is not directly embodied by headbanging or other beat-oriented dance motions. Two common backbeat time feels are not present in "Whiplash": the half-time backbeat and the blast beat (the latter is defined in the next paragraph). In a half-time feel such as Figures 8.2d and 8.2e, the alternation between kick and snare occurs only once per measure. For half-time backbeats in metal, a time-keeping cymbal is usually played at regular intervals (e.g., on every quarter-note beat), while the kick drum may be coordinated with the guitars instead of strictly marking downbeats (Garza 2021, 19–20).

Backbeats can also be faster than the double-time feel, which tend to afford drastically different qualities of motion. While a double-time backbeat has a kick-snare alternation twice as fast as a normal-time feel, Figure 8.2f is twice as fast again—so that there are two bass drum hits and two snare hits within every quarter-note beat. One could call this a "quadruple-time feel backbeat," but the pace of motion is so fast that it doesn't really feel like a backbeat—it feels like a machine-gun blur of motion. Because of this qualitative transformation, these faster variants of kick-snare alternation are usually called "blast beats" rather than "quadruple-time" or "sextuple-" or "octuple-time feels"; see Garza 2021, 26). Blast beats evoke simultaneous impressions of extreme speed and stasis, and this paradox is essential to the distinct aesthetics of black metal and death metal, in which blast beats often seem to index liminal or sublime experiences beyond the realm of ordinary human action (see Bogue 2004). Blast beats afford extreme motional responses, equally matching both the frenzied motion of fervent headbanging and the absence of motion, whether that's the impassive stasis of "silent men" (Kahn-Harris 2007, 44) or the complete disorientation created by a chaotic blast beat barrage (Walch 2023, 220).[6]

"Whiplash" features another common idiom known as a "push," created when the drums and guitars together place a big accent right before a downbeat, dislocated from the normative place for an accent (right on the downbeat). A push is the core, and arguably only, distinguishing element of the main verse riff in "Whiplash" (Figure 8.5c): this push is created by the guitarists playing a G on the final note of the riff, and the drummer reinforces this off-beat accent with a paired kick drum and crash cymbal hit, but the riff contains nothing else other than the most cliched building blocks of thrash metal, "chugging" low-E 16th notes and a double-time backbeat. The term "push" has been used sporadically across the decades by rock drummers and critics (e.g., MacDonald 2007 [1994], 121), and Jim Riley gives a clear definition in one of his instructional books about the Nashville Number System: "The push ... means that the chord is to be attacked an eighth note earlier, which in this case would be the '&' of the previous measure ... playing the chord on the '&' of beat four propelled the phrase forward" (Riley 2010, 23).[7] Pushes are used in all kinds of popular music styles, where they usually create some feeling of forward propulsion or surprise because they arrive

---

[6] Florian Walch argues that in early grindcore, "The instrumental groove sections invite coordinated motion like headbanging, a potentially communal pleasure in meter that is dashed by the wash of drums and riff fragments in the blast sections" (Walch 2023, 220).

[7] Thanks to Trevor de Clercq for bringing my attention to this source, and thanks to Fred Hosken and Matthew Bannister for helping me trace out this term's historical and recent usage. De Clercq has discussed the push in his own Nashville Number System fake book (2015, 15).

Figure 8.4 Form chart for Metallica "Whiplash" (1983), following the format of Hudson 2021a.

	Time	Section	Guitar Riff	Other Instrumentation	Drum Pattern
Intro	0:00	**Buildup**			snare tattoo
	0:06			sustained guitar note	rolling 16th notes in toms; double-time backbeat implied by accents
	0:30		A	guitars begin riffing	still only toms, double-time backbeat with occasional phrase-ending 332
A	0:41	**Pre-Verse**	A	whole band playing	double-time backbeat (on snare) with occasional phrase-ending 332
	0:53		B		double-time backbeat with push accents
	1:06	**Verse**	B	w/ vocals	double-time backbeat with push accents
	1:19	**Chorus**	C	w/ vocals	alternates between double-time and normal backbeats
		Refrain		"Whiplash!"	roll on toms ending in a push accent timed with "Whiplash!"
A	1:28	**Pre-Verse**	A		double-time backbeat with occasional phrase-ending 332
	1:40	**Verse**	B	w/ vocals	double-time backbeat with push accents
	1:52	**Chorus**	C	w/ vocals	alternates between double-time and normal backbeats
		Refrain		"Whiplash!"	roll on toms ending in a push accent timed with "Whiplash!"
A	2:03	**Pre-Verse**	A		double-time backbeat with occasional phrase-ending 332
	2:17	**Verse**	B	w/ vocals	double-time backbeat with push accents
	2:28	**Chorus**	C	w/ vocals	alternates between double-time and normal backbeats
	2:36	**Refrain**	C'	w/ out vocals	roll on toms ending with massive phrase-ending quarter-note triplet figure
B	2:39	**Bridge**	D		normal backbeat
	2:54	**Guitar Solo I**	D		double-time backbeat
	3:17	**Refrain**		held guitar note, "Whiplash!"	hihat counting off quarter notes, then silence during "Whiplash!"
	3:20	**Guitar Solo II**	D		double-time backbeat with occasional phrase-ending 332
A'	3:32	**Verse**	B	w/vocals	double-time backbeat with push accents
	3:44	**Chorus**	C	w/vocals	alternates between double-time and normal backbeats
	3:55	**Playout to Cadence**	C'		slightly altered normal backbeat

Figure 8.5 (a), (b), and (c) Drum pattern variations and shifts in "Whiplash."

"early"—but within metal's aesthetic of heaviness, their physical impact is especially important.

There are several ways in which a headbanging listener might navigate a push, which result in subtly different physical experiences of heaviness—and these interpretive options apply to many other rhythmic irregularities in metal. A push accent could be experienced as a syncopation: if a headbanger keeps moving the same way all the way through, the push accent could be experienced as a surprising off-beat accent, clashing against the bobbing rhythm of their head. But a headbanging listener could also interpret a push accent to imply a change of body motion: the off-beat hit of the push accent could be heard to suggest or specify an "early" headbanging motion. This could be experienced as an adjustment imposed on the body by some outside force—and thus a heavy, embodied impact. If a push accent surprises you in this way, it can be jarring, a heavy, visceral, physical dislocation from the established pattern of headbanging that is unexpected forced upon you by the music. But for a knowledgeable listener (someone who has heard this song before,

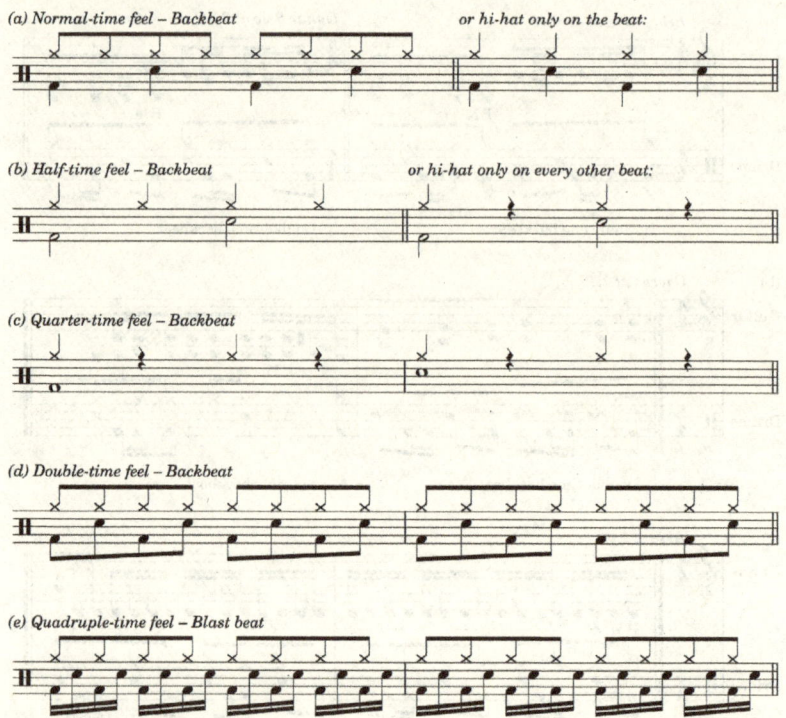

Figure 8.6 Different backbeat time feels, following Garza (2021, Examples 10 and 11).

or is familiar with rock or metal styles), the change in body motion afforded by a push accent may not be a disruption at all, but a familiar idiom. In this case, a push could feel like a jointly enacted deviation from the regular pulse, affording feelings of togetherness through cooperative action, just like the standard backbeat drum pattern. This feeling of togetherness and joint action can add power and gravity (or, in a metal context, heaviness) to anything we do, musical or otherwise. (Of course, such a listener could still choose to experience the push as a disruption of their own body motion, just as someone watching a horror movie can still experience the thrill of a jump scare even when they know it's coming. I explored this type of response in Chapter 1 through Stephen King's concept of "suspension of disbelief.")

But also, a knowledgeable headbanger who moves with the push accent could think of this change in motion as a deviation from the crowd, a perspective which might have its own special sense of impact. To be clear, this would not involve a different physical motion than the hearings described above, but rather a distinct stance or meta-stance toward that motion and toward other listeners. If an average listener follows along with the basic quarter-note pulse as long as they can, then choosing to move in another way could carry a sense of social distinction or a type of performative connoisseurship—not just distinction in some abstract sense, but also in a literal sense of moving differently. Olivia Lucas (2018, 55) observes an analogous distinction at Meshuggah concerts between "'nerds' in the balcony" counting the band's esoteric guitar riff convolutions, and moshers in the pit who headbang to the straight-ahead backbeat. An off-beat accent like a push provides a chance to go against the grain in a way that is musically supported ("dancing the song" as I discussed in Chapter 5), or to demonstrate one's deep knowledge of a particular song or style (which could easily be a kind of "subcultural capital" in the sense of Kahn-Harris 2007). Moving differently from the people around you can have a mild transgressive charge, even when one remains within common conventions for movement in metal communities—and this transgressive charge can be experienced as embodied intensity or power, similar to speaking up in a meeting to contradict someone else's point of view, or showing up to a social occasion in an outfit you know will stick out. If the transgressive charge of moving differently is experienced as an embodied impact in this way, it arguably contributes to an experience of heaviness.

Another Drum Pattern and Headbanging Strategy: Phrase-Ending 332

The backbeat is the dominant drum pattern in "Whiplash," but it is not the only type of drum pattern in play. Another is what I've previously described as a "phrase-ending 332 construction" (Hudson 2022a, 130; see also Hudson 2019). "Whiplash" and many other metal songs often use rhythms which consist of a string of dotted eighth notes, followed by a couple of regular eighth notes that fill out the length of the pattern to an even total (usually a half or full measure of 4/4). Each dotted eighth note is three sixteenth notes long, while each regular eighth note is two sixteenth notes long, so one can represent these patterns as strings of 3s and 2s; the most common ones are 332 and 333322, which are called "tresillo" and "double-tresillo," respectively (Biamonte 2014).

Headbangers move to these 332 rhythms in several ways, which create different experiences of heaviness. Sometimes the 332 rhythm is played by just one or two members of the band; for example, in the chorus of "Whiplash," the guitars play some 332 rhythms but the drummer sticks to backbeats (Figure 8.7a). In these moments, band members and listeners will often headbang normally to the backbeat, but a few might choose to instead join the 332 rhythm. The consequences of this motional choice are similar to those of

Figure 8.7 "Whiplash" phrase-ending 332 constructions, compared with other similar rhythms.

the push accents I discussed earlier in the chapter, but with some additional properties specific to 332 rhythms that I'll describe below.

At other times, all the instrumentalists in the band articulate a 332 rhythm in unison, creating a new kind of rhythmic structure that is completely distinct from the backbeat because it no longer specifies quarter-note or half-note headbanging. Piper (2013, 60) describes this phenomenon in the passage I quoted earlier: "If the last 4/4 measure in a four-bar phrase is accented in a 3+3+2 feel, the banging of the heads will change to match it." This happens most frequently at the end of a phrase or section.[8] For example, in "Whiplash," a phrase-ending 332 construction is used for a pivotal structural point in the

---

[8] Nicole Biamonte describes this use of tresillo rhythm as a "cadential hemiola" (2014, 7.5).

song: the end of the buildup intro when the whole band begins playing (at 0:40, see Figure 8.7b). At this moment, the whole band briefly departs from the regular motion of backbeats and 4/4 time, and instead moves their heads to the 332 rhythm.

The phrase-ending 332 is usually given a particular drumkit realization that distinguishes it from other 332 rhythms: regular quarter notes and back-beat accents on beats two and four are both omitted, and instead the drummer creates a chain of heavy accents in the 332 rhythm by simultaneously striking the kick drum and crash cymbal. As I've previously argued, this blunt kick-cymbal impact is a sonic icon of heaviness that invokes, imitates, and invites the physical impact of headbanging (Hudson 2022a); and in metal I usu-ally feel compelled to nod along with this kind of strike and feel it as a beat whenever it occurs, even outside of familiar patterns like the phrase-ending 332 (e.g., the same paired kick-cymbal strike is sometimes used to empha-size push accents, as in Figure 8.5c). When Metallica's drummer uses these kick-cymbal strikes for a phrase-ending 332, all band members headbang in unison with these strikes in 332 rhythm (in contrast with the band's other uses of 332 rhythm, in which one or more of the band members is usually still headbanging to a quarter-note pulse).

One way to understand the syntax of metal drum patterns is as "grooves" and "fills." Grooves, in this sense, are stable repeating patterns like the back-beat, which provide the foundational structure for particular sections of music (see Attas 2015). Drum fills, on the other hand, are interruptions to, alter-ations of, or variations on those patterns: "the punctuation that drummers use to articulate, organize, and comment on sections of songs" (Walser 2014 [1993], 173). The phrase-ending 332 is a fill, not a groove. Fills like the phrase-ending 332 rarely form the basis for any substantial passage of a song; instead, they are "punctuation" inserted into sections whose primary material is made up of other drum patterns (such as backbeats or blast beats). Drum fills can provide a sense of closure to a section that is ending, and they can create antic-ipatory momentum building up to a new section.[9]

Another rhythmic construction which has the same syntactic role as the phrase-ending 332 is the quarter-note triplet. One appears in "Whiplash" at the end of the third chorus (at 2:39), creating a moment of acceler-ating momentum which propels forwards into the bridge (see Figure 8.7c). Like phrase-ending 332s, quarter-note triplets are often played with paired

---

[9] Drum fills are the drum equivalent of what Susan Fast describes as "cadential figures" in guitar riffs (2001, 117), which I've described previously as "riff turnarounds" (Hudson 2025), since they are not always cadential in the classical sense of the term.

kick-cymbal hits in the drums, and usually have a phrase-ending role. Mark J. Butler (2006), writing about electronic dance music, has pointed out how similar these rhythms can be, differing by only a slight change in proportion from three slightly unequal notes to three exactly equal ones. In "Whiplash," it's even harder to tell the difference between quarter-note triplets and 332 because Metallica often rushes in climactic anticipatory moments (and especially during phrase-ending 332s), part of a tendency throughout their career to prioritize feeling over precision in their playing.

The special timing profile of phrase-ending 332 rhythms gives them an accelerating quality: the felt beat is literally getting faster, because the 2 is shorter than the 3s that precede it. (Later in "Whiplash," Metallica's drummer Lars Ulrich occasionally doubles the speed of his backbeat instead of joining the phrase-ending 332 rhythm, confirming this rhythm's accelerative purpose; see Figure 8.7d.) The acceleration is not only in musical sound, it is physically enacted by headbangers: for anyone who headbangs along with the 332 rhythm in the manner described by Piper, their headbanging will get faster when the rhythm switches from 3s to 2s.

For all the reasons above, headbanging to a phrase-ending 332 creates an increase in heaviness. The accelerating rate of head motion literally increases the number of physical plunges of one's head. But also, this rhythm's inherent acceleration creates a sense of anticipation toward the next downbeat, giving that downbeat's arrival additional impact. These physical impacts are amplified by the distinctive bludgeoning sound of the paired kick-cymbal strikes, and the sonic and physical impacts are in turn amplified by the syntactic specificity and unison movement associated with this construction, which in turn reinforces its sense of anacrusis or anticipation. This creates a feedback loop of mutually reinforcing factors, give the phrase-ending 332 in metal a devastatingly heavy, blunt impact that analogous drum patterns do not have in other rock styles (e.g., compare Figures 8.7b and 8.7c to the lighthearted, lilting phrase-ending 332 at the end of the chorus to the Beatles' "Here Comes the Sun").

Heaviness, Meaning, and the Paradox of Individuality and Community

While headbanging is usually understood as a spontaneous individual dance practice, and listeners have agency in choosing when and how to headbang, this does not mean headbanging is a solitary behavior—instead, it is often understood to be communal (whether or not that community is physically

Intro	0:00 –	Extra Intro	heartbeat sound	
	0:08 Ax4	Buildup Intro	one guitar	toms only
A	0:16 Bx4	Buildup / Preverse	add more guitars	normal-time backbeat
	Bx4		add higher octave guitar	
	0:32 Cx8			normal-time backbeat
	0:48 Dx8	Verse 1		normal-time backbeat
A	1:05 Bx4	Preverse	no vox	normal-time backbeat
	1:13 Dx8	Verse 2		normal-time backbeat
	1:29 Ex4	Chorus	ends one measure early	normal-time backbeat
B	1:43 F	Bridge / New Buildup	one guitar only; faster tempo	no drums
	1:46 F		add other guitars	snare roll
	1:49 Gx8	Guitar Solo		double-time backbeat
	2:01 Fx4			double-time backbeat
A'	2:13 Bx4	Preverse		double-time backbeat
	2:21 Dx8	Verse 3		normal-time backbeat
	2:38 Ex4	Chorus		normal-time backbeat
	2:52 Bx8	Post-Chorus	long scream fading out	normal-time backbeat
	3:08 Ax4	Outro	like intro	toms only

Figure 8.8 Form chart for Sepultura's "Refuse/Resist," following the format of Hudson (2021a).

present in the moment of dancing). To trace the complex interplay between individual and community, and its impact on the meanings of headbanging, I will end the chapter with a close analysis of my experiences headbanging to an entire song, "Refuse/Resist" by the Brazilian metal band Sepultura (Figure 8.8). Headbanging to this song's various drum patterns creates and amplifies experiences of physical impact, but also can be understood as a realization of sentiments expressed in the lyrics, so that headbanging indexes or invokes experiences of rage, rebellion, oppression, resistance, heaviness, and—paradoxically—both individuality and community.

The paradox of individuality and community, of self and other, is present from the start of the song, as "Refuse/Resist" begins with the heartbeat of the then-unborn first child of the band's lead vocalist Max Cavalera. The sound itself is quite affective, even at a biological level; an infant's heartbeat is faster than an adult's, and since listeners often unconsciously synchronize their heartbeat with a beat heard around them, this opening will tend to trigger many listeners' hearts to beat faster, physiologically manifesting a higher level of arousal and excitement. Because of this source, the heartbeat sound can be interpreted as a kind of dedication of the song to the future generations. The song thus opens by foregrounding a specific individual relationship between the songwriter and his unborn son, while recruiting listeners' bodies to resonate communally with the intensity of that relationship.

After this heartbeat, the first musical sound we hear is an ominous riff fragment repeating a single power chord on the lowest open string of the guitar. In

Figure 8.9 Excerpts of Sepultura's "Refuse/Resist" illustrating the main changes in rhythmic feel.

the space at the end of this riff fragment, while the final note fades, the band's drummer Igor Cavalera plays some patterns inspired by Brazilian samba music—a unique style interpolation within metal at the time of the song's release in 1993 (Figure 8.9a). Cavalera's snare and 10-inch tom are tuned higher than normal, to evoke the sounds of the caixa and tamborim drums used in samba ensembles, and he has layered on some extra takes of these drums to evoke samba's large-ensemble drumline sound. Samba music originated within nineteenth-century Afro Brazilian communities and is often associated with survival in the face of oppression and slavery (a practice which was not abolished at the national level in Brazil in 1888). Although samba was reformulated into its modern incarnation in the 1920s, it remains a music of the people, especially associated with Black or mixed-race heritage. The groove created by these samba elements starts to pull my body into motion, but because the drums have not started a full backbeat, I do not yet start headbanging in earnest—so this powerful groove serves as an accelerant burning toward an even higher level of energy, anticipation rather than arrival.

At 0:15, a full riff finally comes in with a regular-time backbeat (97b), and it's time to start headbanging. "Refuse/Resist" is a real neckwrecker—a film of the band's live performance at Donington in 1994 includes some of the most intense crowd footage of headbanging that I've ever seen. The song's official music video alternates between shots of the band performing the song for a wild audience, and clips of rioting and police violence from around the world. One of the most recognizable is a famous image of a man standing in front of a line of tanks outside of Tiananmen square during the 1989 student protests, but many other clips show riots from the 1987 "June Democracy Struggle" in South Korea. This creates a strong visual association between headbangers and protestors, which puts a new spin on historic associations between rock music and rebellion. While rock'n'roll rebellion was originally a youthful resistance against parents, churches, and schools—often with exuberant overtones of partying and youthful fun—Sepultura's incarnation of rebellion is darker, and the stakes are much higher: resistance against fascist governments in the face of lethal force.

Across the next minute or two, Igor Cavalera maintains the regular-time backbeat in the snare, but adjusts the kick drum and cymbal texture to create additional heaviness. For example, the kick drum eighth notes in the verse (Figure 8.9c) create a one-two thumping that has a more pum-meling quality than the rapid sixteenth note kick drums used earlier. There is a distinct sense of higher energy arrival when Cavalera adds a special fill (in synchrony with a new guitar riff) to mark the beginning of a catastroph-ically heavy chorus (Figure 8.9d), during which his brother Max intones the song's title "Refuse ... / Resist ..." over and over again as an instruction or encouragement for the audience. After two verses and choruses, there is a gut-wrenching jump to a higher tempo for the bridge, led by the guitars. When the drummer joins them, he is playing a double-time backbeat (Figure 8.9e) that feels out of control—and somehow every live version I hear feels even faster. Headbangers start absolutely thrashing here, and a wild guitar solo wails in sympathy, but the performers and their audience alike can barely keep up with the tempo. When the band returns to their original speed and drum patterns at the end of the bridge, it feels like an increase in energy, because the sense of re-established control allows one to headbang with more force.

The practice of headbanging, and its collection of strategies for interpreting drum patterns, brings metal fans together in what the sociologist Eviatar Zerubavel (1997) calls a "thought community"—a group united by shared ways of experiencing and being in the world. During Sepultura's song, headbangers can share the experience of resistance against oppressive forces, even though no real political action has been taken. A similar sense that metal music and its imagined community can help individuals transcend their real-life situations is reported by Rosemary Lucy Hill (2016) in her ethnography of female listeners, and is certainly available to fans of all genders (although, as Hill correctly argues, metal's rhetoric of an inclusive imagined community does not always lead to real, in-person inclusion). This community-in-headbanging is evoked by numerous metal songs, such as "Bonded by Blood" (1985) by the San Francisco Bay Area thrash metal band Exodus. Depicting a (mostly) fictional fantasy of blood sacrifice at a metal show ("Murder in the front row," etc.), Exodus's chorus lyrics describe a very real sense of unity in motion, of sharing the same transgressive actions: "And there's blood upon the stage / Bang your head against the stage / And metal takes its price / Bonded by blood!" These shared ways of moving in and perceiving the world—rhythmic constructions, drum patterns, headbanging dance traditions, all considered as embodied practices of rhythm perception—help communities understand each other and experience the world together (Hudson 2022a).

Within this thought community, headbanging is unchoreographed, and listeners have agency to move however they want, creating a delicate or even paradoxical balance between individuality and community. This paradox resonates with Walser's description of a "dialectic" between freedom and control, two core concepts of the genre's ideology and aesthetics.

> Rhythm in heavy metal often seems very simple… But a dialectic of freedom and control, which I will later trace in terms of ensemble and solo sections, is also inscribed rhythmically. Accents and rhythmic deviations, whether performed by the vocalist, the guitar soloist, or the whole band, are all the more significant for being played against the solid pulse that characterizes metal. (Walser 2014 [1993], 49)

Walser mentions different musicians' roles but omits the dancing of the "performing audience" (Butler 2006, 47 and 72; 2014, 13) which is often forgotten in popular music scholarship. The dialectic of freedom and control Walser describes is thus not only a lens for listening, but also for performative dance as headbangers move with different layers of the powerful groove or join the musicians' rhythmic deviations that push against that groove.

Even though unchoreographed headbanging is understood as an unfettered expression of one's individual experience, it is still imagined as a community activity. This resonates with how Hill (2016, 52) identifies a powerful, individualistic "warrior" mythology as a central archetype and ideological force within metal culture, that coexists in seeming contradiction with a sense that the genre is a unified, global, and all-inclusive imagined community. Community in metal music is thus framed as a togetherness of individuals, which is nowhere more visible than in its visceral physical practices of headbanging and moshing. Headbanging may not be strictly synchronized, but headbangers' values, actions, and intentions are similar enough to afford cooperation. While headbanging is always ontologically understood as a spontaneous individual response, it is also clearly a form of mutual investment.

This paradox of a togetherness of individuals is not only musical, but resonates with the politics of protest in Sepultura's song. "Refuse/Resist" seems to elide headbanging to brutal riffs with resistance against brutal oppression. Like headbanging, protest is both an individual action and a communal one; protest is fueled by the agency of individuals who chose to show up and speak out, but it is most effective when it is a collective action. Unlike headbanging, protest can carry great personal risk and is often undertaken for the benefit of a broader community. In both headbanging and protest, the joint action of individuals takes on greater power when individuals act in synchrony, but also begins to exhibit a kind of conformity—individuals begin to lose some of their individuality when they join the action of a crowd, but paradoxically, we continue to understand their actions as personal expression.

There can be a thrill in moving differently from the crowd, but there's a thrill also in the unity and power of synchronization. While these experiences might seem to be opposites, in fact, they both depend on collaborative relationships with an imagined community of other headbangers. Walser argues that musicians and listeners "come to heavy metal with a wide range of personal histories and needs; they ... not only take selectively from the genre but contribute to it" (2014 [1993], 55), and while he was writing about aesthetic discourse, the same argument applies to headbanging, with a more physical sense of "contribution." The lyrics to "Refuse/Resist" don't have much detail, and audiences need not have experienced the same police violence depicted in Sepultura's video to feel that the song resonates with their own struggles, and to experience their headbanging as a form of communal resistance against oppression in all its forms. Headbanging is a type of cooperation that simultaneously embraces opposites of togetherness and individualism, both of which add to the music's energy and impact—or, in other words, its heaviness.

9

How Song Forms Create Ritual Spaces for Experiencing Heaviness

It all starts with ominous, loping tom-toms, dead space hanging tensely between each group of five wallops. Some of the kids recognize the song immediately—"Down with the Sickness" (2000), the breakout single by the Chicago alternative metal band Disturbed. "Can you feel that?" the singer whispers, as the rhythm guitarist joins in, striking back and forth across his down-tuned muted strings to produce a terrific ripping sound, more mechanical than melodic. Energy slowly builds, coming from two sources: band members joining the riff one at a time, building up the song's volume and rhythmic intensity; and my own feeling of growing anticipation for the song's upcoming breakout moment. "Oh, shit," the singer curses under his breath—a scripted moment in the recording but one which feels authentic to the flare of restless energy that has just shot through the crowd. I pick up my feet one at a time and brace them more widely for stability. The excitement in the music fills to the brim and overflows as the singer's broken rhythmic howl flies through the speakers: "OOWA-A-A-AH!" The room goes wild. I've been waiting for this moment for all evening at the high school summer camp dance party, hoping I get a chance to do one of my favorite things in the whole world: headbang to heavy metal.

As I explain below, most metal songs begin in a similar way, with a building intro culminating in a pugilistic arrival; and most metal audiences respond in a similar way, too, waiting to headbang or mosh at first but all joining in together for certain sections of the song. While metal bands can be quite creative and unconventional in how they structure their songs, they often draw on a repertoire of sonic cues and patterns of song structure that help their audiences decide when and how to move. In previous research, I've identified several normative aspects of song form in metal music (Hudson 2021a). Here, I argue that these conventional song structures frame the interior of the song as a space set apart from everyday life—a space with its own musical expectations, networks of meaning, modes of listening, and appropriate physical behaviors. This widespread use in metal of specific conventional riff-based

Heaviness in Metal Music. Stephen S. Hudson, Oxford University Press. © Oxford University Press 2026.
DOI: 10.1093/9780197774991.003.0013

song structures affords what I call a "double recall," in which each new song with conventional form reminds listeners of their previous experiences with this form while also cueing them to remember and re-enact their prior experiences of heaviness and extreme dance practices. One can listen to these normative forms as a ritual of heaviness, remembering and recreating metal's extreme physical experiences to renew one's affiliation with the metal genre.

First, I should give a few disclaimers, the most important of which is: I intend my arguments to include all metal fans, not just those in the mosh pit. In metal, both audiences and performers engage in headbanging and other extreme dance practices, so while I may use words like "fans" and "listeners," I intend to include performers on stage, too. No matter what someone's role is at an event, by dancing, they are creating their own extreme embodied experience—they are creating heaviness. Additionally, I want to be careful not to prioritize or center dancing at live concerts too much. Plenty of metal fans do not attend live concerts regularly, and even those that do may prefer to stand still rather than dance.[1] While headbanging and moshing are the most outwardly visible expressions of intense physical experience, I believe this intense physicality is felt even when fans listen more contemplatively. In other words, while I talk about metal songs creating a ritual space for extreme physical experiences like moshing and headbanging, actually dancing is not required to enter this ritual space. It's as much a mindset as a physical practice—an understanding that the music implies intense physicality, a feeling of physical power and impact experienced during listening. One final disclaimer is that the norms I describe are most common in mainstream heavy metal styles (as documented in Hudson 2021a), but are less universal in more experimental or extreme subgenres (as I will explore in Chapter 10).

Architectonic Form: Building from Riffs to a Full Song

The most universal convention of metal song structure is the riff: repeating riffs form the foundation of almost every part of almost every metal song. A riff is not just any repeating passage of music (Scotto 2024): it is a distinctive musical idea that repeats immediately to form the foundation for a section,

---

[1] Rosemary Lucy Hill discusses the problems of privileging live performance in her study of gender and metal, arguing that many female fans of metal who do not attend live performances are excluded and ignored by subculture methodologies which emphasize physical participation in group events (Hill 2016, 28–31). But I think Hill would agree that this is not exclusively a women's issue: there are plenty of male fans, too, who listen primarily at home and do not participate in the subculture.

and in metal, riffs are usually played on distorted guitars at high volume. Riffs are "autotelic" (Hughes 2003, 15), meaning that they often lead to their own beginning, creating a loop or cycle.

Riffs do not merely repeat: their repetition is often shaped by familiar riff-based formal processes, out of which a conventional large-scale song form emerges. Through these conventional processes, riffs form a frame that sets off the song as a stylized ritual space, with distinct boundaries that help participants know when to engage in the genre's extreme dance practices. Music theorists call this way of thinking about form "architectonicism" (Cooper and Meyer 1960, 2): large-scale song form does not exist independently from the small-scale details that comprise the form's "content"; instead, form gradually emerges through the activity of smaller bits, as they slowly accumulate into larger and larger shapes—and, vice versa, the feeling or quality of each small-scale bit is shaped by where it falls within the large-scale form. Figure 9.1 shows a hierarchy of parts of song structure, with each level shaping the feeling and function of the next higher level. Riffs, then, are the fundamental building blocks of this architectonic song structure, and as they are sequenced together, they create spaces for experiences of physical impact.

Riffs themselves can vary in size and complexity. The first riff of Sleep's "Dopesmoker" is a rambling, shambling monstrosity; its 40-second length stretches way beyond the capacity of what psychologists call "echoic memory"—a kind of 3–4-second, ultra-short-term memory that enables easy, immediate recognition—making it hard to remember how the riff goes, or even notice where it starts to repeat. Most riffs are much shorter; Led Zeppelin's "Wanton Song" is based on a riff that is only a twentieth of the clock duration of "Dopesmoker's" opening riff. Most riffs are unison (or at least nearly so—bass players' parts are often simplified), but some exceptions are more polyphonic. For example, the first riff in "Cafo" by Animals as Leaders layers a virtuosic sweep-picked figure played by one guitarist over a highly syncopated series of palm-muted power chords played by another; the sweep-picking layer adapts a lead guitar soloing technique usually used as a one-off flourish and repeats it as a riff, a stunt which advertises their lead guitarist Tosin Abasi's peerless technique and consistency. A later riff in "Cafo" (at 2:25) features a torrent of 92 sixteenth notes running through various scale fragments and arpeggios; the riff from "Wanton Song," on the other hand, features only one note (played in two different octaves). The length and complexity of a riff contribute to what Calder Hannan (2022) calls a metal song's "structural density" (which makes a song feel more overwhelming or more difficult to listen to), while shorter and simpler riffs tend to make fast-paced songs that require less effort to follow.

Biggest	compound AABA	whole song form
	Supersection	either a Verse/Chorus rotation, or a Bridge
	Section	such as Verse, Chorus, Pre-Chorus, etc.
	Module	several contiguous repetitions of a riff
Smallest	Riff	distinct melodic/rhythmic idea that repeats

Figure 9.1 Architectonic levels of song structure, from riffs to full songs (adapted from Hudson 2021a).

No matter a riff's size, it is usually looped to form the primary structure for a substantial passage within a song. Riffs are often repeated a number of times that is a power of two, to create "modules" that serve as building blocks for metal song forms (Pillsbury 2006, 20–22). It's rare to hear a riff repeated three or five times, and when it does happen, it usually feels surprising, unbalanced, or disruptive. The end of a module can be marked in a number of ways, the most obvious of which is a substantial change in instrumentation (like the entrance of vocals) or drum pattern (such as switching from normal-time to half-time backbeats). The end of a module is sometimes marked by a drum fill or a "riff turnaround" (Hudson 2025) which replaces part of the riff with new material that creates a sense of extra momentum. Susan Fast observes that these kind of figures can create some ambiguity as to what hierarchical level of size counts as "the riff": in her analysis of "Wanton Song," she observes that either the one-measure motive or the four-measure block of three motives plus a riff turnaround (Figure 9.2) could both be considered with equal validity to be the basic pattern of the song (Fast 2001, 117).

At the next largest level of scale, a string of riff modules in metal music can often be understood through conventional song section terminology like verse, chorus, and bridge.[2] Each of these sections could comprise one module, or several modules together. For example, Kittie's "Brackish" (2000) uses only

---

[2] De Clercq (2012) provides an authoritative study of song section labels in popular music and their definitions throughout the literature.

Figure 9.2 Riff repetition and riff turnarounds in Led Zeppelin's "Wanton Song," 0:00–0:28. Reprinted from Hudson (2025).

one riff for each section, and this economical structure is central to the song's hard-hitting directness. Metallica's "… And Justice for All" (1988), on the other hand, uses at least six different riffs or variants of riffs and two or three distinct riff turnarounds before the first verse starts, contributing to its long-winded, expansive song form.

Across a complete metal song, sections are most often organized into "supersections" that form what music analysts have described as "compound AABA song form" (see Hudson 2021a). "AABA" means that the main body of the song breaks into a recurring cycle of sections (labeled A) and a contrasting middle (labeled B); "compound" means that A is comprised of multiple sections (usually including at least a verse and a chorus, but often others as well). If a metal song has a guitar solo (a requirement in certain subgenres) or a "breakdown" section devoted to moshing (more on this later), these will usually occur in the contrasting B supersection, not the A.[3] Compound AABA is not only the norm not only in metal, but also in popular music more broadly since the late 1960s; John Covach (2005) coined the term to distinguish this form from simple "verse-chorus" forms which had no contrasting B supersection, but David Temperley (2018, 153–54) has pointed out that almost all verse-chorus forms have such a contrasting B supersection, so the terms "verse-chorus form" and "compound AABA form" are redundant for most practical purposes.

---

[3] David Easley (2011, 148fn22) makes a similar observation about hardcore punk, which breakdowns often happen in the middle of a song (i.e., in the contrasting B section), but also explains that songs which end with a breakdown may resemble Brad Osborn's "terminally climactic form" (2013).

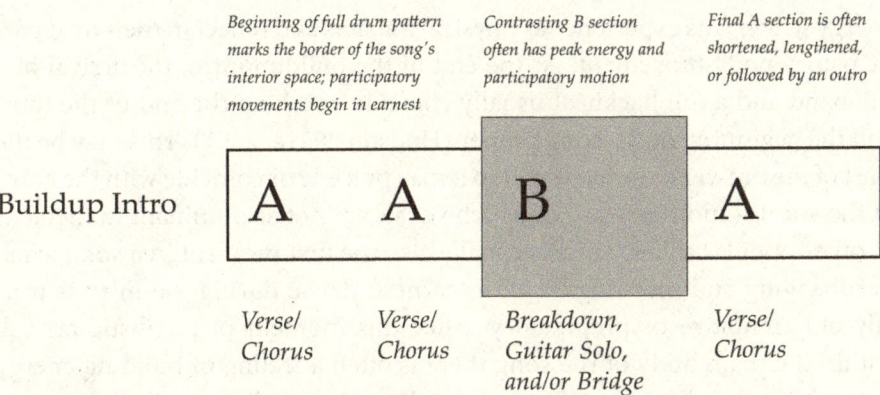

Figure 9.3 Diagram of compound AABA in metal music (reprinted from Hudson 2023b).

Metal-Specific Idioms of Riff-Based Structure: Cycles of Energy

But there are some characteristic riff-based processes in metal's compound AABA forms which distinguish them from pop and rock. The first is the degree to which metal songs spotlight the riff: while instrumental parts merely serve to accompany the voice in many pop songs, in metal they usually have equal importance to the vocals, or even more. Like "Down with the Sickness," metal songs usually feature an extended riff-based "buildup intro" (Attas 2015) in which a song begins with reduced instrumentation, often only a single guitar (Hudson 2021a, 2.2). Other instruments then gradually join in, sometimes while the same riff is repeated, but sometimes while the band switches to new riffs. Metal songs also often feature a consistent "pre-verse" section, in which the guitars play the main verse riff (or, less often, another riff) prior to the entry of vocals in each verse (Hudson 2021a, 2.4). It's not uncommon for there to be a complete break in texture with a new riff-based buildup at the beginning of the contrasting B supersection, or a recurrence of the song's opening buildup intro as a "re-intro" at the end of the B supersection (Hudson 2021a, 2.6). In other words, metal songs often use riffing as a frame for other parts of the song, which leads to a higher proportion of instrumental-only modules without vocals. This riff-based framing can make metal songs feel more stylized, theatrical, or ritualistic compared to mainstream pop music in which there often is singing continuously through almost the entire track.

   Within the main body of a metal song, sequences of sections often feel like they are building in energy from one to the next, creating the "cycles of energy" (Pillsbury 2006) that I discussed in Chapter 8—patterns of building energy which fans experience as physical impacts and reflect in their own participatory body movement. At the end of the buildup intro, the arrival of a full band and a full backbeat usually coincide, marking the end of the intro and the beginning of the song proper (Hudson 2021a, 2.2.1). This may be the start of the pre-verse, or the verse, so it may precede or coincide with the entry of the vocals (another sense in which vocals are not as dominant in metal as in other popular styles). This is usually also the first moment in a song when headbanging and moshing begin in earnest: dance during the intro is usually only tentative or preparatory. After this moment of pugilistic arrival, within the main body of the song there is often a feeling of building energy throughout the verse (and, often, a prechorus) that climaxes in the chorus. This same sequence of sections and pattern of building energy usually repeats in each A supersection, forming a "verse/chorus energy cycle" (Pillsbury 2006, 13) that is usually expressed in timbre and loudness (Scotto 2016), and in drum patterns and dance (Hudson 2022a).

Each time we hear a metal riff, we are invited to return to the world of riffing, a world with patterns and behaviors that are different from everyday life (and from most other forms of music, too). In her exposition on riffs, Susan Fast draws on the work of several philosophers to articulate this idea that musical time lies outside of everyday reality:

> John Blacking and Claude Lévi-Strauss have both suggested (separately) that the organization of time in music takes the body out of ordinary or everyday time into what Blacking calls "virtual time," what Lévi-Strauss characterizes as the "obliteration of time" leading to "a kind of immortality." An analogy can be made with what anthropologist Victor Turner, theorizing the use of time in ritual and theater, calls the "subjunctive." Ritual or theater removes one from the "indicative," the world of "actual fact," to a world of "as if." The effect that these authors suggest this has on the body is to release it from the everyday and open up the possibility of a different reality, a liberatory experience. (Fast 2001, 129)

This kind of thinking has been developed in one direction by Mariusz Kozak (2020), who argues that musical time has no objective existence but is something enacted by each individual listener. Elizabeth Margulis (2014, 55–75) has explored similar concepts but focused on musical repetition, expanding on some of the same philosophical sources as Susan Fast, but grounding these phenomena in empirical results from psychology and cognitive science research.

Drawing on these frameworks, I argue that a familiar process like riffing does not just take us out of the everyday, it transports us over and over to the same extraordinary space. Richard Schechner, a leading theorist of performance art, theater, and religious ritual, has argued that repeating an act associates it with a distinct sense of space: the conventions of that space bracket the performance off from normal daily life, facilitating certain kinds of actions and experiences and discouraging others.

> Being tossed around a mosh pit at a rock concert is very different from applauding a performance of the American Ballet Theatre's *Giselle* at New York's Metropolitan Opera House. Dance emphasizes movement, theatre emphasizes narration and impersonation, sports emphasize competition, and ritual emphasizes participation and communication with transcendent forces or beings. (Schechner, 2013 [2002], 33)

The space specified by metal's sonic conventions is indeed different from that conjured by other styles of music. Olivia Lucas observes how unique it was when moshing occurred outside of this musical frame at a Meshuggah concert:

> Below me, in the pit, something incredible is happening: the impatient jostling and shifting of the crowd has erupted into a full mosh pit before the band has even come onto the stage. A physical anacrusis to an anticipated downbeat, the show has *begun before the beginning*; [. . .] (Lucas 2018, 2)

Metal's conventions of riff-based form create a sounding musical frame that brackets off this space of different rules and behaviors from regular daily life— a space of extraordinary physical experiences, fantastical lyrics and visual imagery, and spectacular tropes of power and opposition.

"Being tossed a mosh pit at a [metal] concert" is a space with its own (usually implicit) rules and conventions, affordances for behavior and meaning— and these dimensions of moshing have been analyzed by Sherril Dodds (2011) and Gabrielle Riches (Riches 2011; Riches et al. 2014). Riches describes moshing as a "liminal experience" because "rules and regulations governing everyday life are suspended [and ...] new rules are implemented" (Riches 2011, 317). Moshing can be thought of as controlled chaos, a simulation of violence in which unspoken rules ensure that no actual injury occurs. But even though the violence is only simulated, it still violates the norms of behavior expected in everyday society, where the full-body collisions of moshing are unacceptable. Within the sonic boundaries of a metal song, however, these everyday rules are suspended—enabling participants to experience relatively uninhibited physical play, and to create a degree of corporeal contact and closeness with strangers, that is not usually allowed in public.

Bridges, Breakdowns, and Guitar Solos as Sites of Ritual Action

The contrasting B supersection of metal's conventional compound AABA form often has special features which can afford experiences of transcendence, transportation, or transformation. In classic rock compound AABA forms, the B part is just a single bridge section, perhaps as short as eight measures, which provides contrast with the A supersection's verse/chorus cycle.[4] But in metal the B supersection often contains multiple sections, and these often include section types which do not appear elsewhere in the song, the most important of which are guitar solos and breakdowns.[5] For easier reading, I'll call the whole B supersection the "bridge," because it has a similar function as the bridge in a standard rock form: contrast to and transition with the verse/chorus cycle. But unlike bridges in rock and pop music, metal's contrasting B sections tend to be much longer, more climactic, and more elaborate—to the point that the bridge can be more of a focus or energetic peak than the song's chorus.

This feeling of contrast and transition often gives metal bridges a feeling of altered or alternate reality that contributes to a sense that the bridge is some kind of peak stage of the song-as-ritual, although the type of energy and formal structure in this peak stage varies widely depending on the metal sub-genre and its norms for composition. Strong rhythmic contrasts sometimes mark a section within the bridge as the "mosh part" of a song (Pillsbury 2006, 13), such as Anthrax's "Caught In A Mosh" (1987). During the 1990s, mosh parts were conventionalized as "breakdowns," a section type marked by a pummeling downshift to a half-time backbeat, combined with a riff with a syncopated or otherwise striking rhythm, during which audience members inclined to mosh throw themselves into a complete frenzy.[6] Breakdowns are spaces where participants experience transcendent peak intensities or work out frustrations through the physical release of unrestrained motion and

---

[4] For more on the history and emergence of conventional rock compound AABA form, see Temperley 2018 and Appen and Frei-Hauenschild 2015.

[5] Elsewhere, I've listed more section types in metal that are common in (and unique to) B sections (Hudson 2021a, 2.5.1).

[6] Steven Gamble (2019) provides an ethnography and musical analysis of breakdowns, which I will engage further in Chapter 10.

body contact. For example, in Pantera's "This Love" (1992), the verses are first-person narration and the chorus is a second-person imperative command ("You keep this love"). But the only lyrics during the bridge are an exasperated exclamation without any clear subject or object—"No more head trips!"—after which a pummeling breakdown provides a vent for this frustration. On the other hand, heavy bridges are not always so cathartic. Metallica's ballads, including "One" and "Fade to Black," have several dark bridge verses in which the song's protagonist despairs or gives up a struggle that they had pursued in the verses (for an analysis of this AAB form type, see Hudson 2023b, 16–20).

But not all bridges have the heavy, brutal quality of a breakdown. Bridges reach breathtaking vistas or exuberant escape velocities as often as they drag into pounding, unyielding descents. Robert Walser describes a "heavy metal dialectic" characterized the "freedom" of virtuosic guitar solos straining against the more repetitive framework (or "control") established by the accompanying riffs (I quoted Walser's definition in Chapter 8). Walser elaborates,

> The feeling of freedom created by the freedom of motion of the guitar solos and fills can be at various times supported, defended, or threatened by the physical power of the bass and the violence of the drums. The latter rigidly organize and control time; the guitar escapes with flashy runs and other arrhythmic gestures. The solo positions the listener: he or she can identify with the controlling power without feeling threatened because the solo can transcend anything (Walser 2014 [1993], 54).

Walser argues that this heavy metal dialectic is central to the metal genre, but it's important to remember here that Walser was writing in the early 1990s and focusing mostly on classic heavy metal and glam metal styles. The dialectic does not apply evenly across all metal subgenres, especially in extreme metal, in which guitar solos are both less common, and less transcendent when they do happen (Kahn-Harris 2007, 30). But transcendent guitar solos can happen in extreme metal styles too, as in "Twisted Truth" (1991) by the Dutch death metal band Pestilence. This song's verse lyrics allude to hypocritical interpretations of religious values (the "twisted truth" of the title), set to ugly and primitive death metal riffs; but the two wordless guitar solos are majestic, heartfelt, and surprisingly melodic lamentations—perhaps representing the original "untwisted" truth.

These inherent qualities of contrast and transcendence in the bridge, and its increased length and importance in metal songs, make metal bridges likely places for experiences of climax and transformation—a dynamic which is dramatized in songs about ritual (Hudson 2023b, 11–16). The theater theorist Richard Schechner argues that rituals are performances, and calls "performances where performers are changed 'transformations' and those where performers are returned to their starting places 'transportations'" (Schechner 1981, 91). Many metal songs about ritual (including "Into the Coven" by Mercyful Fate, and "Ritual" by Ghost) are transformations, in that a central character in the lyrics performs a ritual that irrevocably transforms them during the course of the song. This transformation event usually happens within the altered reality of the bridge, and when the subsequent final A section differs from the previous ones (as is conventional), this altered A' seems to reflect the permanence of the character's transformation (see Figure 9.4).

The pattern of compound AABA song form is analogous to the form of many rituals, as described by the French ethnographer Arnold van Gennep (2019 [1908]). Gennep identifies three phases in ritual action: the preliminal, the liminal, and postliminal. In the preliminal phase, an initiate breaks with everyday practices and routines, sometimes enacting a kind of metaphorical "death," leaving them vulnerable and open to change. In the liminal phase, the initiates must complete a ritualized task to pass over some kind of threshold, taking on a new identity or power. In the postliminal phase, the initiate slowly returns to the mundane world as a changed person.

Compound AABA often has a similar shape: the first two A supersections (preliminal) bring performers and listeners into the extraordinary musical world of riffing; the B supersection (liminal) is literally "liminal" in that it is a transition from one A to another, but also in that it often contains the most

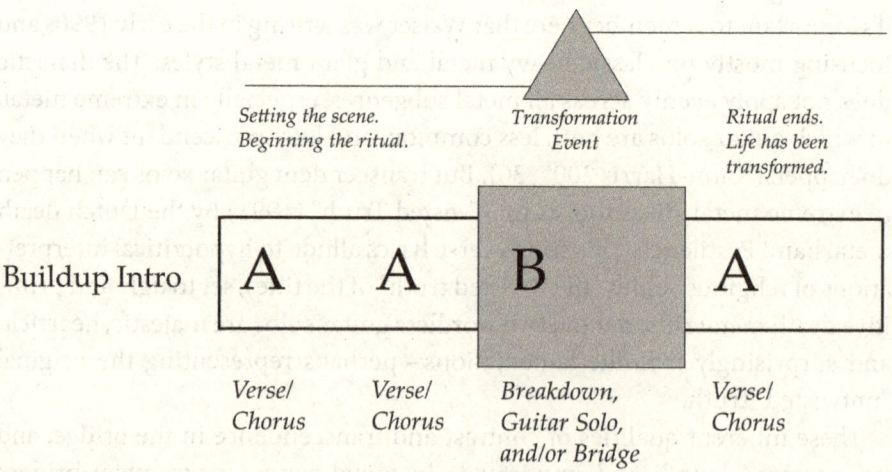

Figure 9.4 Diagram of compound AABA songs about ritual (reprinted from Hudson 2023b).

transcendent sonic and physical excesses of the whole song; and the final A section (postliminal) brings the open-ended, autotelic cycle of riffing to a satisfying closure. Whether we are headbanging with the riffs or moshing against them, the musical codes of the bridge frame it as a particularly transcendent or climactic space. Compared with the rest of the song, we might feel like *something different* happens, or the song takes us *somewhere else*. Fans participate in this transcendence or climax by dancing harder, or by imagining heavier physicality—more power with more impact. In short, we can experience the act of listening and dancing to metal music as a kind of ritual, even when the songs are not explicitly about ritual.

Experiencing Metal Idioms in Terms of Patterns and Exemplars

How do we learn about such conventions, and how do we make use of them in constructing our experiences? Consider an analogy between musical structure and linguistic grammar, a comparison that has structured human thinking about music for centuries. Language and music are both perceived and produced by human brains—and in the case of texted, sung music, these two domains have quite a lot of overlap in the form of the sound and the physiology of its expression—so it stands to reason that there might be many underlying similarities in our cognition of musical and linguistic structures. As in language, in music we develop gut-feeling expectations for what "should" happen next, and sometimes we infer explicit grammatical rules; but we also experience rules and patterns by reliving or recalling iconic, memorable exemplars.

The generative grammar approach to linguistics, championed by Noam Chomsky (1965), sought to describe how the infinite set of possible sentences could be described or "generated" by a finite set of abstract rules (rules which, it is usually acknowledged, may not directly correlate with how any real speakers actually understand language, either explicitly or implicitly). Usage-based linguistics was conceived in the late twentieth century in a response to generative linguistics. In this newer paradigm, the practical matter of learning rules inductively through use was elevated to become the primary site for theorizing about language. By analogy, we might say that each listener is building their own subjective understanding of "riffing" inductively, encountering instances of riffs "in the wild," rather than learning about riffs in terms of generalizations about the whole metal tradition, the way a language's grammar might be summarized in a textbook.

Ronald Langacker, who first coined the term "usage-based linguistics" (Langacker 1987), explains the significance of this paradigm by considering how we understand and learn a common linguistic schema. Langacker argues that we first encounter individual instances of a broader schema or pattern, and that some of these individual instances become encoded as "units," or "familiar, thoroughly mastered structures—cognitive routines" (Langacker 2002, 263). For example, as children we might initially encounter specific terms like "actor" or "actress" and learn these as automatic, hard-coded, immediate references requiring no further processing.

But when we inductively generalize to a broader rule for constructing gendered nouns "-er/-or" and "-ress," Langacker argues that our individual instances of "actor" and "actress" do not lose their automatic, hard-coded status—the more abstract schemas like "-er/-or" or "-ress" do not supplant the individual exemplars in our cognition, but simply offer an additional option in a growing network of cognitive concepts (which will also include instances of exceptions to the rule, like "fighter" but not "fightress").

> The coexistence in the grammar of the schema and instantiations affords the speaker alternate ways of accessing a complex but regular expression with unit status: it can simply be activated directly, or else the speaker can employ the schema to compute it. Moreover, the schema is available for the computation of novel instantiations [. . .]; if such an expression is frequently employed, it may very well become established as a unit and thus be incorporated per se in the grammar. (Langacker 2002, 264)

Musical structures, whether they are formal processes like "riffing," individual idioms like eighteenth-century voice-leading patterns (Gjerdingen 2007), or large-scale structures like sonata form or compound AABA form, can also be described as "schemas" in similar terms (Gjerdingen and Bourne 2015). We learn about how each of these patterns works inductively and in context, but following Langacker, if we come up with abstract generalizations about how a given pattern or form works, these generalizations do not replace our immediate experience of individual exemplars.

In other words, as each of us learns about metal riffing and riff-based metal song forms, we can develop generalized expectations for what "should" happen in a song or how particular sonic cues might orient us within a normative map of riff-based song form. But we also continue to experience song structure through recalling and reliving hard-coded exemplars that are important to us—whether those exemplars are some of the first metal songs we encountered, or songs that we have listened to over and over, or songs that we have learned are considered to be famous or pivotal.

Double Recall of Form Conventions and Physical Experiences

Each time a metal song uses conventional riff-based formal processes, it is both a reference to an existing convention of form and a performance of that convention—a reanimation of that convention as cycles of energy. Diana Taylor describes a sense that many performative actions (like wedding vows, or "discovery" of an uncontacted tribe) are "always in quotations, a copy of a lost copy" (Taylor 2003, 55). Metal's riff-based formal processes also have "an air of quotations" without a specific origin or source: riffing conventions have developed gradually from blues and rock, infused with classical music and other influences, from Beethoven to B. B. King (Walser 2014 [1993], 102–7; Fast 2001, 116, 147). To anyone who listens to enough riff-based rock or metal, the small-scale conventional moves between riffs that create cycles of energy are always (and have always been) vaguely familiar, even in moments where the riffs and timbres are radically new.

On the other hand, rather than saying "there is no single original source," it might be more meaningful to say (building on Langacker's arguments) that we each understand metal's conventional structures and formal patterns in terms of our own variety of sources drawn from our individual listening histories. My understanding of how a buildup intro goes and what it's supposed to feel like developed from a foundation shaped by the millennial nu-metal or alternative metal songs that were my gateway into metal music, like Disturbed's "Down With the Sickness" (2000)—which I heard constantly on the radio as a teenager—or Korn's "Here to Stay" (2002)—the opening track of the second album I ever bought. Korn opens the song with one guitar panned all the way to the right, and so distorted you can barely hear the notes, before the rest of the band joins in all at once to make a wall of rumbling sound with more definite pitch.[7] Other listeners likely have their own points of reference for how a metal song begins, but for me, "Here to Stay" and "Down With the Sickness" are among the most memorable and definitive examples.

Whenever I hear a buildup intro, I feel a sense of "here we go again," returning to the same feelings, repeating the same physical behaviors in anticipation of a similar buildup and pugilistic arrival. This experience is a double recall, in which I recall and anticipate a particular conventional

---

[7] Eric Smialek (2016a, 108–109) calls this as a "panned entry," and describes it as part of what is essentially a buildup intro, which he identifies as a common song-opening strategy in nu-metal music, but which is in fact relatively common in most metal subgenres (Hudson 2021a, 2.2).

musical structure (the buildup intro) at the same time as I recall and re-perform physical behaviors from my prior encounters with heaviness, to create a ritual-like experience of return and re-enactment. Within this ritual-like space, metal's heavy embodied listening practices (whether liminal dance practices like headbanging or moshing, or less overt stances of listening for a sense of physical power and impact) form "a repertoire of embodied practice/knowledge" (Taylor 2003, 19) for creating, remembering, and re-performing heaviness (I explore this sense of repertoire further in Chapter 7).

This "air of quotations" or sense of circular reference resonates with a sense of self-reference that metal sociologist Keith Kahn-Harris describes as an integral part of the genre. In unpacking the seeming paradox that metal celebrates "trueness" or unmediated authenticity, while having entirely fantastical and blatantly unreal lyrics, Kahn-Harris proposes that "Heavy metal's aesthetics are the aesthetics of essentialism" (Kahn-Harris 2016, 26). He explains later, "That essentialism is a tautological essentialism that points toward heavy metal itself. Metal is metal, its meaning is metal, its ideal metaller is essentially metal, and it is essentially metal" (Kahn-Harris 2016, 31). A few conventions for building a compound AABA form out of riffs occur over and over again in metal music, and this recurrence of form participates in the tautological essentialism Kahn-Harris describes, a sense that each metal song is channeling metal itself.

The combination of these ideas feels rather paradoxical: Metal is ultimately always about the same thing—itself—but in a practical sense "what metal is" is different for everyone because they encounter metal through their own unique "listening biography" (Margulis et al. 2009). Langacker anticipates this type of problem, arguing: "The specific array of instantiations having the status of units doubtless varies from speaker to speaker (and changes with experience for an individual speaker), but this is not considered problematic" (Langacker 2002, 264). In other words, we all come to understand approximately the same ideas of song structure (a buildup intro, or a breakdown, or a guitar solo), but through the lens of (perhaps wildly) different primary exemplars. This reflects a broader tension between the individual and the communal that has threaded throughout this book: it's striking how formulaic metal music can be (and how much group experiences and blurring of the self are valued), despite the genre's prevailing rhetoric of individualism and free-thinking rebellion. At the same time, the conventionality of these formulas is not a negative aspect of the genre, but a positive trait which enables the kind of ritualistic listening experiences I have described.

Double Recall in Ghost's "Cirice"

The music video for "Cirice," the single which earned the Swedish pop-oriented heavy metal band Ghost the 2016 Grammy for Best Metal Performance, uses conventional compound AABA song form to tell a parable of initiation into the metal community. This serves as a ritual of heaviness through double recall: a chance for fans (1) to recall and replay metal's conventions of song form, anticipating and experiencing the unfolding of the verse/chorus energy cycle and transformational bridge; and (2) to recall and replay the genre's (imagined and real) power and impact within the ritual space of this conventional song form, reliving their prior peak experiences of heaviness and renewing their own commitments to the genre.

The buildup intro ushers viewers into the world of heavy metal. As a single acoustic guitar plays the eerie first riff, the music video shows a girl named "Cirice" walking up to a Catholic primary school to attend a talent show, accompanied by an older female chaperone. As other guitars begin to play sustained tones (0:24; these timecodes refer to the music video, not the album version), Cirice walks through the lobby and into the auditorium. An older gentleman appears onstage to announce the beginning of the show and receives applause, and then at the same time as the full rhythm section joins the riff for the song's pugilistic arrival (0:47), the first talent act begins. It doesn't seem like a coincidence that at the moment the metal song proper begins, the first talent act is a young man with long blond hair dressed in black—who would not look out of place at a metal show.

A	0:00	Intro	Ax4	acoustic guitar, panning back and forth
			Ax4	add sustained guitar and synth notes
			Ax4	add bass, power chords, and back beat on open hi-hat
	1:11	Preverse	Bx3	full back beat with snare
	1:22	Verse 1	Bx2	Strophe 1 of vocals
			Cx2	" "
			Bx2	(link function - no vocals)
			Bx2	Strophe 2 of vocals
			Cx2	" "
	2:15	Chorus	Dx2	piano and vocals only
A	2:39	Preverse	Bx2	as before
	2:50	Verse 2	Bx2	Strophe 1 of vocals
			Cx2	" "
			Bx2	(link function - no vocals)
			Bx2	Strophe 2 of vocals
			Cx2	" " (vocals only this time)
	3:32	Chorus	Dx2	whole band
B	3:56	Bridge	D'	one guitar only
	4:03	Guitar Solo	D'x2	whole band
	4:27	Keyboard Solo	E	
	4:40	Melodic Break	C'	quiet organ chords, ride cymbals, vocals like the end of Verse
A'	4:53	Double Chorus	Dx4	ends slightly differently than before
	5:41	Interrupted Cadence	___	ends abruptly before the final note of the album version

Figure 9.5 Form chart of Ghost "Cirice."

The song's intro and verses act out a common trope of metal's rhetoric and its fans' personal listening histories: alienation from the mainstream. Cirice appears bored by the first few acts, while her chaperone and the rest of the audience are visibly delighted. But at the start of the pre-verse (1:11), a child-actor version of the band Ghost appears on stage. The lead singer jumps into the shot from the right (1:22) just in time to sing the first lines of the verse, "I feel your presence amongst us / you cannot hide in the darkness." Cirice appears interested in the show for the first time, while the rest of the audience shakes their heads in disapproval or disgust. At the end of verse 2 (3:22), Ghost sings "Can't you see that you're lost / Can't you see that you're lost without me / I can feel the thunder that's breaking in your heart," and reaches out to Cirice, mirroring many fans' reports that their initial encounters with metal music were strangely compelling, as if they felt the music reaching out to them and offering something that was missing from their lives (which I discuss at the end of Chapter 3). Deena Weinstein (1991) has described metal as a "proud pariah" genre; the assumption that metal is distasteful to mainstream society, and its obverse (that metal fans hate mainstream music) are central stances throughout the genre, even though this stance sometimes clashes with the reality that in many parts of the world today metal is generally considered acceptable or even respectable.[8]

In the song's bridge, the music video enacts a wild fantasy of heaviness's impact: the music begins to have a malevolent effect over the audience. As the guitar solo begins (4:04), the audience begins writhing and raving, invoking demonic possession tropes from classic horror films. One man unbuttons his shirt to reveal that the band's monogram (a G combined with an inverted cross) has appeared on his chest. At the end of the guitar solo (4:27), which was in the G natural minor scale, the band modulates to a D phrygian dominant scale—a scale which has, in Western music, traditionally been associated with the exotic and the supernatural. When the bridge ends, the audience returns more or less to normal, glancing at one another uneasily. This bridge section, then, explicitly realizes the sense of altered or alternate reality that is common in metal bridges, and is the site of transformative action for the song's protagonist, like many other metal songs about ritual (Hudson 2023b).

At the end of the song's bridge (4:45), a man gets up from the audience to interrupt the performance (thus, presumably, interrupting the music's sinister effects). But Cirice jumps out of her chair, seems to shout "NO!" (although

---

[8] One need look no further than the Finnish band Lordi, whose music video fantasy "Hard Rock Hallelujah" about heavy metal being the music of outcasts topped the charts in their own country and won the 2006 Eurovision song contest. The band members became national celebrities, and their hometowns bestowed great honors on them, like Rovaniemi renaming their city center "Lordi Square."

we cannot hear her), and seems to suddenly realize latent telekinetic powers. She gesticulates at the man from a distance, choking him until he falls to the ground, then turns on the audience, closing the exits and casting waves of invisible power that slowly force them into the corner. This scene obviously echoes the climax of *Carrie* (1976), a classic horror film based on a Stephen King novel. In the song form, we have returned from the supernatural bridge to the more mundane world of the A supersection, but Cirice has changed: she has encountered heavy metal, realized that she enjoys it and that others don't, and discovered that her enjoyment gives her a kind of transgressive status that gives her some kind of power over others (metaphorically, of course, except within the music video's fantasy).

Eventually, the man succeeds in pulling a plug out of the wall and ending the performance, nullifying Cirice's telekinetic abilities. It appears that it was only within the boundaries of the song form that Cirice or the band had these unnatural abilities to affect the audience. Two adults—perhaps parents of the lead singer—stand up and clap wildly; notably, they were both the only adults smiling and enjoying the band's show, and the only ones unaffected by the sinister powers within the bridge. But the music has impacted them in a different way: they were blown away by the performance, judging by how enthusiastically they (alone) cheer for the band. This dramatizes metal's myths of polarizing reception, with fans buying into the music's impact and experiencing thrills that others don't seem to be able to appreciate; while, on the other hand, metal's critics allege that this music has some kind of sinister, subversive, or satanic power. (But in reality metal has no such power, of course . . . or does it? Suspending disbelief on this point can lead to additional thrills, as discussed in Chapter 2.)

Various scenes of the music video form a fantasy of the music's embodied impact. The physical impacts experienced by Ghost's audience in the music video might evoke fans' own experiences of headbanging, moshing, and other forms of raving enthusiasm—inviting them to relive highlights of their previous experiences of heaviness, and perhaps inspiring them to increase their own physical commitment within whatever mode of listening they have chosen. Viewers might also imagine what it would feel like to have metal music provide them with surges of telekinetic power, feeling a corresponding surge in the energy cycles of "Cirice" when they see the main character exercising her newfound abilities. This imagery, viewers' vicarious simulation of Cirice's actions, and their own participatory investments of feeling and/or motion, all add to and amplify listeners' experiences of heaviness.

All in all, the story of this music video—Cirice discovers metal and is initiated as a fan—and the song's highly conventional riff-based compound AABA form also invite and structure performance of heaviness and metal identity by the song's listeners. Listeners can headbang or make other metal-appropriate poses and dance moves, investing their own energy in the performance to amplify their experiences of heaviness and create stronger cycles of energy. And as they watch Cirice discover metal, they might be remembering their own personal listening histories, reliving their own experiences of metal's heavy impacts, and renewing their own commitments to the genre.

10

Feeling Different Heavinesses in Different Song Forms and Subgenres

Metal music has been plagued throughout its history by critiques that it is repetitive and predictable.[1] While many sympathetic writers have defended metal by discussing specific artists' complexities and innovations, Allan F. Moore was bold enough in 1993 to double down on this critique and claim repetition as a positive trait. After comparing heavy metal to hard rock along dimensions like lyrics and blues influences, Moore came to musical form and proclaimed that "heavy metal is perhaps the most formulaic of rock styles (and hence, the rock style that permits the subtlest play of significances)" (Moore 1993, 132). In Chapter 9, I explored how the conventionality of metal's riff-based compound AABA song forms allows the act of listening to have a sense of recurrence, remembering, and re-enactment, creating musical spaces within song form for ritual-like experiences of heaviness.

But what about the "subtle play of significances" Moore describes? One way to identify a "play of significances" within any formulaic style is to compare individual differences in how those formulas are realized. This is expressed clearly in Leonard Meyer's conception of "style": "*Style is a replication of patterning, whether in human behavior or in the artifacts produced by human behavior, that results from a series of choices made within some set of constraints*" (1989, 3; italics in original). From this perspective, compound AABA structure is not merely the most common pattern in metal music that provides coherence to the genre as a whole—the repetition of this formula also structures the divergence of distinct subgenres and subtler differences of style and feeling.

These differences of style are not static, inert characteristics of song form, but are brought to life by listeners (including the performers onstage) through embodied motion. Music theorists writing on the perception of rhythm—including Justin London (2012), Mark J. Butler (2006), and Mariusz Kozak

---

[1] Several parts of this chapter were previously printed as the article "Compound AABA Form and Style Distinction in Heavy Metal" (Hudson 2021a).

Heaviness in Metal Music. Stephen S. Hudson, Oxford University Press. © Oxford University Press 2026.
DOI: 10.1093/9780197774991.003.0014

(2020)—have shown that listeners construe their own experiences of rhythm and time through the manner of their attention and embodied participation. As listeners move through these diverse variations of riff-based compound AABA, they help constitute those forms as "cycles of energy" (Pillsbury 2006) through which they experience different qualities of temporal flow and different feelings of heaviness.[2]

A genre is often understood as an "imagined community" (Hill 2016, citing Anderson 1983) that is thought to correspond directly to a particular group of people who share a common demographic identity, or a particular philosophy, attitude, or approach toward life. (It is worth noting that these groups are often not as inclusive or well-defined as they are imagined to be; see Hill (2016, 47–82) and Brackett (2016, 16–26). Metal's diverse collection of subgenres is also an imagined field of social distinctions. As fans identify styles in listening, and as they embody different qualities of motion and time, they are navigating this network of imagined types of people, and (for the duration of the song, at least) posing as a member of one of these imagined groups.

In this chapter, I begin by drawing on music theory to explain the relationship between broader song-form norms, individual compositions, and distinct styles, and I explain why these styles map on to imagined communities. I then spend the rest of the chapter exploring a series of short case studies, to map out parts of metal's topology of subgenres through the lens of common song form strategies.

Theorizing Songwriters' Choices and the Listening Experience

All composers (including metal songwriters) work in response to established patterns of musical form, choosing from a variety of conventional options (or choosing to diverge from all conventional options). Meyer describes these choices as "strategies" within the framework of "rules" that make up the style.

> Strategies are compositional choices made within the possibilities established by the rules of the style. For any specific style there is a finite number of rules, but there is an indefinite number of possible strategies for realizing or instantiating such rules. (Meyer 1989, 20)

---

[2] There are many other musical qualities which shape cycles of energy and the temporality they create—including timbre (Scotto 2016), lyrical imagery, pitch, and drum patterns (Kozak 2021; Hudson 2022a)—but the contributions of song form have not been investigated as much.

In mainstream metal styles, the majority of songs use compound AABA (Hudson 2021a), a convention that can be considered a "rule" for the style in Meyer's terms. But I prefer "defaults" (Hepokoski and Darcy 2006) to Meyer's term "rule," because "rule" implies a single correct option, and there are often a number of common options for any given aspect. For example, compound AABA is certainly the "default" form in metal music, but there are other conventional forms which metal songwriters have used (including twelve-bar blues form, and "simple verse" forms which only loop the same section), in addition to unique forms which "break the rules."

Many musical analyses attribute narrative or semantic meaning to a series of musical events which happen during a piece. For example, a change from a major to a minor key could signify a shift of emotions, like the arrival of a tragic character, or a narrative shift from goal-striving to failure. From this perspective, a songwriter's decisions about any musical aspects are evaluated as meaning-bearing communication. The main terms of the discipline of music theory (such as "topic for discourse," "sign," "symbol," etc.) often seem to be inherently biased toward this kind of one-way, composer-to-listener communication or representation. In previous research, I've explored a few ways in which metal songs can carry or "act out" narrative, although with a lot of caveats about subjectivity and the inscrutability of artists' intentions (Hudson 2023b).

But as far as I can tell, metal songwriters and fans hardly ever talk about their music in this way. Instead of hermeneutic interpretation of what happens across a song's form, discourse about metal tends to focus more on what kind of song it is as a whole: what style it has, how the individual parts are executed, and what experiences of heaviness it offers. This resonates with how James Hepokoski and Warren Darcy have described the choices faced by the composers of classical sonatas in the eighteenth century. Hepokoski and Darcy describe the interplay of style and strategy as "dialogic form," meaning that individual compositions are both composed and heard in dialogue with a norm. But this does not mean that composers make each decision as an explicit statement about that norm.

> Surely the most common decisions were made efficiently, expertly, and tacitly on the basis of norms that had been internalized (rendered automatic) through experience and familiarity with the style. Still, even before a sonata form was begun, a composer might, consciously or not, confront an array of initial questions acting as a filter for all that followed: . . . how long or 'grand' a movement? how complex? how 'original'? how 'intense' or 'challenging' to listeners? what is the expected audience? (Hepokoski and Darcy 2006, 9)

The questions at the end of this quotation suggest a different "play of significances" than semantic, iconic, and/or narrative representation. Instead, a composer's choices position a piece within an imagined geography of real or imagined aesthetic binaries, style trends, and types of listener. Similarly, the strategies a metal band uses for realizing compound AABA are more likely to represent their style and identity, their relative social and aesthetic positioning within the broader genre, and the kind of experiences they want to create for their listeners, rather than some sort of narrative or message.

Listeners experience music within a similar imagined geography of aesthetic binaries, trends, and listening communities. Hill (2016, 47–82) posits that the way we imagine ourselves fitting into the metal genre fundamentally shapes our experience of the music. Fans imagine themselves to be part of groups of other fans, regardless of whether those groups exist in any demographic sense, or would include them. These imagined affiliations are an essential component of our "listening stances" (Berger 2009)—the mindset, ideology, and listening practices with which we approach music, which shapes the kind of experiences we have when we listen.

Many bands develop consistent strategies of compound AABA form, and comparative analysis can show correlations between the bands' formal strategies and aspects of their artistic image or genre positioning. My purpose is not to establish absolute style distinctions or category boundaries, because metal listeners are not scripted by genre myths or style binaries, but make their own "preferred," "negotiated," or "oppositional" readings (see Hill 2016, 16). Instead, these are relative distinctions between different strategies for creating musical form, illustrating the kind of genre work that listeners do all the time as they group artists within overlapping and contestable boundaries (I explore this kind of genre work more in Chapter 7).

Vamp and Celebration in Hard Rock and Classic Heavy Metal

Some heavy metal bands use vamp in a way that resonates with the gospel music tradition of Black American churches, although the structure and connotations of such climactic repetition differ slightly in metal. (This comparison is not entirely opportunistic, as gospel music was an ancestral influence on heavy metal, by way of rock'n'roll.) Braxton Shelley (2019, 194; 2021) describes vamp in contemporary gospel music as "a complex of music, text, and escalatory procedures composed to facilitate religious experience," in which the audience participates in a climactic repetition and escalation at the end of a song. Shelley argues that by participating in the vamp through what he calls "the gospel stance," singers and audience both access a space of spiritual transcendence removed from the everyday world.

Hard rock and heavy metal bands often use vamps with a similar climactic structural function, and similar connotations of celebration, and comparable expectations of audience participation (singing, headbanging, etc.). But within the ideological fields of metal, there is no spiritual elevation; the closest available analogue is the Dionysian celebration "embodied in the unholy trinity of sex, drugs, and rock and roll" (Weinstein 1991, 35). (And in extreme metal styles, even this Dionysian celebration does not exist.) Vamps in metal music generally do not have the sense of escalation or accumulation that Shelley describes; they are song-ending overflows, redlined maximum excess, intoxication rather than transcendence.

It seems like no coincidence that Guns N' Roses promotes an image that they are the ultimate party band, and most of their songs on their debut album end with a vamp (only 3 of 12 songs do not: "Out Ta Get Me," "Sweet Child O' Mine," and "Rocket Queen"). Similarly, AC/DC, a band known for anthemic sing-along choruses which repeat the title of the song over and over ("I'm on a Highway to Hell," etc.; see Figure 10.1), rarely brings the verse back in the third rotation. Instead, most AC/DC songs feature extended versions of the chorus material (either a double chorus, or a vamp, or two statements of the chorus separated by some other riff)—often with the whole band and audience singing the song's title as a refrain. Almost all AC/DC songs are about the classic Dionysian trifecta of sex, drugs (well, usually just alcohol), and rock and roll. A number of NWOBHM bands use vamps in a similar way; for example, on Saxon's 1980 album *Wheels of Steel*, five out of nine tracks end with a vamp, with lyrics that celebrate a black-leather-wearing biker character

Intro	0:00 **Buildup Intro**	Ax1	one guitar
		Ax1	add drums; normal-time backbeat
A	0:17 **Verse 1**	Ax4	add vox to drums and one guitar
	0:53 **Chorus**	Bx4	add bass, backup vox, all guitars
A	1:12 **Verse 2**	Ax4	same as before
	1:47 **Chorus**	Bx4	same as before
B	2:04 **Bridge**	Cx2	no vocals
	2:12 **Guitar solo**	Bx4	like chorus, but without vox
A'	2:28 **Double Chorus / Vamp**	Bx4	lead guitar continues soloing / comping;
		Bx4	repeating title lyrics over and over

Figure 10.1 AC/DC "Highway to Hell."

archetype that was characteristic of heavy metal's earlier decades (Clifford-Napoleone 2016, Chapter 2).

It is also no coincidence that bands who avoid Dionysian themes do not use vamps nearly as often. Deena Weinstein describes a "battle for the soul of the genre" between "Dionysian" and "Chaos" themes, a spectrum which can be crudely (but mostly accurately) superimposed on Moore's hard rock–heavy metal continuum (Moore 1993; see my Chapter 3). Hard rock bands like AC/DC and Guns N' Roses use Dionysian topics (and vamp) much more frequently than thrash metal bands, like Exodus, Metallica, and Slayer. Occasionally these more "chaotic" bands use terminal repetition strategies, but the resulting affect is usually the opposite of celebration. For example, Slayer's "Raining Blood" features a driving acceleration at the end, a climactic crush which feels more like terror than exultation; and the protracted repetitions at the end of Metallica's "For Whom The Bell Tolls" (1984) have a slow and heavy rhythmic feel, combined with ominous lyrics and title which describe someone who is trapped by their mortal and material circumstances, rather than transcending them.

Metallica Versus Megadeth

Metallica have articulated one of the most historically influential and easily perceivable aesthetic and social postures on compound AABA formal strategy in the metal genre. Their lead singer and rhythm guitarist, James Hetfield, argued:

> Diamond Head, for example, had a pretty unique way of putting songs together. It wasn't the traditional verse-chorus-verse-chorus-middle eight and then out. They had middle breakdowns, new riffs that came in at weird places, and their songs kind of took you on journeys. Budgie and Mercyful Fate were also pretty inventive ... those bands taught us that there were more than three parts to a song—that you could have a song with different parts, each of which could almost be its own song. You can really hear their impact on ... *And Justice for All* [1988], which was where we really started to go over the top with that type of songwriting. (Kitts 1998, quoted in Aglugub 2007, 64)

Metallica rejects the simplistic strategy "verse chorus verse chorus middle 8 then out," but praises bands which find ways to innovate within this template. Metallica's songs follow their own prescription. Metallica used some form of compound AABA on virtually every song from their 1980s albums, but they gradually used more and more modules within each verse-chorus cycle, aligning themselves with bands they viewed as more sophisticated and innovative (Hudson 2021a, 5.2). This convention-based approach to formal innovation matches Metallica's everyman image and consistent focus on commercial success (Smialek 2016b), but also matches a "thinking man's metal" image discussed by Pillsbury (2006, Chapter 3).

In addition to associations with sophistication and innovation, Metallica's approach toward expanding compound AABA form also appealed to listeners through visceral embodied impact. In his study of Metallica, Glenn T. Pillsbury argues that "rhythmic intensities do not signify nearly as strongly by themselves, rather the *changes* in intensity provide the crucial context for their signification" (Pillsbury 2006, 20; original emphasis). Within Pillsbury's conception of these changes as "cycles of energy," a riff or groove is not just a sonic loop, but felt and experienced as a cycle of embodied motion (embodied through headbanging and other participatory dance/listening practices). When Metallica added new sections, they added what Hetfield describes as "middle breakdowns, new riffs that came in at weird places" so that their songs "took you on journeys." For example, on "Blackened" (1988), instead of a steady transition directly from verse to chorus, Metallica added a frenetic fast break in between (1:36–1:43) that switches to a double-time backbeat, a dramatic and unexpected left turn, after which the band returns to a normal-time backbeat for a relatively conventional chorus (1:43). Similar sudden changes in texture and tempo throughout "Blackened" (Figure 10.2) and Metallica's other songs from this period can be experienced as bodily disruptions: whatever headbanging or other motion a listener was performing as an expression of the previous section must be cast aside or adapted to fit the new section (listener's agency within such shifts is explored in Chapter 8). Thrash metal bands valorized these dramatic rhythmic shifts and their physical impacts, and they become even more important and more common in later death metal and metalcore.

Metallica's consistent adherence to the overarching compound AABA plan contrasts with the more anarchic formal plans of Megadeth, a band formed by guitarist Dave Mustaine after he was ejected from Metallica in 1983. Megadeth's second album *Peace Sells... But Who's Buying?* (1986) doesn't have a single song that can be read as a perfect compound AABA form, although six of eight tracks use many of metal's smaller-scale conventional form processes, like buildup intros or pre-verses. Two tracks on this album ("Wake Up Dead" and "Good Mourning/Black Friday") are entirely through-composed: each

Intro	0:00 **Extra Intro**	Ax4	fading in
	0:40 **Buildup Intro**	Bx4	one guitar x2, then add drums (four on the floor)
		Bx4	all together
A	1:12 **Pre-verse?**	Cx4	normal-time back beat
	1:20 **Verse 1**	Cx8	
	1:35 **Link**	Bx2	double-time back beat
	1:42 **Chorus**	Dx2	normal-time back beat
	1:55 **Link**	B'	double-time back beat with double-kick 16th notes
A	1:59 **Verse 2**	Cx8	normal-time back beat
	2:13 **Link**	Bx2	double-time back beat
	2:20 **Chorus**	Dx2	normal-time back beat
B	2:35 **Bridge / New Buildup**	Ex2	one guitar plus drum accents
		Ex2	all togethr, normal-time back beat
	3:06 **Bridge Verse**	E'x2	
	3:29 **Bridge**	Ex2	
	3:43 **Bridge Verse 2**	E'x2	
	4:06 **Melodic Break**	Fx8	
	4:31 **Guitar Solo**	Gx8	
		Hx2	faster normal-time back beat
		Ix2	
	5:32 **Re-intro**	Bx4	original tempo normal-time back beat
A	5:50 **Verse 3**	Cx8	
	6:05 **Link**	Bx2	double-time back beat
	6:12 **Double Chorus**	Dx2	normal-time back beat
		B'	

Figure 10.2 Metallica "Blackened."

song has three completely different verses, and none of the riffs recur elsewhere in the song.

Even for Megadeth songs that do fit into compound AABA form, this formula provides an ill-fitting account of the song's structure. For example, it is possible to hear Megadeth's "The Conjuring" (1986) as a kind of verse-chorus form with a bridge, but only by stretching this way of hearing to its limit. There is a passage of verse 1—verse 2—prechorus—chorus which could be interpreted as the first two A sections of a compound AABA form (Figure 10.3). But Megadeth skips the prechorus and chorus sections in the first rotation, making it sound more like development of new material and less like a repeated verse-chorus cycle; and furthermore, this whole passage of two verses and a chorus only lasts for one minute of sound, after which the song spends twice as much time on what I've labeled as the contrasting bridge, and then ends there. While the song presents potential verse and chorus material early on, this material takes up so little time (and is never clearly cycled or reprised) that the familiar functions of verse and chorus are not clearly established. Instead, the overwhelming majority of the song's duration is occupied by normally auxiliary sections, intro and bridge.

Disruption as Embodied Impact Within Death Metal

Around 1990, a group of increasingly extreme metal bands built on Megadeth's innovations to distinguish themselves even further from classic heavy metal, veering even further away from conventional compound AABA, verse-chorus song forms—and this group included many early pioneers of the style that became known as "death metal." Death metal bands acquired a reputation for jettisoning verse-chorus form to make complex songs that were hard to follow, resonating with the genre's widespread repudiation of anything mainstream or "pop." But I argue that this trend has been exaggerated: death metal bands' song forms often retain substantial continuities to conventional metal song structures.

One of the most prominent writers to make this claim that death metal avoids verse-chorus form is Michelle Phillipov, in her compelling book *Death Metal and Music Criticism* (2012). Phillipov argues that death metal leaves behind the verse-chorus format for something more chaotic and unpredictable.

> While thrash and heavy metal also departed from mainstream rock and pop insofar as the music is primarily riff-driven (rather than driven by melody), songwriting in these two genres is still largely structured within a verse-chorus format. As part of its pursuit of maximum extremity, death metal takes thrash and heavy metal's focus on the riff to a new level: rather than a structuring rhythmic device used within an otherwise conventionally recognizable song form, the riff is death metal's primary unit of songwriting. (Phillipov 2012, 82)

But there is lots of "death metal" that has verse-chorus structure still—specifically, a wide range of bands in more melodic death metal styles ranging from Amon Amarth to Arch Enemy (Smialek 2016a, 209), as well as plenty of songs by famous death metal bands ranging from Cannibal Corpse to Death (Dekovich 2022, 181–97). Phillipov's claim that death metal bands avoid verse-chorus structure, then, actually represents a relatively partisan stance toward what counts as death metal, excluding many of the genre's most popular bands like Entombed, Amon Amarth, Arch Enemy, and Death.

For example, Death's "death metal" credentials are unimpeachable—they are often credited with releasing the first true death metal album, and were recognized as an innovator in the genre for decades until the untimely death of their founder, frontman, and songwriter Chuck Schuldiner—but their song forms often include a version of verse-chorus structure. Michael Dekovich (2022, 189) observes that the band's most common song organization (in fact, the structure they use almost exclusively after their first album) is a compound

Intro	0:00 **Buildup Intro**	Ax1	two guitars only
		Ax1	add bass pulsing
	0:26 **Intro Verse**	Ax2	add hihat and vocals
	0:54 **More Buildup**	Bx4	add lead guitar fills, no vocals
		A'x4	
A	1:31 **Verse 1**	Cx2	
	1:44 **Link**	Dx2	no vocals
A	1:57 **Verse 2**	Cx2	
	2:09 **Pre-Chorus**	C'x2	
	2:21 **Chorus**	Ex4	
B	2:32 **Bridge / New Buildup**	Fx4	one guitar + ensemble punches
		Gx2	one guitar + ensemble punches
	3:06 **Breakdown**	Gx4	whole band together
	3:30 **Bridge Verse 1**	H H H' H"	
	3:41 **Link**	Gx1	
	3:46 **Bridge Verse 2**	H H H' H"	
	3:56 **Link**	Gx1	
	4:02 **Bridge Verse 3**	H H H' H"	
	4:12 **Link**	Gx1	
	4:18 **Bridge Verse 4**	H H H' H"	
	4:28 **Link**	Gx1	
	4:34 **Bridge Verse 5** (instr)	H H H' H"	
	4:46 **Cadential Ending**		singer shouts the song's title

Figure 10.3 Megadeth, "The Conjuring."

ABA form, a simple variation of compound AABA. One of Dekovich's examples is "Spiritual Healing" (1991), which I've charted in Figure 10.4, showing that this song features many recognizable riff-based metal formulas. Compared with compound AABA, an ABA structure makes it somewhat harder to identify a verse or chorus, since no sections recur until two-thirds of the way through the song; and in "Spiritual Healing" there are plenty of dramatic, disorienting shifts in tempo and texture to distract listeners from the song-form pattern. But the song still utilizes many of the basic conventions of riff-based metal song forms—like most of Death's compositions.[3]

Even Phillipov's primary examples of formal disruption, the early albums of the English death/grindcore band Carcass, which do indeed often abandon verse-chorus structure, are still less disruptive and more conventional than Phillipov makes it sound. Phillipov argues that Carcass uses disrupted,

---

[3] Only two Death songs are through-composed instead of using compound ABA song form (Dekovich 2022, 189).

Intro		0:00 **Build-up Intro**	Ax4	drums only play accents
A		0:19 **Preverse**	Bx2	full non-backbeat drum pattern; slow tempo
		0:30 **Verse 1A**	Bx4	
		0:56 **Preverse**	Cx2	slightly faster, normal-time back beat
		1:07 **Verse 1B**	Cx2	
		1:17 **Preverse / New Buildup**	Dx1	much faster, thrash metal style; no drums
		1:22 **Verse 1C**	Dx2	add double-time back beat with double-kick drum 16th
		1:30 **Interlude**	Dx4	
		1:52 **Interlude / Fast Break**	Ex4	even faster double-time back beat
		2:11 **Prechorus**	Fx2	
			F'x2	with vox this time
			Fx2	
			F'x2	with vox this time
		3:02 **Breakdown**	Gx2	slower; 332 drum pattern; similar to a preverse
		3:16 **Chorus**	Gx2	normal-time backbeat
B		3:30 **Bridge**	Hx2	Dekovich labels this a "decoy chorus"
		3:41 **Bridge Chorus?**	H'x2	features song title in lyrics
		3:49 **Guitar Solo I**	H"x2	Chuck Schuldiner's solo
		4:09 **Guitar Solo II**	H"'x2	James Murphy's solo
A		4:29 **Preverse**	Bx2	full non-backbeat drum pattern; slow tempo
		4:40 **Verse 2A**	Bx4	
		5:05 **Preverse**	Cx2	slightly faster, normal-time back beat
		5:17 **Verse 2B**	Cx2	
		5:27 **Preverse / New Buildup**	Dx1	much faster, thrash metal style; no drums
		5:32 **Verse 1C**	Dx2	add double-time back beat with double-kick drum 16ths
		5:38 **Interlude**	Dx4	
		6:02 **Interlude / Fast Break**	Ex4	even faster double-time back beat
		6:20 **Prechorus**	Fx2	
			F'x2	with vox this time
			Fx2	
			F'x2	with vox this time
		7:10 **Breakdown**	Gx2	slower; 332 drum pattern; similar to a preverse
		7:25 **Chorus**	Gx2	normal-time backbeat

Figure 10.4 Death "Spiritual Healing."

discontinuous song forms that match the jumbled narratives and dismembered bodies depicted by their lyrics.

> While some conventional identificatory mechanisms are featured in the music and lyrics, Carcass's unpredictable use of the voice, the evolutionary randomness of the song structures as well as the rhythmic irregularity of the songwriting imparts an overall "messiness" to the music that not only complements the grisly fantasies of the lyrics, but also disrupts the establishment of any consistent, stable locus of listening. Appreciating this kind of death metal requires finding pleasure in constant disruption and disequilibrium. This results in the construction of disrupted or fractured listening subjectivities that parallel musical and lyrical depictions of disrupted and fractured bodies. (Phillipov 2012, 113).

But many aspects of the song's form are in fact relatively conventional and continuous. Carcass retains the normative structuring principle that

Intro	0:00 **Riff Fragment**		
A	0:03 **Pre-Verse / Buildup**	Ax1	one guitar only
	0:06 **Verse 1**	Ax4	half-time back beat *
		A'x4	no vox
	0:29 **Pre-Chorus**	Bx4	half-time back beat *
		Cx2	blast beat *
		Dx4	double-time back beat *
	1:16 **Chorus**	Ex4	half-time feel *
	1:23 **Interlude**	Fx4	no vox; normal-time feel
	1:34 **Chorus**	E'x2	half-time feel *
B	1:45 **Sustained note**		
	1:47 **New Build / Breakdown**	Gx2	rhythm section only; normal-time feel
	2:00 **Guitar Solo**	G'x4	add lead guitar
	2:14 **Bridge Verse**	Hx4	blast beat
	2:24 **Bridge Chorus**	Ix4	normal-time feel
A	2:35 **Reintro / Pre-Verse**	Ax1	one guitar only
	2:37 **Verse 2**	Ax4	half-time back beat *
		A'x4	no vox
	2:59 **Pre-Chorus**	Bx4	half-time back beat *
		Cx2	blast beat *
		Dx4	double-time back beat *
	3:46 **Chorus**	Ex4	half-time feel *
	3:54 **Interlude**	Fx2	no vox; normal-time feel
	4:05 **Chorus**	E'x2	half-time feel *.

Figure 10.5 Carcass "Excoriating Abdominal Emanations"; asterisk indicates a stanza of lyrics.

metal songs are structured as a series of modules that each repeat a riff two, four, or eight times. They often have a recurring cycle of sections forming an A supersection, and even have somewhat identifiable verse/chorus section functions; for example, "Excoriating Abdominal Emanation" (1989; the lyrics are somehow even more gruesome than the title) features a sequence of twelve different modules from 0:03–1:34 that repeats from 2:35 to the end of the song (Figure 10.5), which can be heard as something analogous to a verse/chorus energy cycle, but which has six separate stanzas of vocals, requiring more distinctions than are available within the conventional set of section labels "verse," "pre-chorus," and "chorus" (although these labels can still be applied). Carcass uses lots of tempo changes and texture shifts; but metal has had lots of tempo changes and texture shifts ever since Metallica's early thrash metal, although it is true that Carcass's are relatively exaggerated. These exaggerated shifts create a heightened sense of unpredictable chaos and jarring bodily impacts, even though the song's underlying formal structure is not itself particularly fragmented or disruptive.

Admittedly, a small number of death metal artists depart more completely from the structural formulas of mainstream heavy metal. Calder Hannan's 2022 analysis of "Ohmnivalent" by the technical death metal band Anomalous describes "structural density" caused by several factors including extreme speed, lack of repetition, lack of clear section divisions, and constantly shifting time signatures or drum patterns. Behold … the Arctopus is another band that has experimented extensively with sections that have no simply repeating "riff" but instead feature a stream of developing, shape-shifting riff-like motives. These bands tend to be labeled as "technical" and "progressive" death metal, and remain extremely unpopular (no track by either band has received more than 100,000 all-time plays on Spotify) and are even controversial within the death metal community, although they are revered by a select few. The majority of death metal bands (and, not coincidentally, the more popular ones) build their songs in more conventional ways that are more accessible to listeners (even when they do not use compound AABA form), stringing together squarely built riff modules into energy cycles that feature identifiable, familiar section types, like verse, chorus, breakdown, and guitar solo.

Fetishizing the Climax: Breakdowns in Metalcore

The style of metalcore is stereotypically centered around "breakdowns," a section which marks the climactic peak of a song's energy and invites intense participatory movement. These sections are sonically marked by a downshift to a half-time backbeat, and a sudden clearing of the texture to focus on a unison riff with a limited pitch palette and an arresting, especially heavy rhythm. Breakdowns emerged out of 1990s death and groove metal (early examples include Anthrax's "Caught in a Mosh" and Pantera's "This Love"). Originally, breakdowns—or "mosh parts" as Pillsbury (2006) describes them—exclusively happened in the B supersection. This aligns with the tendency (described in Chapter 9) for the B supersection to be a transcendent, climactic zone in any metal song (the B supersection also often contains other extraordinary section types like guitar solos and melodic breaks).

As breakdowns became more and more common in the metalcore subgenre, its sonic cues and the expected audience response became more specific and stylized. Breakdowns occur in virtually every song by iconic metalcore bands such as Parkway Drive or Bring Me the Horizon, and have become virtually obligatory in the metalcore subgenre. Steven Gamble (2019, 346) argues that "Breakdowns appear to be on many metalcore listeners' minds a lot of the time, and much of the pleasure of their listening appears to relate specifically to these structures." Breakdowns in this sense are "imagined climaxes," moments of peak energy that listeners seek out, anticipate, and curate into online lists and compilation videos of "best breakdowns." Metalcore has thus developed a unique temporality, stylized and ritualistic, with constant anticipation of these clearly-defined climaxes.

But this stylization and conventionalization of breakdowns has made metalcore deeply controversial in the broader metal community (although metalcore's use of clean vocals also plays a role; see Chapter 6). For example, in a discussion about breakdowns, one Reddit user argues that breakdowns (and the metalcore fans who liked them) are clichéd and inauthentic: "This shit sounded like obnoxious bros throwing tantrums over predictable, lock step breakdowns and formulaic riffs, and trying to act 'hard'" (JamZward 2013). Breakdowns have been a flash point in debates over the status of several recent subgenres and styles, including djent and deathcore.

But as the B-section breakdown became conventionalized and "expected," metalcore bands (especially in the newer deathcore substyle) began to use them in other parts of the song form to create jarring interruptions analogous to the tempo and texture shifts in death metal. Jan-Peter Herbst and Mark Mynett (2023a, 196) show how "To The Hellfire" by the deathcore band Lorna Shore features four breakdowns in different places throughout the song (Figure 10.6). In the first A supersection, the breakdown occurs between

Section	Time	Label	Form	Description
Intro	0:00	**Buildup Intro**	A	Clean acoustic guitars only
	0:15		A'	Clean electric lead and distorted power chords
	0:30		A''	add four-on-the-floor hi-hat and vox
A	0:44	**Verse 1A**	A''x2	add quadruple-time drums (blast beat)
	1:14	**Verse 1B**	Bx4	normal-time back beat
	1:29	**Breakdown**	Cx4	slower, half-time back beat
	1:47	**Prechorus**	Dx2	original tempo blast beat
	2:02	**Chorus**	Ex8	normal-time back beat
	2:34	**Post-chorus**	Fx4	normal-time back beat, then blast beat
A	2:49	**Verse 2A**	A''x2	blast beat
	3:15	**Breakdown 2**	Gx2	slower, half-time back beat
	3:30	**Prechorus**	Dx2	original tempo blast beat
	3:45	**Chorus**	Ex8	normal-time back beat
	4:14	**Post-chorus**	Fx4	blast beat
B	4:29	**Bridge / New Buildup**	A	clean acoustic and electric guitars only
	4:43	**Guitar solo**	A'x2	all together; blast beats
	5:23	**Breakdown 3**	H	slower, normal-time back beat
	5:50	**Breakdown 4**	H'	even slower

Figure 10.6 Lorna Shore "To the Hellfire," adapted from Herbst and Mynett (2023a, Table 1).

Verse 1B and the prechorus; but in the second A supersection, there is no Verse 2B, and the breakdown occurs immediately after Verse 2A, disrupting the order of the first verse-chorus cycle. At the end of the song, Lorna Shore uses a third breakdown as a terminal climax (Osborn 2013), which is subsequently upstaged by a fourth breakdown that is even slower—breaking down the breakdown even further, interrupting the interruption, transcending what first-time listeners probably already thought was a transcendent climax. The song ends then ends here, instead of returning to the normal "non-breakdown" space.

With these multiple breakdowns distributed throughout the song, Lorna Shore is literally breaking down compound AABA form. An analogy could be made to how the Romantic composer Beethoven deconstructed Classical sonata form, but unlike Beethoven's disruptions of convention, the use of extra breakdowns in deathcore isn't a "musical critique" (Spitzer 2006) of previous genres or philosophies, just a search for additional heaviness. In the case of "To the Hellfire," the band's breakdowns disrupt the conventional form so completely and heavily that the song literally grinds to a halt. While "To The Hellfire" still has an underlying skeleton of compound AABA, verse-chorus structure, the breakdowns fragment the teleology (Nobile 2022) of a conventional verse-chorus energy cycle. This reorganizes the temporality of compound AABA, making it hard to orient to the verse-chorus teleology or even maintain a sense of a contrasting B supersection. Instead, the song's form seems to be entirely oriented around the buildup to breakdowns that emerge somewhat unpredictably from the sections around them, without following a fixed, predictable pattern.

The conventionalization of breakdowns as a climactic section in metalcore has allowed a second sense of breakdown to emerge: a set of sonic features for cueing extreme physical release which is invoked more flexibly in a much wider variety of subgenres and styles. For example, the Swedish progressive extreme metal band Meshuggah often has sections that evoke the intensity, motional feeling, and brutal affective style of breakdowns, but constantly throughout a song instead of only as a climax. "Rational Gaze" (2002) begins and ends with a section that clearly resonates with breakdown markers: a half-time backbeat underpinning a unison riff that only uses two different pitches, with an off-kilter syncopated rhythm (Figure 10.7). This section also comes back after the verse(s?). There is another breakdown with unique material in the bridge verse, and most of the song's other sections, also have similarly brutal riffs and half-time backbeats. Like many other Meshuggah songs, it feels like the entirety of "Rational Gaze" inhabits the breakdown ritual space,

A	0:00 Breakdown	Ax2	half-time back beat
	0:32 Preverse	Bx2	add lead guitar sustained notes
	0:45 Strophe 1	Bx2	with vox
	0:58 Strophe 2	Bx2	
	1:13 Counter-Strophe	B'x2	beat moves from hi hat to china cymbal
	1:28 Strophe 3	Bx2	as Strophe 1, 2
	1:42 Strophe 4	Bx2	
B	1:57 Breakdown	Ax2	as in the Intro, but add vox
	2:26 Bridge	Cx2	add lead guitar sustained notes
	2:55 Bridge Verse	Dx1	hi hat accents only
		Dx1	half-time back beat
	3:09 Guitar Solo	Ex6	
	3:38 Bridge Verse	E'x2	
		___	long sustained note...
A'	4:14 Breakdown / Vamp	Ax5	

Figure 10.7 Meshuggah "Rational Gaze."

turning the breakdown from a single climactic section into a kind of plateau of extraordinary intensity that suspends time, denying the energy cycle orientation of a conventional verse-chorus form.[4]

Slowing Down Time in Doom Metal

Doom metal, which has for decades lurked in the shadows as other subgenres of metal took the main stage, cultivates qualities of heaviness and experiences of temporality that are orthogonal to the developments that I've traced through thrash metal, death metal, and metalcore/deathcore. While those styles tend to favor quick tempos and jarring changes of tempo and texture, creating disorienting interruptions and chaotic collisions, the heaviness of doom metal is more ponderous. This slower form of heaviness can range from a relaxed, introspective tranquility to a suffocating feeling of terror and, well, doom.

A key determinant of this ponderousness is the drummer's tempo and time feel. Doom metal tends to use slower actual tempos (beats per minute) than many other metal styles, but it also uses more expansive forms of the backbeat. Where a half-time backbeat is a special effect in many metal styles,

---

[4] Olivia Lucas argues that Meshuggah songs "tend not to have identifiable verses, choruses, etc." and that "individual song segments do not typically indicate to listeners 'where' in the song they are" (Lucas 2018, 8).

Figure 10.8 Electric Wizard "Funeralopolis," 0:00–2:15.

reserved for breakdowns and other climactic moments, in doom metal the half-time backbeat may even be more common than normal time. Even at the same metronome tempo and the same rate of headbanging, a half-time backbeat *feels* qualitatively slower, giving doom metal a more relaxed pace by default (or more depressive, depending on the affectual connotations cued by other musical parameters).

But another important factor in doom metal's aesthetic of slow heaviness is its elephantine construction. The basic riffs in doom metal seem to often be longer than the riffs in other styles; the average doom metal riff seems to be about four measures long, and they often have multiple distinct rhythms and parts within the riff. For example, while many longer riffs in metal re-peat the same rhythmic figure multiple times, the first riff in Electric Wizard's "Funeralopolis" (2006) uses several unique rhythmic figures, ranging from long sustained notes to loping triplets—but each expressing an irrepressible, though laboriously slow, pulse (Figure 10.8). A single statement of the riff is some 11 seconds long—the length of an entire chorus in a fast metal song like Exodus' "Bonded By Blood" (1985).

Another aspect of many doom metal songs that contributes to this ele-phantine quality is their monumental renditions of compound AABA. In "Funeralopolis," Electric Wizard repeats each riff in blocks of four or more, creating gargantuan riff modules as the basic building blocks of its songs, each of which lasts 45 seconds or more (Figure 10.9). At 3:43, by which many metal songs would already be finished, Electric Wizard is just starting verse 2. Verse 2 then spills out even longer than verse 1, and then after kicking into a higher tempo for a long-winded, many-sectioned bridge, Electric Wizard ends the song with a virtually interminable vamp-chorus that lasts for two whole minutes, if you include the drawn-out final note. Another strategy, used in Candlemass's "Bewitched" (1987), is to have slightly less gargantuan indi-vidual sections, but repeat the verse/chorus cycle a third time before the B sec-tion. Both songs expand compound AABA from a standard 3-minute length

Intro	0:00 **Buildup Intro**	Ax8	bass, half-time back beat
	1:30	Ax4	whole band together, distorted power chords
A	2:15 **Verse 1**	Bx4	
	3:00 **Link**	Ax2	
	3:22 **Chorus**	Ax2	
A	3:43 **Verse 2**	Bx12	the last couple are instrumental
B	4:48 **Bridge / New Buildup**	Cx2	bass only, faster tempo, normal-time back beat
		Cx2	whole band together
	5:03 **Bridge Verse**	Cx4	
	5:18 **Bridge Chorus**	Dx4	
	5:35 **Bridge**	Cx4	
	5:49 **Bridge Verse**	Bx4	
	6:04 **Bridge Chorus**	Dx4	
	6:20 **Guitar Solo**	Dx4	
		Cx4	
	6:55 **Vamp**	Cx4	whole band together
		Cx4	even louder; add comping lead guitar
		Cx16	add refrain, until last 2
		____	long sustained note, slowly fades

Figure 10.9 Electric Wizard "Funeralopolis."

A	0:00 **Buildup Intro**	Ax2	Guitar and bass only
	0:32 **Verse A**	Bx2	one guitar only, high pass filter
		Bx2	whole band together with acoustic guitars, half-time back beat
	1:36 **Chorus A**	Cx4	
A'	2:34 **New Buildup**	Ax2	gutiar and bass plus synth
		Ax2	whole band together with louder electric lead
	3:45 **Verse B**	Ax2	
	4:17 **Vamp**	Cx2	no vox
	4:50 **Chorus B**	Cx2	
		Cx2	add distorted guitar
	5:54 **Vamp**	C'x2	no vox, add more power chords and distortion

Figure 10.10 Pallbearer "Where the Light Fades."

to well over 6 minutes, with only a few long riffs structured in Brobdingnagian scale. Death metal songs can run this long, too, but often reach it by inserting dozens of new, contrasting riffs and sections, while doom metal is more monolithic in its construction.

Occasionally, doom metal bands use epic forms that stray from the predictable orbits of verse/chorus structure to trace out more inscrutable leviathan forms. For example, Pallbearer's "Where the Light Fades" has a meandering song form that confounds any attempt to hear verse-chorus structure (Figure 10.10). There are two verse-like sections, but they use completely different riffs; the buildup intro inexplicably recurs after the first verse-chorus pair; there are two chorus-like sections but they use different lyrics and are different lengths, and the second one emerges in the middle of a longer vamp that gradually increases in volume. It's a surprisingly simple song, entirely set in the same half-time back-beat, with only three distinct riffs each reused a few times across a handful of sections—but its disorienting song form, combined with its glacial pace, gives it a dream-like, mystical quality of time, and makes it hard to remember it clearly.

The peak achievement of this formless strain of doom metal is Sleep's leg-endary "Dopesmoker" (2003),[5] a 63-minute-long song based on a seem-ingly endless, directionless sequence of mammoth-sized riffs. There is only one stylistically appropriate way to hear meter in this song's drum pattern: a compound-meter normal-time backbeat at a tempo of thirty-two beats per minute (compare to Garza 2021, Example 13). This is insanely, inhumanly slow—so slow that the musicians have to nod to a subdivision of the beat listeners feel, in order to perform the rhythms accurately. It takes 40 seconds to complete a single statement of each riff in "Dopesmoker," which, as I said in Chapter 9, is beyond the capacity for normal human short-term melodic memory.[6] While each riff repeats four or eight times to form a module, no riff ever recurs later in the song. These factors combine to create what feels like an endless, meandering journey.

The languorous and long-winded parameters that are taken to such extremes in "Dopesmoker" are characteristic of the difference in experience between doom metal and other subgenres. In doom metal, everything is gradual, avoiding jarring changes in texture or rhythm. At concerts, there is no moshing or other frantic dance styles; instead, headbangers move slowly but dig deeply. The heavy physical impacts of doom metal are even and predictable, but no less powerful for it—analogous to the unrelenting force of immovable weights, or glacial movements like the changing of seasons, rather than spontaneous com-bustion or murderous violence or jackhammering machines.

Conclusion

The French philosopher Jacques Derrida (1992) proposes that songs par-ticipate in genres, rather than belonging to them. The word "participate" is

---

[5] Sleep's original recording was rejected by their label, and several different cuts have been released under two different titles, "Dopesmoker" and "Jerusalem." I am referencing the 2022 remastered version by Third Man Records, which is widely available on streaming services, and which is based on the cut released in 2003 by Tee Pee Records.

[6] For example, this is slower than the lower threshold for accurate beat entrainment given by Justin London (2012).

doubly useful, because it also describes listeners who participate in these form and style conventions through active listening and dance. Listeners participate in compound AABA form by investing in physical feelings of energy and performances of motion which Pillsbury calls "cycles of energy," which they act out through moshing and headbanging (Hudson 2022a). They also participate in genre and style conventions by making distinctions between different bands (see Chapter 7). These style distinctions and physical energy are a kind of "meaning" that is signified by the music's form, among other parameters.

In connecting embodied experiences of cycles of energy to this type of "meaning," I am inspired by the musical topic theorist Wye J. Allanbrook. As I did above, Allanbrook (1983, 3) warns that musical meaning encompasses more than just programmatic representation or narrative. She argues that dance topics in Mozart's operas involve physical experience: every musical figure in the classical style does not merely symbolize dance but recruits the listener's body into a certain character of motion (Allanbrook 1983, 8). Like the dance topics of classical music, metal often evokes specific kinds of motion that we hear representing human actions and feelings; and in listening, it often feels like metal invites us to participate in this motion, even if only through vicarious imagination.

Different metal styles and their characteristic qualities of motion are often heard to represent different imagined communities. We imagine distinct style communities whether or not they are demographically real. Allanbrook anticipates Brackett's distancing between types of music and types of people, in a way that productively maps on to my arguments: "Even the most rustic court dances, the gigue and the pastorale, are only secondhand rustic ... The dancer does not dance them to express himself, but to catch the naively frank and free manners of country people" (1983, 63). This secondhand quality is analogous to what I called a "hypothetical quality" in Zohren's suggestion that "Hardcore Thrashers will be somewhat disappointed" by Metallica's 1984 album (see Chapter 7). To participate in the motion of a particular style of metal, we don't need to personify that style ourselves; in joining the movement of a song, we can imagine ourselves posing as "Hardcore Thrashers," whether or not that group actually exists or would include us. This exposes the fallacy of conceiving of a genre as a "subculture," which implies a one-to-one homology between style and listener community. In today's internet streaming music market, almost everyone listens to many styles, posing as a member of those style's imagined communities, "trying on" different kinds of motion and different experiences of heaviness.

My point in this conclusion is perhaps just a minor expansion of Allanbrook's, or even just a clarification of an idea she left implicit: our sympathetic "resonance" with familiar forms and their characteristic affects is a form of participation. Arnie Cox (2011) points toward this clearly, proposing in his "mimetic hypothesis" that the perception of music often involves covertly simulating the actions one imagines would be used to create that sound, creating a kind of vicarious or sympathetic feeling of motion. In metal this participation is often literal and explicit, not just sympathetic feeling but performed motion and physical pose, such as headbanging, moshing, and fist-pumping. In experiencing metal styles as different ways of moving, we join the style's characteristic motional trajectories; or, if we physically do not join, like the "silent men" which Kahn-Harris describes at extreme metal concerts (2007, 44) or the skeptic who aloofly derides metalcore fans and their breakdowns, we are still placing ourselves within the same tableau, hearing that motion while enacting stillness beside it.

We participate in our perception of musical structure and meaning, a process which Harris Berger (2009) theorizes as "stance" (which I introduced in Chapter 1). Styles are stances, or at least stance-like, "sedimented quasi-stances" (Berger 2009, 30)—not just symbols (as in Agawu 1991), but also relative social distinctions that we participate in as we use these distinctions to imagine style categories and communities. Vamp is not just a static sign representing celebration—fans perform celebration as we shout along to AC/DC's proliferative refrain, "We're on a Hiiiigh-way to Hell!" Black metal's grim, inhuman, and sublime stasis is something we join, bracing our legs, baring our teeth, and raising one hand in a dramatic claw gesture. The majestic cathedrals of progressive metal song structure are not only signifiers of complexity, but an arcade hallway we stumble down, starry-eyed as we pass underneath each arch and vault. It's possible that all musical signs and semiotics are equally performative, but this performance is especially visible and tactile in metal. Metal music moves through time in many ways—and as we experience that motion in listening, headbanging, and moshing, we imagine how both the music and ourselves fit within a diverse field of styles and values and communities, willing these categories and distinctions into (new or continued) existence.

Epilogue

The Promise of Post-Extreme Metal

Metal music is in the middle of a quiet revolution, but you might not know it. All kinds of (usually unwritten) rules and expectations about what metal is supposed to be, and who and what can count as metal, are starting to gently fade into the background. One of these, gender, was explored in Chapter 6: women vocalists were once the exception in metal, but it is no longer exceptional (or even particularly remarkable) for a woman to sing metal—even if she uses clean-toned, high-pitched, "girly" vocal style (that particular glass ceiling has been effectively demolished by artists like BABYMETAL and Poppy). Simply put, metal may still be dominated by men, but it is not not feminine anymore. Two more unwritten rules, about Blackness and progressionism, deserve further discussion.

Metal is Not Not Black

There have always been Black artists and fans within the genre, but this has never undermined the perceived "Whiteness" of metal. And there is no indication that racism is disappearing from the genre—to the contrary, many racist artists continue to be tolerated and celebrated, despite numerous voices of concern and criticism (Creek 2024). However, the underlying assumption that metal is White is no longer valid, if it ever was. In 2016, Keith Kahn-Harris argued,

> [. . .] heavy metal is highly globally diverse, but with a small but growing number of exceptions, whatever metal is, it is generally "not Black" and reproduces an implicit Black–White duality in order to shun the Black half. The most controversial metal subgenres and artists are often those that draw on what is perceived to be Black culture. (Kahn-Harris 2016, 27)

While this represents a lot of what has historically been said about metal, I'm not sure it could be said today—and I'm also not sure what has historically been said was really the full truth, in the first place.

Heaviness in Metal Music. Stephen S. Hudson, Oxford University Press. © Oxford University Press 2026.
DOI: 10.1093/9780197774991.003.0015

One counterexample to the idea that metal is "not Black" is, of course, the blues. Blues has usually been understood as a part of Black culture (or a translation or legacy of Black culture), and while the extreme metal paradigm perpetuated a narrative of "leaving the blues behind," various musical and ideological legacies from the highly racialized blues scene from which metal emerged have persisted in even the most extreme metal. No matter how extreme metal gets, it can never completely leave the blues behind. The genre's foundational ideologies and aesthetics will forever be connected with this racialized history. But one doesn't have to dig to such archaeological depths to find the blues in metal. The more Sabbathian strains of doom and stoner metal have kept these blues legacies alive within the metal underground all the way to the present. Blues guitar stylings were also revalorized as a badge of honor in the 1990s "groove metal" of bands like Pantera and Black Label Society. Blues and rock have always been part of metal's history, and with metal's penchant for heritage and retrospection, I expect that blues and blues-rock features will continue to be perennially reinfused into the genre.

Additionally, a range of commercially and critically successful bands have been writing music which is explicitly about Black people and their experiences, and combining specifically Black styles including blues, gospel, reggae, rap, and R&B with a range of metal styles including thrash metal, black metal, and metalcore. Body Count and Skindred have each been climbing the charts by fusing metal with either rap or reggae, respectively, since the 1990s. More recently, Zeal & Ardor have combined old-fashioned gospel and work songs with black metal to create songs about the horrors of slavery and segregation—brutal topics that unbelievably have never previously been tackled by metal bands, even though many other horrific episodes of human history have been more deeply mined—and they have been well received at the large metal festivals across the world.[1]

Metal Is No Longer Progressionist

Metal appears to no longer be dominated by the "teleological treadmill of increasing brutality" (Wallmark 2018), or by strict requirements to oppose more mainstream pop and rock music, as I discussed in Chapters 3 and 4. This is evident in an opinion essay that was making the rounds as I was writing

---

[1] Zeal & Ardor's take on these topics is somewhat problematic, though, and they have been criticized for their superficial and inaccurate representations of American Black culture and history (Dawes 2023).

this book, "Metal's Stadium Class Is Less Metal Than Ever" by Eli Enis, a journalist writing for *Stereogum* (Enis 2024). Enis laments that none of the newer bands poised to become perennial headliners is extreme or heavy in the manner of the genre's canonical bands, echoing a long tradition of premature proclamations about the genre's impending doom, dating back at least to the *Creem* October 1979 cover story "Is Heavy Metal Dead?" But I don't think this is a failure of the genre to produce true metal that can succeed on the largest stages: instead, it represents a fundamental shift in the genre's values. Some of the most exciting bands of the last two decades have not been breaking new ground in terms of extremity, but recombining older established sounds into new expression, with diverse approaches and results, such as Ghost, Baroness, Mastodon, Opeth, and Gojira.

Additionally, styles which were previously opposed to metal are being brought into the genre increasingly often, with less and less controversy. Rap metal is having a comeback, to the surprise of almost everyone—but this time, we have all been spared the reactionary indignation sparked by its 1990s debut. Some of this rap metal is revisiting and recombining nu-metal styles, but some artists, like the Nova Twins and Sleep Token, are breaking new ground. There have been lots of EDM-metal hybrids, especially in the goth/industrial dance club scene and the "Neue Deutsche Härte" or "Tanzmetall" subgenre that developed in Germany at the end of the millennium (e.g., Eisbrecher, KMFDM, and Rammstein). The darker end of synthwave has a lot of metal in it, alongside gated reverb and post-disco synth leads (e.g., Carpenter Brut, Dance With The Dead, and Perturbator), and four-on-the-floor electro-house-style beats can be found in the work of a number of power metal bands (e.g., Battle Beast, and Nightwish's breakthrough hit "Wish I Had an Angel").

One of the most surprising and notable genre hybrids is that in recent years, there has been more and more jazz in metal—actual jazz played by genuine acoustic jazz instruments like trumpet and saxophone, not the alleged "jazz influence" of progressive death metal bands like Opeth, Atheist, or Cynic. The Swedish heavy metal band Ghost featured a prominent sax solo in their 2018 summer hit "Dance Macabre." The math metal band Polyphia featured Brazilian bossa nova guitar stylings on "Playing God," and a jazz trumpet solo as the outro for their intergenerational collaboration with Steve Vai, "Ego Death." These might both seem to some readers like tokenistic genre inclusions, by bands whose gentle timbres and melodicism have caused many to question whether they are even "metal" at all. But one that is harder to deny is Periphery's "Wildfire." The chorus to this song (2:12–2:50) is constructed as a long multi-measure progression of power chords, instead of featuring a conventional 2- or 4-measure metal riff; and after a particularly brutal breakdown, between two metal versions of this chorus, the band plays a gentle acoustic jazz arrangement of the same theme (4:27–5:37), revealing an unexpected but convincing overlap between smooth jazz and progressive metalcore.

Since these shifts are happening among the most prominent newer metal bands, and not at the fringes of the genre, I think it's fair to characterize much of the metal scene from the last twenty years as "post-extreme metal." By "post-extreme metal" I do not mean that extreme metal no longer exists, or is no longer important—just like "post-metal" now coexists in the same world as "metal," and has not usurped the status of its forebear. Plenty of bands are still pushing the envelope of extremity, and I find it thrilling when they succeed. But metal no longer *has* to be extreme to innovate and be taken seriously within the genre.

Conclusion

In addition to the tendencies discussed above, metal has often been described as apolitical, or even divorced from reality, but even this may be beginning to change. Keith Kahn-Harris suggested:

> For all the seeming essentialism inherent in the equation of heavy metal and white, masculine heteronormativity, this equation is in the final analysis epiphenomenal to a greater essentialism. That essentialism is a tautological essentialism that points toward heavy metal itself. [. . .] To be metal is to be "true" to oneself, to "live for metal," to be deeply committed to the scene: all these aspects though assume a kind of productive vacuity at the heart of what metal is. (Kahn-Harris 2016, 31)

Part of what created this "vacuity at the heart of what metal is" surely must be the erasure of Blackness within discourse and ideology at the moment that "White blues" became "heavy metal," which disconnected many references to Black Americans and their music and culture, and left these references as empty signifiers. But as the mandate of "leaving the blues behind" fades into the background, perhaps this tight tautological essentialism can uncurl, opening the genre back up to more continuous historical narratives that emphasize the influence and persistent legacies of Black American music and aesthetics—and of highly racialized White conceptions of musical Blackness.

But metal already seems to be embracing the political in other directions, too. Robert Walser said,

> Metal is a fantastic genre, but it is one in which real social needs and desires are addressed and temporarily resolved in unreal ways. These unreal solutions are

attractive and effective precisely because they seem to step outside the normal social categories that construct the conflicts in the first place. (Walser 2014 [1993], 134)

To the contrary, a growing number of metal songs seem to directly tackle real social needs and desires, in the terms of normal social categories. Quite a few songs relate narratives about struggles with racism: Skindred's "Bruises," Body Count's "Black Hoodie," and most songs by Zeal & Ardor. There are also a number of songs that critique misogyny, including "Someone's Daughter" by Jinjer (discussed at the end of Chapter 7) as well as the blistering "Misogyny" by Benedictum. The Japanese anime *Aggretsuko* (about a shy female red panda who sings death metal songs on her lunch breaks to vent about her horrible boss, who is literally a pig) may be satirical, but it engages with workplace sexism about as directly as a cartoon about anthropomorphic animals can. These are not unreal fantasies which "step outside normal social categories," but real-world engagements.

The post-extreme metal paradigm is increasingly less and less oriented around ideologies of oppositional authenticity, ever-increasing extremity, aggression as a form of masculinity, and the implicit racial exclusion of "leaving the blues behind." If heaviness as an experience of impact is taken to be the central feature of the metal genre—rather than either the "identity triad" of White, heteronormative masculinity (Kahn-Harris 2016, 27), or the pursuit of extremity for its own sake—this opens up a less exclusionary or elite perspective on what, and who, can count as "metal," perhaps with less skepticism and surveillance of musicians and fans with identities outside those categories. Instead, a future of post-extreme metal promises an expanding array of voices, a wealth of new possibilities for cross-stylistic collaborations and influences, and a more self-reflective and retrospective genre that is not afraid to engage with its own past.

Works Cited

Adelt, Ulrich. 2010. *Blues Music in the Sixties: A Story in Black and White*. New Brunswick: Rutgers University Press.

Agawu, Kofi. 1991. *Playing With Signs: A Semiotic Interpretation of Classic Music*. Princeton, NJ: Princeton University Press.

Agawu, Kofi. 2003. *Representing African Music: Postcolonial Notes, Queries, Positions*. New York, NY: Routledge.

Aglugub, Raymond David. 2007. "Shape Shift: Riff Variation and Development in the Music of Metallica." Master's Thesis, Boston University.

Allanbrook, Wye Jamison. 1983. *Rhythmic Gesture in Mozart: Le Nozze Di Figaro & Don Giovanni*. Chicago, IL: University of Chicago Press.

Allett, Nicola. 2011. "The Extreme Metal 'Connoisseur.'" *Popular Music History* 6 (1/2): 164–79.

Amott, Michael. 2022. "Arch Enemy's Michael Amott Is 'Not a Fan' of Bands 'That Do the Screaming and the Clean Vocal.'" *Blabbermouth.Net* (blog), September 13, 2022. https://blabbermouth.net/news/arch-enemys-michael-amott-is-not-a-fan-of-bands-that-do-the-screaming-and-the-clean-vocal.

Anderson, Benedict. 1983. *Imagined Communities: Reflections on the Origin and Spread of Nationalism*. New York, NY: Verso Books.

Appen, Ralf von and Markus Frei-Hauenschild. 2015. "AABA, Refrain, Chorus, Bridge, Prechorus—Song Forms and Their Historical Development." *Samples* 13. https://gfpm-samples.de/index.php/samples/article/view/171

Attas, Robin. 2015. "Form as Process: The Buildup Introduction in Popular Music." *Music Theory Spectrum* 37 (2): 275–96.

Austin, J. L. 1975 [1962]. *How to Do Things with Words*. Second edition. Oxford: Oxford University Press.

Bangs, Lester. 1987. "Psychotic Reactions and Carburetor Dung: A Tale of These Times." In *Psychotic Reactions and Carburetor Dung*, edited by Greil Marcus, 5–19. New York, NY: Alfred A. Knopf.

Baur, Steven. 2021. "Towards a Cultural History of the Backbeat." In *The Cambridge Companion to the Drum Kit*, edited by Daniel Akira Stadnicki, Joseph Michael Pignato, and Matt Brennan. Cambridge: Cambridge University Press.

Berger, Harris M. 1999. *Metal, Rock and Jazz: Perception and the Phenomenology of Musical Experience*. Middletown, CT: Wesleyan University Press.

Berger, Harris M. 2009. *Stance: Ideas about Emotion, Style, and Meaning for the Study of Expressive Culture*. Middletown, CT: Wesleyan University Press.

Berger, Harris M. and Cornelia Fales. 2005. "'Heaviness' in the Perception of Heavy Metal Guitar Timbres: The Match of Perceptual and Acoustic Features over Time." In *Wired for Sound: Engineering and Technologies in Sonic Cultures*, edited by P. D. Greene and T. Porcello, 181–97. Middletown, CT: Wesleyan University Press.

Biamonte, Nicole. 2014. "Formal Functions of Metrical Dissonance in Rock Music." *Music Theory Online* 20 (2). https://www.mtosmt.org/issues/mto.14.20.2/mto.14.20.2.biamonte.html.

Blabbermouth. 2024. "Jinjer Releases New Song 'Someone's Daughter.'" *Blabbermouth.Net*, August 1, 2024. https://blabbermouth.net/news/jinjer-releases-new-song-someones-daughter.

Bogue, Ronald. 2004. "Becoming Metal, Becoming Death ..." In *Deleuze's Wake: Tributes and Tributaries*, edited by Ronald Bogue, 83–108. Albany, NY: State University of New York Press.

Boughali, Khalil. 2022. *Thoughts on Black Metal*. English translation (Original French published in 2021). Las Vegas, NV: [Self-published].

Brackett, David. 2005. "Questions of Genre in Black Popular Music." *Black Music Research Journal* 25 (1/2): 73–92.

Brackett, David. 2016. *Categorizing Sound: Genre and Twentieth-Century Popular Music*. Berkeley, CA: University of California Press.

Brown, Andy R. 2015. "Explaining the Naming of Heavy Metal from Rock's 'Back Pages': A Dialogue with Deena Weinstein." *Metal Music Studies* 1 (2): 233–61.

Bueller, Ferrous. 2017. "Yer Metal Is Olde: Death—Scream Bloody Gore." *Angry Metal Guy* (blog), July 15, 2017. https://www.angrymetalguy.com/yer-metal-is-olde-death-scream-blo ody-gore/.

Burns, Lori. 2023. "Female Subjectivities in the Words, Music, and Images of Progressive Metal: The Case of Tatiana Shmayluk (Jinjer)." *Music Theory Online* 29 (4). https://mtosmt. org/issues/mto.23.29.4/mto.23.29.4.burns.html.

Burns, Lori. 2025. "Beyond 'Beauty and the Beast': Division of Work, Sonic Expression, and Musical Subjectivity in Metal Duets with Clean and Harsh Vocals." In *The Routledge Handbook of Metal Music Composition: Evolution of Structure, Expression, and Production*, edited by Lori Burns and Ciro Scotto. London: Routledge.

Butler, Mark J. 2006. *Unlocking the Groove: Rhythm, Meter, and Musical Design in Electronic Dance Music*. Bloomington, IN: Indiana University Press.

Butler, Mark J. 2014. *Playing with Something That Runs: Technology, Improvisation, and Composition in DJ and Laptop Performance*. Oxford: Oxford University Press.

Chaker, Sarah and Florian Heesch. 2016. "Female Metal Singers: A Panel Discussion with Sabina Classen, Britta Görtz, Angela Gossow, and Doro Pesch." In *Heavy Metal, Gender and Sexuality: Interdisciplinary Approaches*, edited by Florian Heesch and Niall Scott, 133–46. London: Routledge.

Cheng, Tzu-Han and Chen-Gia Tsai. 2016. "Female Listeners' Autonomic Responses to Dramatic Shifts Between Loud and Soft Music/Sound Passages: A Study of Heavy Metal Songs." *Frontiers in Psychology* 7 (182). https://www.frontiersin.org/articles/10.3389/ fpsyg.2016.00182/full.

Chomsky, Noam. 1965. *Aspects of the Theory of Syntax*. Cambridge, MA: The MIT Press.

Christe, Ian. 2003. *Sound of the Beast: The Complete Headbanging History of Heavy Metal*. New York, NY: HarperCollins.

Clarke, Eric F. 2005. *Ways of Listening: An Ecological Approach to the Perception of Musical Meaning*. Oxford: Oxford University Press.

Clercq, Trevor de. 2012. "Sections and Successions in Successful Songs: A Prototype Approach to Form in Rock Music." PhD Dissertation, Rochester, NY: University of Rochester.

Clercq, Trevor de. 2015. *The Nashville Number System Fake Book*. Milwaukee, WI: Hal Leonard.

Clercq, Trevor de. 2016. "Measuring a Measure: Absolute Time as a Factor for Determining Bar Lengths and Meter in Pop/Rock Music." *Music Theory Online* 22 (3). http://mtosmt.org/iss ues/mto.16.22.3/mto.16.22.3.declercq.html.

Clifford-Napoleone, Amber R. 2016. "Metal, Masculinity, and the Queer Subject." In *Heavy Metal, Gender and Sexuality: Interdisciplinary Approaches*, edited by Florian Heesch and Niall Scott, 39–51. New York, NY: Routledge.

Cone, James H. 1972. *The Spirituals and the Blues: An Interpretation*. New York, NY: The Seabury Press.

Cooper, Grosvenor and Leonard Meyer. 1960. *The Rhythmic Structure of Music*. Chicago, IL: University of Chicago Press.

Cope, Andrew L. 2010. *Black Sabbath and the Rise of Heavy Metal Music*. Farnham, Surrey: Ashgate.

Covach, John. 2005. "Form in Rock Music: A Primer." In *Engaging Music: Essays in Music Analysis*, edited by Deborah Stein, 65–76. Oxford: Oxford University Press.

Cox, Arnie. 2011. "Embodying Music: Principles of the Mimetic Hypothesis." *Music Theory Online* 17 (2). http://www.mtosmt.org/issues/mto.11.17.2/mto.11.17.2.cox.html.

Creek, Meghan. 2024. "Persistence and Resistance: Examining the White Racial Frame in Metal Music." PhD Dissertation, College Park, MD: University of Maryland.

Cronon, William. 1991. *Nature's Metropolis: Chicago and the Great West*. New York, NY: W. W. Norton & Company.

Cross, Charles R. 2005. *Room Full of Mirrors: A Biography of Jimi Hendrix*. New York, NY: Hyperion.

Cusick, Suzanne G. 2006. "Music as Torture / Music as Weapon." *TRANS: Revista Transcultural de Música*, no. 10.

Daughtry, J. Martin. 2014. "Thanatosonics: Ontologies of Acoustic Violence." *Social Text* 32 (2): 25–47.

Davis, Angela Y. 1998. *Blues Legacies and Black Feminism: Gertrude "Ma" Rainey, Bessie Smith, and Billie Holiday*. New York, NY: Random House.

Davis, Donna. 1983. "Metallica Interview with Donna Davis." *MTV*. https://www.youtube.com/watch?v=ayO0p1D-p4k.

Dawes, Laina. 2012. *What Are You Doing Here?: A Black Woman's Life and Liberation in Heavy Metal*. Brooklyn, NY: Bazillion Points Books.

Dawes, Laina. 2022. "'Freedom Ain't Free:' Race and Representation(s) in Extreme Heavy Metal." PhD Dissertation, New York, NY: Columbia University.

Dawes, Laina. 2023. "'Righteous Violence': Zeal & Ardor's Application of African-American Folk Music in Black Metal." In *Black Metal Rainbows*, edited by Daniel Lukes and Stanimir Panayotov, 119–34. Oakland, CA: PM Press.

Dekovich, Michael. 2022. "Formal Dialectic in Heavy Metal Music." PhD Dissertation, Eugene, OR: University of Oregon.

Derrida, Jacques. 1992. "The Law of Genre." In *Acts of Literature*, edited by Derek Attridge, translated by Avita Ronell, 221–52. New York, NY: Routledge.

Desmond, Jane C. 1997. "Embodying Difference: Issues in Dance and Cultural Studies." In *Meaning in Motion: New Cultural Studies of Dance*, edited by Jane C. Desmond, 29–54. Durham, NC: Duke University Press.

Dixon, Brenda. 1990. "Black Dance and Dancers and the White Public: A Prolegomenon to Problems of Definition." *Black American Literature Forum* 24 (1): 117–23.

Dodds, Sherril. 2011. *Dancing on the Canon: Embodiments of Value in Popular Dance*. Berlin: Springer.

Doe, Bernard. 1984. "Metallica: Lightning Raiders." *Metal Forces* (8). http://www.metalforcesmagazine.com/site/feature-metallica-mf8/.

Drott, Eric. 2013. "The End(s) of Genre." *Journal of Music Theory* 57 (1): 1–45.

Easley, David B. 2011. "'It's Not My Imagination, I've Got a Gun on My Back!': Style and Sound in Early American Hardcore Punk, 1978–1983." PhD Dissertation, Tallahassee, FL: Florida State University.

Eidsheim, Nina Sun. 2019. *The Race of Sound: Listening, Timbre & Vocality in African American Music*. Durham, NC: Duke University Press.

Ekeroth, Daniel. 2008. *Swedish Death Metal*. Brooklyn, NY: Bazillion Points Books.

Enis, Eli. 2024. "Metal's Stadium Class Is Less Metal Than Ever." *Stereogum* (blog), April 12, 2024. https://www.stereogum.com/2258777/metal-sleep-token-bad-omens-spiritbox/columns/sounding-board/.

Fales, Cornelia. 2002. "The Paradox of Timbre." *Ethnomusicology* 46 (1): 56–95.

Farber, Jim. 2013. "Black Sabbath's No. 1 Hit with Their First Album in 35 Years Shocks Ozzy Osbourne." *New York Daily News*, August 2, 2013. https://www.nydailynews.com/entert ainment/music-arts/ozzy-osbourne-black-sabbath-hit-no-1-article-1.1414859.

Fast, Susan. 2001. *In the Houses of the Holy: Led Zeppelin and the Power of Rock Music*. Oxford: Oxford University Press.

Fast, Susan. 2010. "Bold Soul Trickster: The 60s Tina Turner." In *She's So Fine: Reflections on Whiteness, Femininity, Adolescence and Class in 1960s Music*, edited by Laurie Stras, 203–34. Farnham, Surrey: Ashgate.

Fellezs, Kevin. 2011. "Black Metal Soul Music: Stone Vengeance and the Aesthetics of Race in Heavy Metal." *Popular Music History* 6 (1/2): 180–97.

Fischer, Jillian. 2021. "If It Growls Like a Nazi … : The Role of Noise and Affect in National Socialist Black Metal." American Musicological Society, Chicago, November 12, 2021.

Fisher, Rudolph. 1999. "The Caucasian Storms Harlem." In *Keeping Time: Readings in Jazz History*, edited by Robert Walser, 60–65. Oxford: Oxford University Press.

Gamble, Steven. 2019. "Breaking Down the Breakdown in Twenty-First-Century Metal." *Metal Music Studies* 5 (3): 337–54.

Gamble, Steven. 2022. *How Music Empowers: Listening to Modern Rap and Metal*. London: Routledge.

Garza, Jose M. 2021. "Transcending Time (Feels): Riff Types, Timekeeping Cymbals, and Time Feels in Contemporary Metal Music." *Music Theory Online* 27 (1). https://mtosmt.org/iss ues/mto.21.27.1/mto.21.27.1.garza.html.

Gennep, Arnold van. 2019 [1908]. *The Rites of Passage*. Translated by Monika B. Vizedom and Gabrielle L. Caffee. Second edition. Chicago, IL: The University of Chicago Press.

Gentner, Deidre. 1983. "Structure-Mapping: A Theoretical Framework for Analogy." *Cognitive Science* 7: 155–70.

Gibson, James J. 1966. *The Senses Considered as Perceptual Systems*. New York, NY: Houghton Mifflin.

Gibson, James J. 1978. "The Ecological Approach to the Visual Perception of Pictures." *Leonardo* 11 (3): 227–35.

Gjerdingen, Robert O. 2007. *Music in the Galant Style*. Oxford: Oxford University Press.

Gjerdingen, Robert O. and Janet Bourne. 2015. "Schema Theory as a Construction Grammar." *Music Theory Online* 21 (2). https://mtosmt.org/issues/mto.15.21.2/mto.15.21.2.gjerdingen _bourne.html.

Gossow, Angela. 2008. "Arch Enemy Vocalist Angela Gossow: 'When it Comes to Combining Clean with Death Vox, Alissa from The Agonist is the Best I Have Heard So Far.'" *BraveWords* (blog), June 4, 2008. https://bravewords.com/news/arch-enemy-vocalist-ang ela-gossow-when-it-comes-to-combining-clean-with-death-vox-alissa-from-the-agon ist-is-the-best-i-have-heard-so-far.

Gracyk, Theodore. 1996. *Rhythm and Noise: An Aesthetics of Rock*. Durham, NC: Duke University Press.

Gus. 2017. "Buzzsaw: An Oral History of the HM-2 Pedal." *CVLT Nation* (blog), September 13, 2017. https://cvltnation.com/buzzsaw-an-oral-history-of-the-hm-2-pedal/.

Hagstrom-Miller, Karl. 2010. *Segregating Sound: Inventing Folk and Pop Music in the Age of Jim Crow*. Durham, NC: Duke University Press.

Hainaut, Bérenger. 2020. "Bestial Vocalities? Characterizing Black Metal's Noisy Voices." *Volume!* 17 (1): 145–61.

Halberstam, Jack. 1998. *Female Masculinity*. Durham, NC: Duke University Press.

Hall, Stuart. 1993. "What Is This 'Black' in Black Popular Culture?" *Social Justice* 20 (1/2): 104–11.

Hamilton, Jack. 2016. *Just Around Midnight: Rock and Roll and the Racial Imagination*. Cambridge, MA: Harvard University Press.

Hanenberg, Scott J. 2020. "Using Drumbeats to Theorize Meter in Quintuple and Septuple Grooves." *Music Theory Spectrum* 42 (2): 227–46.

Hannan, Calder. 2018. "Difficulty as Heaviness: Links Between Rhythmic Difficulty and Perceived Heaviness in the Music of Meshuggah and The Dillinger Escape Plan." *Metal Music Studies* 4 (3): 433–58.

Hannan, Calder. 2022. "Structural Density and Clarity, Technical Death Metal, and Anomalous's 'Ohmnivalent.'" *Music Theory Online* 28 (1).

Hannan, Calder. 2024. "Perspectives on Tactus Transformations in Metal." PhD Dissertation, New York, NY: Columbia University.

Harker, Brian. 2008. "Louis Armstrong, Eccentric Dance, and the Evolution of Jazz on the Eve of Swing." *Journal of the American Musicological Society* 61 (1): 67–121.

Harris, Keith. 2000. "'Roots'?: The Relationship Between the Global and the Local Within the Extreme Metal Scene." *Popular Music* 19 (1): 13–30.

HawkMoon. 2002. "Finally Something Good - 85% [Review of Arch Enemy's Wages of Sin (2001)]." *Encyclopedia Metallum; The Metal Archives* (blog), September 10, 2002. https://www.metal-archives.com/reviews/Arch_Enemy/Wages_of_Sin/450396/HawkMoon/170.

Headlam, Dave. 1997. "Blues Transformations in the Music of Cream." In *Understanding Rock: Essays in Musical Analysis*, edited by John Covach and Graeme M. Boone, 59–92. Oxford: Oxford University Press.

Hebdige, Dick. 1979. *Subculture: The Meaning of Style*. London: Methuen.

Heesch, Florian. 2018. "'Voice of Anarchy': Gender Aspects of Aggressive Metal Vocals. The Example of Angela Gossow (Arch Enemy)." *Criminocorpus, Revue Hypermédia* 11. https://journals.openedition.org/criminocorpus/5726.

Heesch, Florian and Niall Scott, eds. 2016. *Heavy Metal, Gender, and Sexuality: Interdisciplinary Approaches*. New York, NY: Routledge.

Heidemann, Kate. 2016. "A System for Describing Vocal Timbre in Popular Song." *Music Theory Online* 22 (1). https://www.mtosmt.org/issues/mto.16.22.1/mto.16.22.1.heidemann.html.

Heller, Michael C. 2015. "Between Silence and Pain: Loudness and the Affective Encounter." *Sound Studies* 1 (1): 40–58.

Hepokoski, James and Warren Darcy. 2006. *Elements of Sonata Theory: Norms, Types, and Deformations in the Late-Eighteenth-Century Sonata*. Oxford: Oxford University Press.

Herbst, Jan-Peter. 2017. "Historical Development, Sound Aesthetics and Production Techniques of the Distorted Electric Guitar in Metal Music." *Metal Music Studies* 3 (1): 23–46.

Herbst, Jan-Peter. 2018. "Heaviness and the Electric Guitar: Considering the Interaction Between Distortion and Harmonic Structures." *Metal Music Studies* 4 (1): 95–113.

Herbst, Jan-Peter and Mark Mynett. 2022. "What Is 'Heavy' in Metal? A Netnographic Analysis of Online Forums for Metal Musicians and Producers." *Popular Music and Society* 45 (5): 633–53.

Herbst, Jan-Peter and Mark Mynett. 2023a. "Lorna Shore's 'To the Hellfire': A Study in Heaviness." *Metal Music Studies* 9 (2): 189–213.

Herbst, Jan-Peter and Mark Mynett. 2023b. "Mapping the Origins of Heaviness Between 1970 and 1995." In *The Cambridge Companion to Metal Music*, edited by Jan-Peter Herbst, 29–42. Cambridge, UK: Cambridge University Press.

Herbst, Jan-Peter and Mark Mynett. 2023c. "Toward a Systematic Understanding of 'Heaviness' in Metal Music Production." *Rock Music Studies* 10 (1): 16–37.

Herbst, Jan-Peter and Mark Mynett. 2025. *Heaviness in Metal Music Production*. New York, NY: Routledge.

Herskovits, Melville J. 1941. *The Myth of the Negro Past*. New York, NY: Harper & Brothers Publishers.

Hill, Rosemary Lucy. 2016. *Gender, Metal and the Media: Women Fans and the Gendered Experience of Music*. London: Palgrave Macmillan.

Hill, Rosemary Lucy and Heather Savigny. 2019. "Sexual Violence and Free Speech in Popular Music." *Popular Music* 40 (2): 237–51.

Hudson, Stephen S. 2019. "Feeling Beats and Experiencing Motion: A Construction-Based Theory of Meter." PhD Dissertation, Evanston, IL: Northwestern University.

Hudson, Stephen S. 2021a. "Compound AABA and Style Distinction in Heavy Metal." *Music Theory Online* 27 (1). https://mtosmt.org/issues/mto.21.27.1/mto.21.27.1.hudson.html.

Hudson, Stephen S. 2021b. "Thirty-One Years Later: A Review of Metallica's 'Black Album' and Its Legacy on Alternative Metal and Alt-Right Politics." *Metal Music Studies* 7 (3): 475–78.

Hudson, Stephen S. 2022a. "Bang Your Head: Construing Beat Through Familiar Drum Patterns in Metal Music." *Music Theory Spectrum* 44 (1): 121–40.

Hudson, Stephen S. 2022b. "Review of Making Sense of Recordings: How Cognitive Processing of Recorded Sound Works by Mads Walther-Hansen, Oxford University Press 2020." *Intégral* 35: 103–8.

Hudson, Stephen S. 2023a. "Review of Focal Impulse Theory, by John Paul Ito, and Enacting Musical Time, by Mariusz Kozak." *Journal of Music Theory* 67 (1): 187–98.

Hudson, Stephen S. 2023b. "Song Form and Storytelling in Mainstream Metal." *Metal Music Studies* 9 (1): 7–26.

Hudson, Stephen S. 2025. "Recognizing Tonal Momentum and Echoes of Past Styles in Riff Turnarounds." In *The Routledge Handbook of Metal Music Composition: Evolution of Structure, Expression, and Production*, edited by Lori Burns and Ciro Scotto. New York, NY: Routledge.

Hughes, Tim. 2003. "Groove and Flow: Six Analytical Essays." PhD Dissertation, Seattle, Washington, DC: University of Washington.

Hurston, Zora Neale. 1995. "Characteristics of Negro Expression." In *Zora Neale Hurston: Folklore, Memoirs, and Other Writings*, edited by Cheryl Wall, 835. New York, NY: Library of America.

Islander. n.d. "No Clean Singing—About." *No Clean Singing* (blog), n.d. https://www.noclean singing.com/about/.

Ito, John Paul. 2020. *Focal Impulse Theory: Musical Expression, Meter, and the Body*. Bloomington, IN: Indiana University Press.

JamZward. 2013. "Why Is 'Metalcore' Music So Frequently Ridiculed?" *Reddit.com*. https://www.reddit.com/r/OutOfTheLoop/comments/1t90lq/why_is_metalcore_music_so_frequently_ridiculed/.

Johnson, Imani Kai. 2023. *Dark Matter in Breaking Cyphers*. Oxford: Oxford University Press.

Johnson, Jasmine Elizabeth. 2012. "Dancing Africa, Making Diaspora." PhD Dissertation, Berkeley, CA: University of California, Berkeley.

Johnson, Rick. 1980. "Van Halen—'Women and Children First.'" *Creem*, July 1980: 53.

Kahn-Harris, Keith. 2007. *Extreme Metal: Music and Culture on the Edge*. Oxford: Berg Publishers.

Kahn-Harris, Keith. 2010. "Black Sabbath and the Rise of Heavy Metal Music by Andrew L. Cope (Farnham: Ashgate, 2010)." *Popular Musicology Online*, ["Review articles" issue]. http://www.popular-musicology-online.com/issues/review%20articles/harris.html.

Kahn-Harris, Keith. 2016. "'Coming Out': Realizing the Possibilities of Metal." In *Heavy Metal, Gender and Sexuality: Interdisciplinary Approaches*, edited by Florian Heesch and Niall Scott, 26–38. New York, NY: Routledge.

King, Stephen. 2010. *Danse Macabre*. Gallery Books.

Kitts, Jeff. 1998. "Metallica Plays the Heavy Hits & Kills 'em All." *Guitar World*, December 1998.

Kozak, Mariusz. 2020. *Enacting Musical Time: The Bodily Experience of New Music*. Oxford: Oxford University Press.

Kozak, Mariusz. 2021. "Feeling Meter: Kinesthetic Knowledge and the Case of the Backbeat in Recent Progressive Metal." *Journal of Music Theory* 65 (2): 185–237.

Lady Enslain. 2009. "Interview with Angela Gossow: Nummirock, June 20, 2009." *Enslain*, 2009. http://www.enslain.net/interviews/archenemy.html.

Lakoff, George and Mark Johnson. 1980. *Metaphors We Live By*. Chicago, IL: University of Chicago Press.

Langacker, Ronald W. 1987. *Foundations of Cognitive Grammar*. Vol. 1. Stanford, CA: Stanford University Press.

Langacker, Ronald W. 2002. *Concept, Image, and Symbol: The Cognitive Basis of Grammar*. Second edition. Berlin: Mouton de Gruyter.

Lena, Jennifer C. 2012. *Banding Together: How Communities Create Genres in Popular Music*. Princeton, NJ: Princeton University Press.

Lena, Jennifer C. and Richard A. Peterson. 2008. "Classification as Culture: Types and Trajectories of Music Genres." *American Sociological Review* 73 (5): 697–718.

Lilja, Esa. 2009. *Theory and Analysis of Classic Heavy Metal Harmony*. Helsinki: IAML Finland.

London, Justin. 2012. *Hearing in Time: Psychological Aspects of Musical Meter*. Second edition. Oxford: Oxford University Press.

Lucas, Olivia R. 2014. "Maximum Volume Yields Maximum Results." *Journal of Sonic Studies*, no. 7. https://www.researchcatalogue.net/view/84314/87805.

Lucas, Olivia R. 2018. "'So Complete in Beautiful Deformity': Unexpected Beginnings and Rotated Riffs in Meshuggah's *obZen*." *Music Theory Online* 24 (3). https://mtosmt.org/issues/mto.18.24.3/mto.18.24.3.lucas.html.

MacDonald, Ian. 2007. *Revolution in the Head: The Beatles' Records and the Sixties*. Third edition. Chicago, IL: Chicago Review Press.

Malone, Jacqui. 1996. *Steppin' on the Blues: The Visible Rhythms of African American Dance*. Urbana, IL: University of Illinois Press.

Margulis, Elizabeth Hellmuth. 2014. *On Repeat: How Music Plays the Mind*. Oxford: Oxford University Press.

Margulis, Elizabeth Hellmuth, Lauren M. Mlsna, Ajith K. Uppunda, Todd B. Parrish, and Patrick C. M. Wong. 2009. "Selective Neurophysiologic Responses to Music in Instrumentalists with Different Listening Biographies." *Human Brain Mapping* 30 (1): 267–75.

Maultsby, Portia. 2015. "The Translated African Cultural and Musical Past." In *African American Music: An Introduction*, edited by Portia Maultsby and Mellonee V. Burnim, Second edition, 3–22. New York, NY: Routledge.

McCleary, John. 2004. *The Hippie Dictionary: A Cultural Encyclopedia of the 1960s and 1970s*. Berkeley, CA: Ten Speed Press.

Menninghaus, Winfried, Valentin Wagner, Julian Hanich, Eugen Wassiliwizky, Thomas Jacobsen, and Stefan Koelsch. 2017. "The Distancing-Embracing Model of the Enjoyment of Negative Emotions in Art Reception." *The Behavioral and Brain Sciences* 40 (e347): 1–63.

Meyer, Leonard B. 1989. *Style and Music: Theory, History, and Ideology*. Philadelphia, PA: University of Pennsylvania Press.

Miller, Jason. 2022. "What Makes Heavy Metal 'Heavy'?" *The Journal of Aesthetics and Art Criticism* 80: 70–82.

Moore, Allan F. 1993. *Rock, the Primary Text: Developing a Musicology of Rock*. Buckingham: Open University Press.

Moore, Allan F. 2002. "Authenticity as Authentication." *Popular Music* 21 (2): 209–23.

Moores, J. R. 2021. *Electric Wizards: A Tapestry of Heavy Music, 1968 to the Present*. Reaktion Books.

Mynett, Mark. 2012. "Achieving Intelligibility Whilst Maintaining Heaviness When Producing Contemporary Metal Music." *Journal on the Art of Record Production*, no. 6.

Mynett, Mark. 2017. *Metal Music Manual: Producing, Engineering, Mixing, and Mastering Contemporary Heavy Metal*. London: Taylor & Francis.

Narváez, Peter. 2001. "Unplugged: Blues Guitarists and the Myth of Acousticity." In *Guitar Cultures*, edited by Andy Bennett and Kevin Dawe. Oxford: Berg Publishers.

Nink, Theresa and Florian Heesch. 2023. "Metal Ballads as Low Pop? An Approach to Sentimentality and Gendered Performances in Popular Hard Rock and Metal Songs." *Arts* 12 (1): 38.

Nobile, Drew. 2022. "Teleology in Verse-Prechorus-Chorus Form, 1965–2020." *Music Theory Online* 28 (3). https://mtosmt.org/issues/mto.22.28.3/mto.22.28.3.nobile.html.

Novak, David. 2013. *Japanoise: Music at the Edge of Circulation*. Durham, NC: Duke University Press.

Osborn, Brad. 2010. "Beats That Commute: Algebraic and Kinesthetic Models for Math-Rock Grooves." *GAMUT* 3 (1). https://trace.tennessee.edu/gamut/vol3/iss1/4/.

Osborn, Brad. 2013. "Subverting the Verse-Chorus Paradigm: Terminally Climactic Forms in Recent Rock Music." *Music Theory Spectrum* 35 (1), 23–47.

Overell, Rosemary. 2012. "'[I] Hate Girls and Emo[Tion]s: Negotiating Masculinity in Grindcore Music." *Popular Music History* 6 (1/2): 198–223.

Patacas, Jorge. 2008. "Entrevista: ARCH ENEMY." *RISE!* (blog), May 18, 2008. http://risemetal.com/2008/05/18/entrevista-arch-enemy/.

Phillipov, Michelle. 2012. *Death Metal and Music Criticism: Analysis at Its Limits*. Plymouth: Lexington Books.

Pidgeon, John. 1985 [1976]. *Eric Clapton: A Biography*. Revised edition. London: Vermillion.

Pillsbury, Glenn T. 2006. *Damage Incorporated: Metallica and the Production of Musical Identity*. New York, NY: Routledge.

Piper, Jonathan Nicholas. 2013. "Locating Experiential Richness in Doom Metal." PhD Dissertation, San Diego, CA: University of California, San Diego.

Purcell, Natalie J. 2003. *Death Metal Music: The Passion and Politics of a Subculture*. Jefferson, NC: McFarland & Company.

Radano, Ronald M. 2003. *Lyin' Up a Nation: Race and Black Music*. Chicago: University of Chicago Press.

Rapport, Evan. 2014. "Hearing Punk as Blues." *Popular Music* 33 (1): 39–67.

Rapport, Evan. 2020. *Damaged: Musicality and Race in Early American Punk*. Jackson, MI: University Press of Mississippi.

Reyes, Ian. 2013. "Blacker Than Death: Recollecting the 'Black Turn' in Metal Aesthetics." *Journal of Popular Music Studies* 25 (2): 240–57.

Riches, Gabby. 2011. "Embracing the Chaos: Mosh Pits, Extreme Metal Music and Liminality." *Journal for Cultural Research* 15 (3): 315–32.

Riches, Gabrielle, Brett Lashua, and Karl Spracklen. 2014. "Female, Mosher, Transgressor: A 'Moshography' of Transgressive Practices within the Leeds Extreme Metal Scene." *IASPM @ Journal* 4 (1): 87–100.

Riley, Jim. 2010. *Song Charting Made Easy: A Play-along Guide to the Nashville Number System*. Milwaukee, WI: Hal Leonard.

Rockwell, Joti. 2012. "What Is Bluegrass Anyway? Category Formation, Debate and the Framing of Musical Genre." *Popular Music* 31 (3): 363–81.

Rossi, Roberta Ilaria. 2013. "Noora Louhimo—Battle Beast." *Femme Metal Webzine* (blog), June 12, 2013. https://www.femmemetalwebzine.net/interviews/noora-louhimo-battle-beast/.

Schaller, Milan K. 2025. "'We Are the Varangian Guard': Musical Rhetoric and Literary Reference in Turisas's Varangian Way Albums." In *The Routledge Handbook of Progressive Rock, Metal, and the Literary Imagination*, edited by Chris Anderton and Lori Burns, 191–203. New York, NY: Routledge.

Schechner, Richard. 1981. "Performers and Spectators Transformed and Transported." *The Kenyon Review* 3 (4): 83–113.

Schechner, Richard. 2013. *Performance Studies: An Introduction*. Third edition. New York, NY: Routledge.

Schippers, Mimi. 2002. *Rockin' Out of the Box: Gender Maneuvering in Alternative Hard Rock*. Rutgers, NY: Rutgers University Press.

Schippers, Mimi. 2007. "Recovering the Feminine Other: Masculinity, Femininity, and the Gender Hegemony." *Theory & Society* 36 (1): 85–102.

Schwartz, Roberta Freund. 2007. *How Britain Got the Blues: The Transmission and Reception of American Blues Style in the United Kingdom*. Farnham, Surrey: Ashgate.

Scotto, Ciro. 2016. "The Structural Role of Distortion in Hard Rock and Heavy Metal." *Music Theory Spectrum* 38 (2): 178–99.

Scotto, Ciro. 2024. "What is a Riff? A Structural Definition and its Analytical Consequences for Process and Form in Heavy Metal." In *The Routledge Handbook of Metal Music Composition*, edited by Ciro Scotto and Lori Burns, 51–68. New York, NY: Routledge.

Sharpe-Young, Gary. 2007. *Metal: The Definitive Guide*. London: Jawbone Press.

Shelley, Braxton D. 2019. "Analyzing Gospel." *Journal of the American Musicological Society* 72 (1): 181–243.

Shelley, Braxton D. 2021. *Healing for the Soul: Richard Smallwood, the Vamp, and the Gospel Imagination*. Oxford: Oxford University Press.

Small, Christopher. 1987. *Music of the Common Tongue: Survival and Celebration in Afro-American Music*. London: John Calder.

Smialek, Eric. 2016a. "Genre and Expression in Extreme Metal Music, ca. 1990–2015." PhD Dissertation, Montreal, QC, Canada: McGill University.

Smialek, Eric. 2016b. "The Unforgiven: A Reception Study of Metallica Fans and 'Sell Out' Accusations." In *Global Metal Music and Culture: Current Directions in Metal Studies*, edited by Andy R. Brown, Karl Spracklen, Keith Kahn-Harris, and Niall Scott, 106–24. London: Routledge.

Smialek, Eric and Méi-Ra St-Laurent. 2018. "Unending Eruptions: White-Collar Metal Appropriations of Classical Complexity, Experimentation, Elitism, and Cultural Legitimization." In *The Routledge Companion to Popular Music Analysis*, edited by Ciro Scotto, Kenneth M. Smith, and John Brackett, 378–98. London: Routledge.

Spitzer, Michael. 2006. *Music as Philosophy: Adorno and Beethoven's Late Style*. Bloomington, IN: Indiana University Press.

Stewart-Baxter, Derrick. 1953. "Wynonie Harris and Blind Boy Fuller." *Jazz Journal* 6 (9): 13.

Stras, Laurie. 2006. "The Organ of the Soul: Voice, Damage, and Affect." In *Sounding Off: Theorizing Disability in Music*, 173–84. New York, NY: Routledge.

Strausbaugh, John. 2001. *Rock 'til You Drop: The Decline from Rebellion to Nostalgia*. New York, NY: Verso Books.

Strohl, Matthew. 2019. "Art and Painful Emotion." *Philosophy Compass* 14 (1): e12558.

Swiniartzki, Marco. 2023. *Heavy Metal Und Gesellschaftlicher Wandel: Sozialgeschichte Einer Musikkultur in Den Langen 1980er Jahren*. Bielefeld: Transcript Verlag.

Taylor, Diana. 2003. *The Archive and the Repertoire: Performing Cultural Memory in the Americas*. Durham, NC: Duke University Press.

Temperley, David. 2018. *The Musical Language of Rock*. Oxford: Oxford University Press.

Tsai, Chen-Gia, Li-Ching Wang, Shwu-Fen Wang, Yio-Wha Shau, Tzu-Yu Hsiao, and Wolfgang Auhagen. 2010. "Aggressiveness of the Growl-Like Timbre: Acoustic Characteristics, Musical Implications, and Biomechanical Mechanisms." *Music Perception* 27 (3): 209–22.

Turner, Tina and Kurt Loder. 1986. *I, Tina: My Life Story*. New York, NY: William Morrow & Co.

Waksman, Steve. 2008. "Review: Damage Incorporated: Metallica and the Production of Musical Identity by Glenn Pillsbury; Extreme Metal: Music and Culture on the Edge by Keith Kahn-Harris." *Journal of Popular Music Studies* 20 (2): 194–201.

Waksman, Steve. 2009. *This Ain't the Summer of Love: Conflict and Crossover in Heavy Metal and Punk*. Berkeley, CA: University of California Press.

Waksman, Steve. 2011. "Kick Out the Jams!: The MC5 and the Politics of Noise." In *White Riot: Punk Rock and the Politics of Race*, edited by Stephen Duncombe and Maxwell Tremblay, 30–37. New York, NY: Verso Books.

Walch, Florian. 2023. "Extreme Metal Across the Digital Divide: Music, Technology, Genre." PhD Dissertation, Chicago, IL: The University of Chicago.

Wald, Gayle. 2009. "Rosetta Tharpe and Feminist 'Un-Forgetting.'" *Journal of Women's History* 21 (4): 157–60.

Wallach, Jeremy, Harris M. Berger, and Paul D. Greene. 2011. "Affective Overdrive, Scene Dynamics, and Identity in the Global Metal Scene." In *Metal Rules the Globe: Heavy Metal Music Around the World*, 3–33. Durham, NC: Duke University Press.

Wallmark, Zachary. 2018. "The Sound of Evil: Timbre, Body, and Sacred Violence in Death Metal." In *The Relentless Pursuit of Tone: Timbre in Popular Music*, edited by Robert Fink, Melinda Latour, and Zachary Wallmark, 65–87. Oxford: Oxford University Press.

Walser, Robert. 2014 [1993]. *Running with the Devil: Power, Gender, and Madness in Heavy Metal Music*. Second edition. Middletown, CT: Wesleyan University Press.

Walther-Hansen, Mads. 2020. *Making Sense of Recordings: How Cognitive Processing of Recorded Sound Works*. Oxford: Oxford University Press.

Weinstein, Deena. 1991. *Heavy Metal: A Cultural Sociology*. New York, NY: Lexington Books.

Weinstein, Deena. 1998. "The History of Rock's Pasts Through Rock Covers." In *Mapping the Beat: Popular Music and Contemporary Theory*, 137–51. Oxford: Blackwell Books.

Wenner, Jann S. 2000. *Lennon Remembers*. New edition. London: Verso Books.

Whitely, Sheila. 1992. *The Space Between the Notes: Rock and the Counter-Culture*. New York, NY: Routledge.

Wiederhorn, Jon and Katherine Turman. 2013. *Louder Than Hell: The Definitive Oral History of Metal*. New York, NY: HarperCollins.

Zerubavel, Eviatar. 1997. *Social Mindscapes: An Invitation to Cognitive Sociology*. Cambridge, MA: Harvard University Press.

Zohren, Peter. 1984. "Ride the Lightning (Review)." *Speed Attack* no. 1. https://sendbackmysta mps.org/2013/10/16/speed-attack-1-germany-1984-auf-deutsch/#jp-carousel-4612

Index

For the benefit of digital users, indexed terms that span two pages (e.g., 52–53) may, on occasion, appear on only one of those pages.